Gilles Deleuze

Key Concepts

Edited by Charles J. Stivale

McGill-Queen's University Press
Montreal & Kingston • Ithaca

© Editorial matter and selection, 2005 Charles J. Stivale; individual
contributions, the contributors.

ISBN 0-7735-2984-5   (hardcover)
ISBN 0-7735-2985-3   (paperback)

Legal deposit third quarter 2005
Bibliothèque nationale du Québec

Published simultaneously outside North America
by Acumen Publishing Limited

McGill-Queen's University Press acknowledges the financial support of
the Government of Canada through the Book Publishing Development
Program (BPIDP) for its activities.

Library and Archives Canada Cataloguing in Publication

Gilles Deleuze : key concepts / edited by Charles J.
Stivale.

Includes bibliographical references and index.
ISBN 0-7735-2984-5 (bound).—ISBN 0-7735-2985-3 (pbk.)

1. Deleuze, Gilles. I. Stivale, Charles J. II. Title.

B2430.D454S753 2005   194   C2005-900991-8

Designed and typeset by Kate Williams, Swansea.
Printed and bound by Cromwell Press, Trowbridge

Contents

v

Contributors

Christa Albrecht-Crane is Assistant Professor in English and Communication at Utah Valley State College, where she teaches courses in critical theory, media studies, film theory and writing. Most recently, her other published work has appeared in *JAC* and the *Journal of the Midwest Modern Language Association*.

Ronald Bogue is Professor of Comparative Literature at the University of Georgia. He is the author of *Deleuze and Guattari* (1989), *Deleuze on Literature* (2003), *Deleuze on Cinema* (2003), *Deleuze on Music, Painting, and the Arts* (2003) and *Deleuze's Wake* (2004).

Felicity J. Colman is Lecturer in the Cinema Studies Program at the University of Melbourne and teaches in the areas of contemporary theories of avant-garde, experimental and feminist practices of screen cultures and theory and philosophical analysis. Research interests include experimental cinema and contemporary art practices, sound theory and philosophies of affect. Her doctoral thesis examined temporal and narrative philosophies utilized by American artist Nancy Holt and Robert Smithson's writings, performative and plastic art and experimental film and video works. She is a contributor to the forthcoming *Deleuze Dictionary*.

Tom Conley is Professor of Romance Languages at Harvard University and translator of Deleuze's *The Fold: Leibniz and the Baroque*, author of *The Self-Made Map: Cartographic Writing in Early Modern France* (1996), and *L'Inconscient graphique* (2000). Forthcoming items include *A Map in a Movie* (2005) and a translation of Christian Jacob's *The Sovereign Map: Theoretical Approaches to the History of Cartography* (2005).

Eugene W. Holland is Professor of French and Comparative Studies at the Ohio State University. In addition to numerous articles on Deleuze and Guattari, he is the author of *Baudelaire and Schizoanalysis* (1993) and an *Introduction to Schizoanalysis* (1999), and is currently completing books on *Nomad Citizenship and Global Democracy: Studies in Applied Nomadology* and *Marxist Theory and French Poststructuralism*.

Karen Houle has spent an equal amount of time becoming a writer, a scholar and a parent. She teaches philosophy at the University of Alberta, Edmonton. She has published articles on Spinoza, Foucault, Deleuze and Guattari. Her book, *Ballast* (2000), was nominated for the Lampert Prize for the best first book of poetry, by the Canadian League of Poets.

Gregg Lambert is Associate Professor of English and Director of Graduate Studies at Syracuse University, New York. He has written extensively on the philosophy of Deleuze and is author of *The Non-Philosophy of Gilles Deleuze* (2002) and *The Return of the Baroque in Modern Culture* (2004), among other works.

Melissa McMahon has completed her doctoral thesis on Deleuze and Kant's critical philosophy in the Department of Philosophy, University of Sydney, where she also teaches occasionally. She has published articles on Deleuze and other contemporary European thinkers, as well as numerous translations of pieces by Deleuze, Bergson and others.

Judith L. Poxon is Adjunct Instructor in the Department of Humanities and Religious Studies, California State University, Sacramento. She has published articles on Deleuze and several of the French feminist thinkers, and has co-edited two books on religion: *French Feminists on Religion: A Reader* (2001) and *Religion in French Feminist Thought: Critical Perspectives* (2003).

Gregory J. Seigworth is Associate Professor in the Communication and Theatre Department at Millersville University, Pennsylvania. He has, most recently, co-edited a special issue of the journal *Cultural Studies* (2004) on "philosophies of everyday life" and, in 2000, co-edited an issue of the same journal focused on the work of Deleuze and Guattari. He has previously published essays and articles in a variety of books and in such journals as *Antithesis*, *Architectural Design*, *Cultural Studies* and *Studies in Symbolic Interactionism*.

Jennifer Daryl Slack is Professor of Communication and Cultural Studies in the Department of Humanities at Michigan Technological University. She is the author of *Communication Technologies and Society*

(1984), editor of *The Ideology of the Information Age* (with Fred Fejes, 1987), editor of John Waisanen's posthumous *Thinking Geometrically* (2002), editor of *Animations [of Deleuze and Guattari]* (2003), co-author of *Culture and Technology: A Primer* (with J. Macgregor Wise, forthcoming), and Associate Editor of *Communication Theory*.

Daniel W. Smith is Associate Professor in the Department of Philosophy at Purdue University. He has translated Gilles Deleuze's *Francis Bacon: The Logic of Sensation* and (with Michael Greco) *Essays Critical and Clinical*, as well as Pierre Klossowski's *Nietzsche and the Vicious Circle* (1998) and Isabelle Stengers' *The Invention of Modern Science* (2000).

Patty Sotirin is Associate Professor of Communication in the Department of Humanities at Michigan Technological University. Her work has appeared in such journals as *Text and Performance*, *Organization*, *American Journal of Semiotics*, *Journal of Popular Television and Film* and *Women and Language*.

Charles J. Stivale is Professor of French at Wayne State University, Detroit. Besides guest-editing two issues of *SubStance* (1984, 1991) on Deleuze and Guattari, he has published *The Two-Fold Thought of Deleuze and Guattari: Intersections and Animations* (1998) and *Disenchanting Les Bons Temps: Identity and Authenticity in Cajun Music and Dance* (2003). He has also co-translated Gilles Deleuze's *The Logic of Sense* and coordinates the Pli Deleuze Web Directory, www.langlab.wayne.edu/PliDeleuze/index.html (accessed December 2004).

Kenneth Surin is based in the Literature Program at Duke University, North Carolina.

J. Macgregor Wise is Associate Professor and Chair of the Department of Communication Studies, Arizona State University West. He is author of *Exploring Technology and Social Space* (1997) and *Culture and Technology: A Primer* (with Jennifer Daryl Slack, forthcoming).

Acknowledgements

This collection falls into the general, recent movement to elucidate more fully and directly the ideas and concepts of French philosopher Gilles Deleuze. To paraphrase Deleuze and Guattari at the start of *A Thousand Plateaus*, sixteen of us wrote these essays, and since each of us was several, there was already quite a crowd. Beyond this actual ensemble of authors, we owe thanks to a broad range of individuals and collective assemblages, far too numerous to encompass on this page. Let us, then, limit our thanks to Constantin V. Boundas who, based at Trent University, has been able to foster myriad folds of cooperation, dialogue and powers of life that extend far beyond sylvan Ontario to the works, publications and discussions that animate the global interest in Deleuze.

Charles J. Stivale

Abbreviations

Works by Gilles Deleuze

Dates provided in the text refer to the English-language editions listed in the References using the abbreviations given below, unless otherwise indicated. See References for complete citations in English and in French, including original publication details.

ABC   *L'Abécédaire de Gilles Deleuze*, avec Claire Parnet (1996)
AO   *Anti-Oedipus* (1983)
ATP   *A Thousand Plateaus* (1987)
B   *Bergsonism* (1991)
C1   *Cinema 1: The Movement-Image* (1986)
C2   *Cinema 2: The Time-Image* (1989)
D   *Dialogues* (1987)
DI   *Desert Islands and Other Texts* (2004)
DR   *Difference and Repetition* (1994)
DRF   *Deux régimes de fous: Textes et entretiens 1975–1995* (2004)
ECC   *Essays Critical and Clinical* (1997)
ES   *Empiricism and Subjectivity* (1991)
EPS   *Expressionism in Philosophy: Spinoza* (1990)
FB   *Francis Bacon: The Logic of Sensation* (2003)
FLD   *The Fold: Leibniz and the Baroque* (1993)
FCLT   *Foucault* (1988)
K   *Kafka: Toward a Minor Literature* (1986)
KCP   *Kant's Critical Philosophy* (1984)
LS   *Logic of Sense* (1990)

M   *Masochism: Coldness and Cruelty* (1991)
N   *Negotiations 1971–1990* (1995)
NP   *Nietzsche and Philosophy* (1983)
PI   *Pure Immanence: Essays on a Life* (2001)
PS   *Proust and Signs* (2000)
PV   *Périclès et Verdi: La Philosophie de François Châtelet* (1988)
SPP *Spinoza: Practical Philosophy* (1988)
WIP *What Is Philosophy?* (1994)

Gilles Deleuze, a life in friendship

Charles J. Stivale

In *L'Abécédaire de Gilles Deleuze [Deleuze's ABC Primer]*, the eight-hour video interview with Claire Parnet filmed in 1988–89 and transmitted only in 1995, French philosopher Gilles Deleuze describes his idiosyncratic understanding of the links between friendship, creation and life. Responding to a question from Parnet (in the section "F as in Fidelity"), Deleuze hypothesizes that in order to form the basis for friendship with someone, each of us is apt to seize on a certain indication of an individual's charm, for example, in a gesture, a touch, an expression of modesty or a thought (even before that thought has become meaningful). In other words, friendship can result from perception of the charm that individuals emit and through which we sense that another suits us, might offer us something, might open and awaken us. And a person actually reveals his or her charm through a kind of *démence* or madness, Deleuze says, a certain kind of becoming-unhinged, and as the very source of a person's charm, this point of madness provides the impulse for friendship.

I commence with this angle of approach because, with me, the authors here offer contributions precisely in this spirit, seeking to extend the folds of friendship through which Deleuze lived, wrote and taught. Such glimmers of light and encounters with Deleuze's writing engage readers in an exhilarating, productive, yet disconcerting process of becoming-unhinged that we come to enjoy, indeed to relish, in the energy that reading Deleuze requires. The charm of Deleuze's writing demands of us a kind of thinking otherwise, and thus the contributors here offer to readers, *other-wise*, a guide to specific *works and concepts* developed by Deleuze from a range of disciplinary interests and interdisciplinary connections. In preparing these essays, the authors have been attentive to show not merely what the selected concepts *are*, but especially what these concepts *do*, within and beyond philosophy. Rather than necessarily limit each concept to a fundamental essence, the authors consider the "proximate other(ness)" of the concept(s) engaged, their intersections and linkages with other works, writers and domains of reflection. Above all, the goal of these essays is to encourage students, new and old, to read Deleuze's original texts by showing readers that while his concepts are located within an intricate and sophisticated web of philosophical linkages, they are also accessible and useful for developing critical reflection beyond the domain of philosophy.

In this introduction, I propose to provide a general, albeit unusual conceptual framework for thinking with and through Deleuze's writing. That is, in contrast to the essays here that link selected works to a specific concept, I offer a more general perspective based on the particular concept of friendship that Deleuze develops throughout his written texts and interviews, as a way, subsequently, to describe briefly the book's organization and the place of each essay within it. But first, I consider the trajectory that Deleuze followed in his career from his own perspective on creation and friendship, providing some of Deleuze's own reflections on his intellectual trajectory, alone and with Félix Guattari.[1]

Doing philosophy, with friendship

The conception of friendship that Deleuze proposes in *L'Abécédaire* relates more broadly to his reflections elsewhere. Early in his career, Deleuze followed Marcel Proust in affirming, on one hand, that "friendship never establishes anything but false communications, based on misunderstandings" and, on the other hand, that "there is no intersubjectivity except an artistic one" and that "only art gives us what we vainly sought from a friend" (PS: 42).[2] This iconoclastic perspective helps us better understand Deleuze's statements in *L'Abécédaire* on the fundamental role that "encounters" (*rencontres*) play in life. He sees these as equally important in experiencing intensities and multiplicities through art and literature, in generating thought and thereby in moving beyond philosophy through philosophy. And in his earlier *Dialogues* with Parnet (1977), Deleuze asks a fundamental question in this regard:

> Between the cries of physical pain and the songs of metaphysical suffering, how is one to trace out one's narrow, Stoical way, which consists in being worthy of what happens, extracting something

gay and loving in what occurs, a glimmer of light, an encounter, an event, a speed, a becoming?   (D 66: translation modified)

Deleuze's idiosyncratic definition of his intellectual project in the early years reveals both his modesty and his rapier wit, presented in his 1973 letter to Michel Cressole:

> I belong to a generation, one of the last generations, that was more or less bludgeoned to death with the history of philosophy. The history of philosophy plays a patently repressive role in philoso- phy . . . Many members of my generation never broke free of this; others did, by inventing their own particular methods and new rules, a new approach. I myself "did" history of philosophy for a long time, read books on this or that author. But I compensated in various ways.   (N: 5–6)

His approach was to look at authors whom he judged to challenge the rationalist tradition, notably Lucretius, Spinoza, Hume and Nietzsche, as well as Kant, who Deleuze treated as an "enemy", yet whose work required an effort of discernment and understanding.[3] According to his recollection of this project, Deleuze had to adopt par- ticularly rigorous survival strategies:

> I suppose the main way I coped with it at the time was to see the history of philosophy as a sort of buggery [*enculage*] or (it comes to the same thing) immaculate conception. I saw myself as taking an author from behind, and giving him a child that would be his own offspring, yet monstrous. It was really important for it to be his own child, because the author had to actually say all I had him saying. But the child was bound to be monstrous too because it resulted from all sorts of shifting, slipping, dislocations, and hid- den emissions that I really enjoyed.   (N: 6)

Among the authors that correspond to this image of "doing" history of philosophy, Deleuze cited Nietzsche in his 1962 work and Bergson in his 1966 work. Nietzsche in particular, Deleuze maintained, "extri- cated me from all this", since Nietzsche "gets up to all sorts of things behind your back", giving Deleuze "a perverse taste . . . for saying sim- ple things in [his] own way, in affects, intensities, experiences, experi- ments" (N: 6). Through Nietzsche, Deleuze opened himself to "the multiplicities everywhere within [individuals], the intensities running through them", that is, a depersonalization "opposite [that] effected by the history of philosophy; it's a depersonalization through love, rather than subjection" (N: 6–7). This opening toward depersonalization *and* love led Deleuze towards two projects at the end of the 1960s – *Difference and Repetition* and *The Logic of Sense* – to which one can add his first book on Spinoza. While still heavily laden with many "academic elements", these books were, for Deleuze, "an attempt to jolt, to set in motion something inside me, to treat writing as a flow, not a code" (N: 7). Such a mode of reading, Deleuze argued, is:

> [an] intensive way of reading, in contact with what's outside the book, as a flow meeting other flows, one machine among others, as a series of experiments for each reader in the midst of events that have nothing to do with books, as tearing the book into pieces, getting it to interact with other things, absolutely anything, ... [this] is reading with love [*une manière amoureuse*].
>
> (N: 8–9)

Of course, this is not an easy process, for it is one that situates the "person" along, or in relation to, the "line Outside":

> something more distant than any external world. But it's also something closer than any inner world ... manag[ing] to fold the line and establish an endurable zone in which to install ourselves, confront things, take hold, breathe – in short, think. Bending the line so we manage to live upon it, with it: a matter of life and death.   (N: 110–11)

Deleuze summed up a crucial encounter at this point in his career, at the end of the 1960s, with the phrase "And then there was my meeting with Félix Guattari ..." (N: 7), later describing him as "a man of the group, of bands or tribes, and yet he is a man alone, a desert populated by all these groups and all his friends, all his becomings" (D: 16). Deleuze discussed the importance for his work of this collaboration and friendship in a number of texts, and all suggest the significant connections that Guattari was able to provoke in Deleuze's creative process and, of course, vice versa. For example, in an interview with Robert Maggiori following the 1991 publication of *What Is Philosophy?* and shortly before Guattari's death, Deleuze noted:

> What struck me most [about Guattari] was that since his background wasn't in philosophy, he would therefore be much more cautious about philosophical matters, and that he was nearly more

philosophical than if he had been formally trained in philosophy, so he incarnated philosophy in its creative state.

(Maggiori 1991: 17–18, my translation)

Guattari explained the initial project with Deleuze in 1969 as simply one of "discuss[ing] things together, [of] do[ing] things together" which, for Guattari, meant "throwing Deleuze into the stew [of the post-May 1968 turmoil]" (Guattari 1995: 28). Through what Deleuze described as their "pensée à deux" (Maggiori 1991: 19), which I elsewhere call a "two-fold thought" (Stivale 1998), Deleuze with Guattari developed the major works of the 1970s, *Anti-Oedipus* and *A Thousand Plateaus* (both volumes of *Capitalism and Schizophrenia*), and *Kafka: Toward a Minor Literature*, and then, at the start of the 1990s, their final collaboration, *What Is Philosophy?* In the interim, the 1980s was a decade in which Deleuze pursued a spectacular series of encounters with works and writers in and beyond philosophy – Francis Bacon's art, cinematic creation, Michel Foucault, and François Châtelet, Leibniz and the Baroque, the theatre of Carmelo Bene – and then, at the end of his career, he had a final encounter with literature in *Essays Critical and Clinical*. One might well consider these later works as so many encounters with artistic sensibilities that offer the intensities and charm that Deleuze perceives in friendship.

Encounters with and beyond Deleuze

The angle of approach adopted here, through friendship, helps me join together a range of concepts developed in this volume, for example, "assemblages", "desire", "affects", Deleuzian "style" and, above all, "the fold". To create these connections, I re-enter this conceptual web from another direction, at the end as it were, by attempting to move beyond Deleuze's *tombeau*, a term in French that signifies both the tomb or grave and a form of homage (i.e. a genre of posthumous poetic praise). Rather than plunge into the heart of philosophy, then, I prefer to relax with a comic: Martin tom Dieck and Jens Balzer's *Salut, Deleuze!* (1997), a fictional account of Deleuze's final voyage across the river Acheron to meet his friends on the other side.

Published in Germany (first on a daily basis in the *Frankfurter Algemeine Zeitung*, then as a book), followed by a French translation in Belgium, the *bande dessinée* (graphic art book) *Salut, Deleuze!* [*Hi, Deleuze*] shows this thinker in a refreshingly different light. The authors themselves summarized *Salut, Deleuze!* at the beginning of the sequel published six years later:

In this story, after his death, the philosopher Gilles Deleuze is taken across the Lethe by Charon, the boatman of the dead. On the other shore, Deleuze meets his friends: Michel Foucault, Roland Barthes, and Jacques Lacan. After this, Charon returns in his boat to the shore of the living where he again greets Deleuze. The trip is repeated five times. Five times, Charon and Deleuze argue to determine if repetition is repetition of the same or if it is the possible condition of the metamorphosis of the self. Is it life? Is it death? At the end of the book, Charon salutes his esteemed passenger a final time, believing that it will have been the final crossing. "Death and difference don't go together!" yells the philosopher further as he disappears in the darkness".

(tom Dieck & Balzer 2002: 4)

I draw attention to this text because of its different and intersecting facets of friendship, the idiosyncratic becoming-unhinged of narrative celebration and critique, and the volume's potential to create glimmers of light and encounters for readers with Deleuze's thought.

The scene starts in the country, and the first frame announces the title "Salut, Deleuze!" across a road running into the second frame, where a man stands in the grass, wearing a hat and trench coat, simply saying, "It's nice here." At the top of the third and fourth frames, as if written across the sky, are the words "Gilles Deleuze" (frame 3) "Philosopher, 1925–1995" (frame 4), and the man strolls through the grass towards a river, saying to himself, "Nicer than I thought", and then rings the bell of a small boat house at the river's edge, behind which is a dock and a moored boat. The fifth frame shows the man from behind outlined against the door, while a voice from within says, "Yes, what can I do for you?" to which the man replies, "My name is Deleuze ... You are expecting me." The door opens and a shadowy face from within answers, "It's late", to which Deleuze responds, shadowed in the doorway, "I had trouble finding this place." The response is "Put the money on the table." Frame eight shows a lamp above a small table, a bottle and a glass posed next to a book entitled (in English) "New Adventures of Incredible Orpheus" (tom Dieck & Balzer 1997: 5–7).

Such are the opening frames of a sequence of 36 that shows Deleuze being rowed across a dark river, at night, by a strangely disengaged boatman. For example, as the boatman rows, then gives the oars to Deleuze so he can have a beer, they chat, the boatman commenting, "Down here, time is erased before eternity. That's not so bad. How long do you think I have been doing this?" Deleuze just stares at the boatman, silent, arms resting on the oars, so the boatman asks, "And you? What did you think, before?", a question that gives Deleuze the excuse to present a copy of *Difference and Repetition* to the boatman (*ibid.*: 8–10). But the boatman is interested in something entirely different, asking, "But perhaps you might still have a final statement for me?" and explains "I collect final statements from famous men who have left the stage of life."

Before Deleuze can answer, the greeting "Salut, Deleuze!" comes from the nearby dock. Deleuze looks towards the voices, and there on the dock comes Barthes holding a lamp, followed by Foucault and Lacan, saying "You see, we didn't forget you, dear Deleuze, it's great that you have come! . . . We have to talk!" But before they can, the boatman's words interrupt, "Hey! And your statement?" Flanked by Barthes, Lacan and Foucault, Deleuze faces the boatman and says, "Ah yes, the statement. What to say? . . . What would you say about bringing me some herbs, next time?" As the boatman pulls away into the darkness, the conversation continues on the dock, and the boatman looks over his shoulder back towards the shore of the living with the four friends outlined in the distant light on the far dock. Silently, the boatman arrives at his own dock and steps from the boat carrying his lamp, and then sits reading at his table, where he again hears the "Ding Dong" sound of the doorbell (*ibid.*: 11–13).

Following this opening sequence of 36 frames, the illustrated tale continues with four successive sequences of 36 frames each to render a somewhat offbeat homage, yet also a fascinating critique of Deleuze's book *Difference and Repetition* both formally and substantively.[4] First, that tom Dieck and Balzer engage seriously as well as playfully with Deleuze's possibly most daunting work of philosophy is a gesture of intellectual daring as well as engaged friendship.[5] Secondly, the concluding section of each segment (frames 28–33) brings together the friendships of thinkers who no doubt maintained variously sympathetic relations, but also remained distinctly distanced through much of their actual lives. Hence, the conceit of the three waiting for Deleuze's arrival on the farthest shore is again sprinkled with some gentle fun at the famous French intellectuals' expense.[6]

The two facets of tom Dieck and Balzer's text – the perverse homage and critique of *Difference and Repetition* and the playful celebration of Deleuze's relations with his contemporaries – mirror the very intersections developed in the combination of essays on Deleuze's key concepts in this volume. Just as the authors of *Salut, Deleuze!* fold the concept and practice of friendship into a gentle, but nonetheless precise deflation of the *tombeau* in both of its senses (homage as well as tomb or grave), the authors in this volume productively deploy their knowledge of Deleuze's concepts while pointing out potentials for their extension beyond and, in some cases, against his *oeuvre*. Furthermore, the folds in *Salut, Deleuze!* are enhanced by the detail of the same book title appearing on the boatman's table in the first and final segments: *Salut, Deleuze!*'s sequel, *New Adventures of the Incredible Orpheus*.[7] Likewise, the authors here treat a particular concept by necessarily evoking connections to other concepts in Deleuze's works, beyond a particular text that would appear to explicate that concept, and thereby forecast as well as "backcast", so to speak, the conceptual repertory placed at the reader's disposal.

The creative as well as bibliographical details in *Salut, Deleuze!* point to a practice that Deleuze extolled on numerous occasions: the possibility and necessity to create philosophy by practices that leave philosophy, that is, philosophy by other means (cf. ABC: "C as in Culture"). Martin tom Dieck expresses this well: "So [Deleuze's] philosophy functioned as a source of inspiration to construct stories. Nonetheless ... as a drawing artist, I thus became Deleuzian without wanting to or knowing it was happening" (tom Dieck, "Entretien avec Martin tom Dieck"). Likewise, the authors in this volume offer detailed reflections on particular conceptual arrays that can and do function as sources of inspiration for undertaking creative work, sparking glimmers, making links and encounters of the most vital and productive kinds. This mode of creativity leads me now to shift focus yet again, considering how we might translate this vision in terms of friendship and the conceptual web of philosophical linkages in Deleuze's works.

Folds of friendship

In a rather humorous and also revealing moment in *L'Abécédaire de Gilles Deleuze*, precisely within "C as in Culture", when he discusses going beyond philosophy through philosophy itself, Deleuze refers to his book, *The Fold: Leibniz and the Baroque*, as an example of what can happen in this going-beyond process. Once the book came out in 1988, Deleuze started to receive correspondence from different readers, and not just in academic and philosophical communities. One group that contacted him, a 400-member association of letter folders, told him, "Your story of the fold, that's us!" Deleuze also recounts receiving another letter from some surfers who told him that they never stop inserting themselves into the folds of nature, into the folds of the wave, living there as the very task of their existence. For Deleuze, this type of exchange not only offered the movement he pursued beyond philosophy via philosophy, but also the kinds of *rencontres*, or encounters, that he avidly sought in all of his activities related to culture – theatre, art exhibitions, cinema and literature – in order to engage the very possibility of thought and creativity.

The fold is thus highly important for Deleuze, not merely as a philosophical concept, but as a practical means by which all manner of intersections between ideas and cultural and existential practices can be developed, maintained and appreciated. One could follow a trajectory along which key links between folds and friendship come fully into focus, for example, through Deleuze's observation of the Baroque sensibility in both Stéphane Mallarmé's and Leibniz's works, the interplay of the verbal and the visual, which Deleuze sums up as "a new kind of correspondence or mutual expression, an *entr'expression*, fold after fold," that is, *pli selon pli* (FLD: 31). For Deleuze, this fold after fold serves as the seam along which many new gatherings can take place, most notably, with Henri Michaux's book *Life in the Folds*, with Pierre Boulez's composition inspired by Mallarmé, "Fold After Fold," and with Hantaï's painting method constructed from folding (FLD: 33–4).

Since Tom Conley enlivens these connections in his essay below (Ch. 14), I trace the seam that Deleuze establishes through Mallarmé's practice of diverse poetic expressions of friendship. While the *tombeau*, or elegy, is a circumstantial piece for which Mallarmé gained renown, the *éventails* (poems actually written on fans as gifts) inscribe poetic words for the living, words that fold and unfold, materially opening and closing, fluttering, as the texts appear and disappear on the fans, expressions rippling between the fold of the world and fold of the soul. Some of the other forms of circumstantial texts (or "poetry of the occasion", according to Marian Sugano (1992)) are Mallarmé's messages of thanks inscribed on personal visiting cards (*cartes de visite*); quatrains on postcards containing the actual name and address of the correspondent and sent through the mail; poetic inscriptions on pebbles, Easter eggs and jugs, among many other objects. That Deleuze's reflections on the Baroque and the fold bring these particular kinds of texts so crucially into play suggests that Deleuze also comprehends the many nuances of the fold of and in friendship through the practice of such exchanges.

To follow, then, Deleuze's own line of reflection on the fold, we can observe his diverse practices of intellectual camaraderie. Of course, these forms do not necessarily resemble the precise modes of expression that Mallarmé deployed. Yet, given the means at his disposal, Deleuze produced different sorts of *éventails*, for example, in *L'Abécédaire*, in *Negotiations*, and in the texts and conversations collected by David Lapoujade in *Desert Islands and Other Texts* (2002 in French, 2004 in English).[8] Within the well-known and supportive practice of writing brief profiles of works by contemporaries, an essay by Deleuze entitled "Les plages d'immanence [The Expanses of Immanence]" (1985) appeared in a volume of "Mélanges [Miscellany]" offered as a tribute to the French philosopher, historian and translator Maurice de Gandillac, one of Deleuze's professors at the Sorbonne in the 1940s, and a lifelong friend. Published at the same time that Deleuze was preparing both his *Foucault* and *The Fold: Leibniz and the Baroque*, this essay, only four paragraphs in length, is remarkable, most notably for how it concurs with the practice of folds of friendship while also referring us back (and forwards) to an important reflection by Gandillac on this very theme.

Deleuze's focus in his short essay shifts from his reflections on Leibniz to his former teacher, "to the way in which Gandillac emphasized this play of immanence and transcendence, these thrusts of immanence from the Earth through the celestial hierarchies" (DRF: 245, my translation throughout). For Deleuze, Gandillac's writing provides insight into "an aggregate of logical and ontological concepts that characterized so-called modern philosophy through Leibniz and the German romantics" (DRF: 245), and after citing a number of key works and concepts that he attributes to Gandillac's research, Deleuze addresses the general import of Gandillac's work:

> Recognizing the world of hierarchies, but at the same time causing these expanses of immanence to enter that world, to disturb it more than any direct challenge, this is certainly a life image inseparable from Maurice de Gandillac ... [who] always exercised and reinvented an art of living and thinking [as well as] his concrete sense of friendship. (DRF: 246)

The reference that Deleuze provides here – to a fairly obscure text by Gandillac, his 1945 essay, "Approches de l'amitié [Approaches of Friendship]" – provides yet another pleat in the folds of friendship that I am tracing. Gandillac's development of myriad distinctions in philosophy between love and friendship creates implicit resonances with Deleuze's subsequent reflections on friendship, particularly in *Dialogues* and *L'Abécédaire*. "Pure friendship," says Gandillac, "does not exist any more than pure love," but in contrast to love, friendship remains "the ideal form of the specifically *human* relationship" (1945: 57, original emphasis). Gandillac pursues the paradox of friendship by suggesting:

> I have the right to friendship with anyone, just as that person deserves mine, and we pass each other by without even a glance

> ... Beyond an immediate sympathy, beyond a shared emotion, [friendship] requires a kind of attention of which few humans are capable ... The true connections are established almost without our knowing it; after that, it is up to us to strengthen them.
>
> *(Ibid.*: 58–9)

While friendship may not erase the weight of this oppressive sense of absence, "it involves us in moving past our solitude without losing ourselves in the anonymous status of a false community" (*ibid.*: 62). This move allows us to greet "a friend simply, without drama, without fixed agenda ..., making room for change, for silence, for inspiration, even for absence, this is perhaps the secret of an accord that defies any technique" (*ibid.*: 64). The fundamental *rencontre* (encounter) that founds a friendship, bad ones as well as good ones, implies that there are no guarantees, but this is as it should be: "Friendship would no doubt lose what endows it with real value if we possessed infallible methods for making it succeed" (*ibid.*: 67). These "mortal risks" are precisely those, says Gandillac, that humankind must freely and lucidly accept in order for existence to maintain any value.

Deleuze will, of course, inflect the different principles of friendship to his own experiences, and overlaps and contradictions prevail between his thought and Gandillac's. For example, as I mentioned above, Deleuze tells Parnet in *L'Abécédaire* that friendship for him has nothing to do with fidelity, and everything to do with perception of the charm that individuals emit, and in accord with his understanding of Proust, Deleuze maintains that we become sensitive to that kind of emission of signs, and that in fact, whether one receives them or not, one can become open to them ("F as in Fidelity"). Yet, these perceptions are made up of so many vectors or lines, which Deleuze describes to Parnet in *Dialogues* as "a whole geography in people, with rigid lines, supple lines, lines of flight, etc.", and he asks:

> But what precisely is an encounter with someone you like? Is it an encounter with someone, or with the animals who come to populate you, or with the ideas which take you over, the movements which move you, the sounds which run through you? And how do you separate these things? *(D: 10–11)*

One final overlap lies in the distinction of pure friendship and the human kind, which constitutes yet again a strategy between-the-two that both Gandillac and Deleuze seek in their own ways (as did Mallarmé with his *éventails* and *tombeaux*) in the *rencontres* (encounters), through which we have no guarantees. In this light, the course of gathering or constructing a sheaf of texts and references comes full circle: from Deleuze's conception of the *rencontre* and responses to his book on Leibniz, then into the Leibniz book itself and how the fold develops from the Leibnizian and Baroque perspective; then into Mallarmé's works and their deployment of folds and friendship; into Deleuze's own writings and the particular extension of friendship within the scholarly realm, particularly in his essay on Gandillac; into the latter's essay on friendship and how these perspectives, from the 1940s, are transformed forty years later in Deleuze's thought and practices, particularly as regards the *rencontre* and friendship. These pleats, these glimmers of light and encounters, offer me the opening to bring the authors writing here into these folds as well, since their essays engage with Deleuze's works both as forms of conceptual intersections "in-between", and as folds of friendship, an effective means by which such engagement might be pursued beyond the *tombeau*.

Key concepts

The above reflections bring me to the threshold of this volume. Just as Deleuze, in his final essay, "Immanence: A Life . . .," discussed the singularity expressed by the indefinite article, so too does the fold express the play of *a* life, or *a* child, or *a* work, along the rippling seam or crest of immanence, the expanses of immanence, to recall Deleuze's term. In this sense, then, we can better understand Mallarmé's many poetic and playful gestures of friendship manifested in his *éventails*, his eggs and his postal addresses, to name but a few. No one of these modes of expression represents the fold of friendship in and of itself, but all contribute to *a* work that also deliberately folded into what the poet conceptualized as the Book, but which was, in fact, *a* Book in the sense of the immanence that encompassed all that he expressed poetically. Similarly, the essays in this volume are meant to help readers discern different aspects of the seams and crests, the glimmers and encounters, of Deleuze's writing understood as *a* work, never definitive or closed off, its concepts always in play, in-between. For the authors know full well that by localizing the key concepts in chapters and in words, the essays necessarily undo the very dynamic and generative activity that moves *pli selon pli*, fold after fold. Hence, these essays bring into relief a range of interwoven elements of the Deleuzian corpus, with the relationship of folds to friendship providing one means to conceptualize the in-between, the *entr'expression* of Deleuze's thought.

12

In Part I, "Philosophies", each author situates concepts in relation to the philosophers that inspire Deleuze's reflections. For "force", Kenneth Surin brings forth the term's importance in relation to Deleuze's reworking of Spinoza and Nietzsche. However, rather than limit the understanding of "force" to Deleuze's early work, situated within the history of philosophy, Surin extends this term to encompass Deleuze's collaboration with Guattari in the two volumes of *Capitalism and Schizophrenia*. Gregg Lambert then takes on the concept "expression" and, like Surin, he helps the reader understand how the concept, specific to Deleuze's work on Spinoza, nonetheless extends into subsequent reflections with Guattari on the power of "order-words" and collective assemblages of enunciation in *A Thousand Plateaus*. Melissa McMahon addresses the crucial pair, "difference and repetition", by situating Deleuze's thought on representation in relation to his movement beyond Kant, and then extends these terms to show how they underlie Deleuze's later works alone and with Guattari. Eugene W. Holland studies one of the terms for which Deleuze and Guattari are best known, "desire", showing how they build upon Kant, Marx and Nietzsche in order to deploy a politically and socially charged conceptualization of an often misunderstood key term.

The eight essays in Part II, "Encounters", allow the authors to deploy specific concepts as means to reveal their operation, effectivity, and productivity in other fields. Judith L. Poxon and I engage first with the pair "sense–series", drawing initially on Deleuze's reworking of the structuralist schema in *The Logic of Sense*, and then showing how his innovative re-conceptualization of signs, sense and series operates in the domains of theology and dialogics, specifically Deleuze's attempts with Parnet to create new modes of sense-making through dialogue. J. Macgregor Wise explores the concept of "assemblage", first in terms of its political import in Deleuze and Guattari's works, and then for the ways that an assemblage operates in the realm of technology and across our daily lives. Karen Houle continues this political reflection by explaining how, through "micropolitics", Deleuze and Guattari offer possible means for understanding as well as combating the macropolitical forces in our daily lives, including our work in the classroom. Patty Sotirin considers the controversial term "becoming-woman", first in terms of the specific concept of "becoming", particularly in *A Thousand Plateaus*, and then in the context of feminist politics and feminine practices of "woman's talk" and girls' sociality.

Another term frequently associated with Deleuze and Guattari, "the minor", offers Ronald Bogue an opportunity to show how their engagement with Kafka's works moves beyond the literary into the political and artistic domains of minority expression and experimentation. Christa Albrecht-Crane follows with a no less politically and artistically charged pair of terms, "style and stutter", since these work for Deleuze as a means to describe the subversive power of language and its potential for creating possibly new, possibly effective modes of political and creative expression. Jennifer Daryl Slack engages with the "logic of sensation", explaining how Deleuze's comments on Francis Bacon's painting provides him a way to "do" philosophy otherwise, that is, to reveal how rhythms, sensations, colours and textures constitute means for appreciating the creative force of life. Felicity J. Colman closes this section by deftly addressing the key interrelational concepts proposed in Deleuze's two books on cinema. Her juxtaposition of Deleuze's perspectives drawn from Bergson with the film *Lost in Translation* reveals the manner in which Deleuze proposes a philosophy of cinema that suggests how the latter opens potentials for thought and, indeed, for life itself.

The title of the final part, "Folds", serves as a global descriptor because each of the authors shows us how the specific key terms traverse and weave through Deleuze's works in its entirety in a multiply undulating movement. Gregory J. Seigworth's essay explores not only the different senses of "affect" and "affection", but also how these terms converge and differ in the works of Deleuze's contemporaries. Tom Conley takes up the key term to which I referred above, the processes of "folds" and "folding" that Deleuze addresses, first in the work of Foucault and then from the perspectives of Leibniz, the Baroque and the event. Finally, Daniel W. Smith addresses Deleuze's lifelong project, adopted from his early work on Nietzsche, to develop a symptomatology, at once critical and clinical, as a means for exploring such diverse fields as psychiatry, medicine, literature, art and, of course, philosophy. These different facets of the fold – affect, foldings, the critical and clinical conjoined – help us understand the many concepts proposed in Deleuze's earlier works and fold back on the terms developed in the volume's other essays.

Moreover, the progressive development of key terms has the merit of animating the processes of fold after fold, in the dynamic and recurrent movements of folds of friendship. For the essays in this volume are linked not merely by the authors' engagement in their lives and careers with studying and teaching the works and concepts of Deleuze. They are joined by criss-crossing vectors of friendship, within and ultimately beyond the professional milieu of our initial and continuing exchanges. It is our hope that these encounters, these folds, transform the essays for our readers into practical and creative intersections that then lead them directly into Deleuze's works and, through these, to a greater understanding of the vital energy that his work produces for creation and life.

Notes

1. At the end of the volume, I provide a succinct chronology of Deleuze's life, taken from the website maintained by the Association for the Diffusion of French Thought (ADPF). In lieu of a critical bibliography of secondary works on Deleuze, I refer the reader to the following collections of essays, which offer a broad range of reflections on Deleuze's works: Alliez (1998), Ansell-Pearson (1997), Boundas & Olkowski (1994), Broadhurst (1992), Bryden (2001), Buchanan (1999), Buchanan & Colebrook (2000), Buchanan & Marks (2000), Flaxman (2000), Kaufman & Heller (1998), Massumi (2002c) and Patton (1996).

2. Please consult the list of abbreviations of Deleuze's works at the start of the volume.

3. See also *Dialogues* (D: 12–19) for Deleuze's reflections on this background.

4. Formally, the authors play with the sequence of dialogues and frames by nearly always repeating the same illustration in the same location frame in each sequence, with minor exceptions that gradually add nuances to the same illustrations and thereby create formal differences through repetitions. Substantively, the narrative unfolds as repeated crossings of the river of death, yet with growing debate between the philosopher and Charon, the boatman, who receives the same copy of *Difference and Repetition* during the first four crossings, proceeds to read it (the book appears on the table in his cabin in frame 4 of sequences 2, 3 and 4), and then in each conversation with Deleuze, poses more objections to the philosopher's arguments. As he then rejects the fifth offer of Deleuze's book, the boatman says, "Your eternity has nothing to do with repetition. I am your eternity ... I am the end ... Eternity is the end ... The end and the exit" (tom Dieck & Balzer 1997: 47, frames 25–8), words interrupted by the now familiar, friendly greeting, "Salut, Deleuze!" As I already noted, Deleuze has the final word, but he does so in order to complete the request (from sequence 1) for a last statement: "Even if we wanted it to be so, death and difference do not go together" (*ibid.*: 48, frames 32–3).

5. Yet, the comic book's depiction of Deleuze is not without some gentle malice, as the philosopher all too eagerly promotes his work and then expounds his philosophy, punctuating several statements with the professorial query "You understand?"

6. For example "Lacan already wrote something, but the letter was purloined" (*ibid.*: 30, sequence 3, frame 31), "It's good that you are back, Deleuze ... Foucault was about to read a little poem about the 'I' (a recitation of words from *The Order of Things* 'like a face of sand at the edge of the sea [man will disappear]')" (*ibid.*: 39, sequence 4, frames 30–31) and "Barthes is showing us pictures of his mother" (*ibid.*: 48, sequence 5, frame 31). In an interview available online, tom Dieck responds to the criticism that his depiction of these celebrated philosophers was too caricatural: "The question of knowing whether or not I simplified Deleuze's character hardly interests me. I took him not as a philosopher, but because he had a funny side as a human being [with his glasses and long fingernails], an aspect that I used quite well in the drawings" (tom Dieck, "Entretien avec Martin tom Dieck").

7. This second illustrated volume has five episodes: "The Return of Deleuze" 1 and 2, "Adventures of the Incredible Orpheus" 1 and 2, and "New Adventures of the Incredible Orpheus".

8. Tracing the short period 1972–90, *Negotiations* includes different published letters (e.g. to Réda Bensmaïa, Michel Cressole and Serge Daney), interviews (alone and with Guattari) on topics ranging from *Anti-Oedipus* to "control societies" (with Toni Negri), and a few occasional pieces on cinema and politics. *Desert Islands and Other Texts* is most striking for the texts from Deleuze's early career (1953–74) that are book reviews and prefaces. Not only does he pay homage to the creative strength of literary authors (such as Alfred Jarry, Raymond Roussel and *série noire* [detective novel] writers), he also provides substantive commentary and support of contemporaries such as Kostas Axelos, Hélène Cixous, Michel Foucault, Guy Hocquenghem, Jean Hyppolite and Gilbert Simondon.

PART I

Philosophies

ONE

Force

Kenneth Surin

Deleuze's employment of the concept of *force* (the same in English and French) can be grasped in terms of two distinctive but somewhat over-lapping phases. In the first, associated with the "historical" emphasis on the works on Spinoza and Nietzsche (among others) that marked the earlier part of Deleuze's career, force is understood primarily in terms of its relation to notions of speed and movement. In the case of Spinoza, Deleuze is particularly impressed by Spinoza's philosophical ambition to view all of life as the expression of a fundamental striving or *conatus*, so that the body becomes an ensemble consisting of those forces that it transmits and those forces that it receives. Spinoza, says Deleuze in *Spinoza: Practical Philosophy*, "solicits forces in thought that elude obedience as well as blame, and fashions the image of a life beyond good and evil, a rigorous innocence without merit or culpability" (SPP: 4). This fundamental insight is carried through in Deleuze's work on Nietzsche, where Nietzsche is depicted as someone who follows faith-fully Spinoza's injunction that we think "in terms of speeds and slownesses, of frozen catatonias and accelerated movements, unformed elements, nonsubjectified affects" (SPP: 129).[1]

In the second phase, associated primarily with Deleuze's collabora-tion with Guattari, the notion of force is effectively generalized, so that it expresses a power that ranges over the entirety of the social order. Here another set of definitions and principles comes to the forefront, even if the earlier indebtedness to the archive associated with Spinoza and Nietzsche is retained, so that the notion of force as a movement with its characteristic speeds and slownesses is still operative for Deleuze. This time, however, the emphasis is more on a specific effect of force, namely, *puissance* or "strength" (as opposed to *pouvoir* or "coercive power"). Each of these intellectual phases will be considered in turn.[2]

The physics of forces: Spinoza and Nietzsche

In Spinoza's magnum opus, *Ethics, Demonstrated in Geometrical Order* (1677), each being has an essential and intrinsic disposition to preserve its own being, a tendency Spinoza terms *conatus* (Spinoza 2000: 171). For Spinoza, a being's good is that which adds to its capacity to preserve itself and, conversely, the bad is that which militates against this capacity for self-preservation. Each being's desire (*appetitio*) is precisely for that which conduces to its self-preservation.[3] A being's capacity for action increases, accordingly, in proportion to the strength of its *conatus*; and conversely, the weaker its *conatus*, the more diminished is its capacity for action. A being enhances its capacity for action when it actively transmits its force; its capacity for action is reduced when it is the passive recipient of some other being's forces. Pleasure or joy ensue when the capacity for action is enhanced, and pain when it is diminished, so that for Spinoza pain is passion only and not action, whereas joy is both pleasure and action.[4]

Freedom is promoted when one's scope for action is expanded, and this expansion is, for Spinoza, the outcome of a life led according to reason. In a life guided by reason, especially by knowledge of the third kind, one comes to have knowledge of oneself and of God/nature. In gaining this knowledge, one's mind, which is part of the infinite mind of God, becomes a part of something eternal. The outcome for this kind of knower is beatitude.[5] Deleuze explains the coincidence of power and action for Spinoza in the following terms:

> all power is inseparable from a capacity for being affected, and this capacity for being affected is constantly and necessarily filled by affections that realize it. The word *potestas* has a legitimate use here ... to *potentia* as essence there corresponds a *potestas* as a capacity for being affected, which capacity is filled by the affections or modes that God produces necessarily, God being unable to undergo action but being the active cause of these affections.
> (SPP: 97–8)

This distinction between *potentia* and *potestas* (or *puissance* and *pouvoir*, respectively, in French) is crucially important for Deleuze's subsequent thought, and in particular for the formulation of a materialist ontology of constitutive power, this being one of the primary intellectual objectives of Deleuze and Guattari's *Capitalism and Schizophrenia* project. For Spinoza was, in the eyes of Deleuze (and Guattari), the initiator of this ontology's guiding insights and principles. However, the thinker who in their view created the image of thought that made possible the comprehensive amplification of Spinoza's principles into a full-blown ontology of constitutive power was Nietzsche.[6]

Nietzsche is, of course, credited by Deleuze with numerous philosophical accomplishments, but primary among these is Nietzsche's method of dramatizing thought. In this staging of thought or "dramatology", the speed and slowness with which a concept is moved, the dynamism of its spatiotemporal determinations and the intensity with which it interacts with adjacent entities in a system all become primary. As Deleuze puts it:

> The state of experience is not subjective, at least not necessarily so. Nor is it individual. It is flux, and the interruption of flux, and each intensity is necessarily related to another intensity, such that something passes through. This is what underlies all codes, what eludes them, and what the codes seek to translate, convert, and forge anew. But Nietzsche, in this writing on intensities, tells us: do not trade intensities for mere representations. The intensity refers neither to signifieds which would be the representations of things, nor to signifiers which would be the representations of words.   (DI: 257, translation modified)

The criteria and formal conditions associated with a logic premised on notions of truth and falsity, and indeed of representation generally, constitute a "dogmatic image of thought", and thus for Nietzsche have to be supplanted by a topology and typology in which notions indebted to representation are replaced by such concepts as "the noble and the base, the high and the low", and so forth.[7] Representational thinking is constitutively superintended by the *logos*, and in place of this *logos*-driven thinking Nietzsche advances a conception of sense based on (sense-making) "operators". To quote Deleuze (who at this point is, palpably, a follower of Nietzsche):

> In Nietzsche ... the notion of sense is an instrument of absolute contestation, absolute critique, and also a particular original production: sense is not a reservoir, nor a principle or an origin, nor even an end. It is an "effect", an effect *produced*, and we have to discover its laws of production ... the idea of sense as an effect

21

produced by a certain machinery, as in a physical, optical, sonorous effect, etc. (which is not at all to say that it is a mere appearance) ... An aphorism of Nietzsche's is a machine that produces sense, in a certain order that is specific to thought. Of course, there are other orders, other machineries – for example, all those which Freud discovered, and still more political and practical orders. But we must be the machinists, the "operators" of something.

(DI: 137, original emphasis, translation modified)

The pivot of this Nietzschean image of thought, for Deleuze, is the concept of force (*macht*), and in particular Nietzsche's insight that "all reality is already a quantity of force" (NP: 40).[8] At the same time Nietzsche believes the concept of force "still needs to be *completed*: an *inner* will must be *ascribed* to it, which I designate as 'will to power'" (quoted in NP: 49, original emphasis). It is here that Nietzsche can be said to take to a certain culminating-point Spinoza's conception of the *conatus*.

The will to power (*wille zur macht*) and its relation to force can be understood in terms of the following propositions that can be extracted from Deleuze's "argument" set-out in *Nietzsche and Philosophy*.

- The essence of a force is its quantitative difference from other forces, and the quality of the force in question is constituted by this quantitative difference, and the will to power is thus the principle of the synthesis of forces; the will to power enables the emergence of this quantitative difference from other forces and the quality that is embodied by each force in this relation (NP: 50).
- Force and will should not be conflated; in Deleuze's words, "force is what can, will to power is what wills [*La force est ce qui peut, la volonté de puissance est ce qui veut*]" (NP: 50). Moreover, when two forces are alongside each other, one is dominant and the other is the dominated, and the will to power is thus the internal element of the production of force (NP: 51). Nietzsche understands the will to power in terms of the genealogical element of force. Chance is not eliminated by the will to power, since the will to power would be neither flexible nor open to contingency without chance (NP: 52–3). Also, depending on its original quality, a force is either active or reactive, while affirmation and negation are the primary qualities of the will to power (NP: 53–4); affirmation is not action *per se*, but the power of becoming active, it is the personification of becoming active, while negation is not mere reactivity but a becoming-reactive (NP: 54). As a result, to interpret is to determine

the force that bestows sense on a thing, while to evaluate is to determine the will to power that bestows value on a thing (NP: 54).
- Reactive forces diminish or annul the power of active forces, and every force that goes to the limit of its ability is active, while those who are weak are separated from what they can accomplish (NP: 57–61). All sensibility amounts to a becoming of forces (the will to power is the composite of these forces), and forces can be categorized in the following way: (i) *active force* is the power of acting or commanding; (ii) *reactive force* is the power of being acted upon or obeying; (iii) *developed reactive force* is the power of decomposition, division and separation; (iv) *active force becoming reactive* is the power of being separated, of undermining itself (NP: 63).
- The eternal return indicates that becoming-reactive is non-being, and it also produces becoming-active by generating becoming: the being of becoming cannot be affirmed fully without also affirming the existence of becoming-active (NP: 72). The object of philosophy is liberation, but this philosophy is always "untimely", since it requires the abolition of negativity and the dissipative power of non-being, a task that will be coextensive with the emergence of a new kind of being, one beholden to neither of the two previous forms of being, God and Man.[9]

A Deleuzean ontology will extract one fundamental principle from these theses, namely, that desire is a kind of *puissance* and thus necessarily a type of force. With this principle Deleuze (and Guattari) are in a position to formulate the materialist ontology of political practice associated with their *Capitalism and Schizophrenia* project. In particular, the notion of *judgement*, and the vision of philosophy as the "science of judgement", could now be overthrown in favour of philosophies, political and otherwise, that hinged on conceptions of desire and intensity.

The ontology of constitutive power: the *Capitalism and Schizophrenia* project

By the time the first volume of the *Capitalism and Schizophrenia* project, *L'anti-Oedipe* [*Anti-Oedipus*] (1972), was published, an intellectual and political context had emerged, in France at any rate, that provided enabling conditions for the emergence of the ontological framework developed by Deleuze and Guattari in *Anti-Oedipus* and the project's second volume, *Mille Plateaux* [*A Thousand Plateaus*] (1980).[10]

In (French) philosophy, the then regnant structuralist and phenomenological paradigms had largely run their course and reached a point of exhaustion by the late 1960s. Phenomenology never really managed to detach itself from the Cartesian model of subjectivity and self-consciousness, and when it became clear that not even Heidegger, the later Husserl, Merleau-Ponty and Sartre (to mention only some of the more eminent figures involved in this undertaking) were able to resolve or dissolve the conundrums of transcendental subjectivism, the phenomenological paradigm was increasingly perceived to have struck its equivalent of the proverbial iceberg. Structuralism was able to steer clear of the impasses that afflicted Cartesian subjectivism, but its reliance on Saussure's conception of language required it to posit the linguistic code as something of a transcendental entity in its own right; the code had to be assumed from the outset as a condition for determining meaning. When it became clear that the code could not function as a transcendental principle, and this because it effectively reduced all vehicles of meaning to utterance (images were a particular problem for structuralism because many of their properties could not be accounted for in terms of a model based on utterance), the structuralist paradigm fell into desuetude.[11]

At the same time, conceptions of subjectivity derived from psychoanalysis were found to be problematic. Freud and his more immediate followers viewed the libidinal drives as something that had to be contained or channelled if "civilization" was to be maintained (Freud's *Civilization and its Discontents* (1930) is the canonical text here), and although some of Freud's followers did seek alternative metapsychological frameworks for understanding libidinal intensities, those who strayed too far from Freud's original metapsychological principles were soon denounced by the official Freudian establishment. Foremost among these "deviationists" was Wilhelm Reich, whose call for a "liberation" of the libidinal drives exerted a powerful influence on *Anti-Oedipus*, although it has to be acknowledged that *Anti-Oedipus* is only one of a number of contemporary French works that sought a more expansive conception of the libidinal drives, often involving an extension, more or less radically different in relation to the concept's origin, of Freud's notion of a "polymorphous perversity".[12] The late 1960s and 1970s in France represented a conjuncture in which the various post- or neo-Freudianisms were consolidated into a loose-knit movement, and the *Capitalism and Schizophrenia* project was part of this conjuncture, at least in so far as its vigorous polemic against Freudianism is concerned.

Also important for the conjuncture that enabled the *Capitalism and Schizophrenia* project (and its ontology of political practice) to emerge was the social and political constellation associated with what came to be known as "the events of May 1968". Important for the genesis of this constellation was the perceived failure of the Soviet Communist project after that country's brutal invasions of Hungary in 1956 and Czechoslovakia in 1968, along with the disclosures concerning Stalin's show trials and purges provided by Khrushchev at the Twentieth Communist Party Congress in February 1956. Just as significant for the French left intelligentsia of that period (the mid-1950s to the late 1960s) was the winding-down of the Bandung Project so soon after its inception in 1955; with the collapse of the Bandung Project any hope that a non-aligned Third World could serve as a repository of emancipatory potential rapidly disappeared.[13] In political life, the post-war Gaullist institutional monopoly had pushed the French version of "representative democracy" into a gradual but seemingly inexorable sclerosis, and the post-war compromise between capital and labour, viewed as the basis of a 30-year period of prosperity (*les trente glorieuses*) was also beginning to unravel (as it did elsewhere in the advanced industrial countries of the Western world).[14] These developments marked, collectively, the transition of one phase of capitalist development to another, as the French manifestation of the social-democratic form of capitalism mutated into the globally integrated capitalist dispensation that is in place today. This particular transition is embodied in a number of registers: the emergence of a new subject of labour; the creation of new structures of accumulation; the setting-up of new axes of value; the transformation of the capitalist state; the availability of new forms of opposition and struggle; and so on. These and other parallel developments are taken by Deleuze and Guattari to indicate the need for a new ontology of political practice and constitutive power.[15]

All this amounted to a crisis of utopia for French Marxist and marxisant thought, as the question of the transformations undergone by the regime of accumulation and mode of production became a crucial object of enquiry. In a nutshell, Deleuze and Guattari's analytical treatment of "force" helped them advance a revolutionary conceptualization of the mode of production. Their delineation of the notion of "force" enabled a central focus on the concept of a "machinic process" (*agencement machinique*), which could then be used by them to formulate a full-blown ontology of constitutive power, which in turn could underpin a new "theorization" of the mode of production.

The machinic process is a mode of organization that links all kinds of "attractions and repulsions, sympathies, and antipathies, alterations, amalgamations, penetrations, and expressions that affect bodies of all kinds in their relations to one another" (ATP: 90). The modes of production are constituted by these machinic processes (ATP: 435). This is the equivalent of saying that the modes of production, subtended as they are by machinic processes, are expressions of desire, and thus of force (in the sense of *potentia/pouvoir*); the modes of production are the resultant of this infinitely productive desire or force. As Deleuze and Guattari would have it, it is desire, which is always social and collective, that makes the gun into a weapon of war, or sport, or hunting, depending on extant circumstances (ATP: 89–90). The mode of production is thus on the same level as the other expressions of desire, and it is made up of stratifications, that is, crystallizations or orchestrations of ordered functions, which are these very expressions of desire.[16] Here Deleuze and Guattari bring about a reversal of the typical Marxist understanding of the mode of production: it is not the mode *per se* that allows production to be carried out (as the traditional account specifies); instead, it is desiring-production itself that makes a particular mode the kind of mode that it is. Deleuze and Guattari's recourse to a practical ontology of desiring-production is thus their way of accounting for the organization of productive desire. All this sounds highly recondite, but the principle framed in this part of the *Capitalism and Schizophrenia* project simply elaborates what Marx himself had said, namely, that society has to exist before capitalist appropriation can take place, so that a society or state with already positioned labour has to exist if the realization of surplus-value is to take place. To quote Deleuze and Guattari:

> Marx, the historian, and Childe, the archaeologist, are in agreement on the following point: the archaic imperial State, which steps in to overcode agricultural communities, presupposes at least a certain level of development of these communities' productive forces since there must be a potential surplus capable of constituting a State stock, of supporting a specialized handicrafts class (metallurgy), and of progressively giving rise to public functions. This is why Marx links the archaic State to a certain [precapitalist] "mode of production".[17]   (ATP: 428)

Before any surplus-value can be realized by capital there is politics, that is, force, and this is why the genealogy of force based on Spinoza and Nietzsche (although Hume and Bergson also figure in this genealogy), constructed in the *Capitalism and Schizophrenia* project, is central and unavoidable.

While capitalism is for Deleuze and Guattari an immense set of apparatuses, operating on a planetary scale, that transcodes all reachable spaces of accumulation, its functioning is due to more than just the operation of forces at the level of organizations and formations. The ontology of constitutive power conceptualizes force or *puissance* not just in regard to its role in creating and consolidating a planetary-wide regime of accumulation. This way of conceptualizing also encompasses two complementary facets: on one hand, the ways in which this *puissance* enables at once the emergence and consolidation of the various forms of collective subjectivity; on the other hand, the ways in which these forms make possible the means for capitalism to fashion the kinds of subjectivity (a "social morphology" in Deleuze's words (N: 158)) required for the collective functioning.

Deleuze has in several works connected the notion of force with the concept of a singularity, primarily because it takes a libidinal investment, and thus the activation of a force or ensemble of forces, to constitute a singularity.[18] If the universe is composed of absolute singularities, then production, any kind of production, can only take the form of repetition: each singularity, as production unfolds, can only repeat or propagate itself. In production, each singularity can only express its own difference, its distance or proximity, from everything else. Production, on this Deleuzean view, is an unendingly proliferating distribution of all the myriad absolute singularities. Production is necessarily repetition of difference, the difference of each singularity from everything else.

Capitalism, however, also requires the operation of repetition. A capitalist axiomatics, at the same time, can only base itself on notions of identity, equivalence and intersubstitutivity, as Marx pointed out in his analysis of the logic of the commodity-form. This being so, capitalist repetition is perforce repetition of the non-different, the different in capitalism can never be more than the mere appearance of difference, because capitalist difference can always be overcome, and returned through the processes of abstract exchange, to what is always the same, the utterly fungible. Capitalism, and this is a decisive principle in the *Capitalism and Schizophrenia* project, only deterritorializes in order to bring about a more powerful reterritorialization. When capitalism breaches limits it does so only in order to impose its own limits, which it projects as the limits of the universe. The power of repetition in capitalism is therefore entirely negative, wasteful and lacking in any really productive force. Capitalistic repetition is non-being in the manner set-out by Spinoza. Any collective subjectivity constituted on the basis of this form of repetition will not be able to advance the cause of emancipation. The challenge, at once philosophical and political, posed by the authors of the *Capitalism and Schizophrenia* project has therefore to do with the supersession of this capitalist repetition by forms of productive repetition that are capable of breaking beyond the limits imposed on

27

emancipation by those who rule us. Only force, that is, politics, which is not the same as violence (at least not necessarily), can accomplish this.

For Deleuze, therefore, the ontology of this anti-capitalist power of constitution must take the form of a genealogy of the concept of force. At any rate, it must begin with this genealogy, since Nietzsche and Spinoza were the great discoverers of the scope and nature of force's "social physics". A genealogy of the "social physics" of force adumbrated by Spinoza and Nietzsche augments, philosophically, the critique of capitalism that lies at the heart of the *Capitalism and Schizophrenia* project; indeed, without the first the latter would be impossible.

Notes

1. Immediately before this quotation Deleuze says that "Goethe, and even Hegel in certain respects, have been considered Spinozists, but they are not really Spinozists, because they never ceased to link the plan to the organization of a Form and to the formation of a Subject. The Spinozists are rather Hölderlin, Kleist, and Nietzsche" (SPP: 128–9). Deleuze's book on Nietzsche is *Nietzsche and Philosophy* (NP).

2. An element of artificiality inevitably surrounds such attempts at periodizing an author's work. In 1989 Deleuze provided the following thematically arranged classification for his works: (1) from Hume to Bergson: (2) classical studies; (3) Nietzschean studies; (4) critique and clinical; (5) aesthetics; (6) cinematographic studies; (7) contemporary studies; (8) *The Logic of Sense*; (9) *Anti-Oedipus*; (10) *Difference and Repetition*; and (11) *A Thousand Plateaus*. For this classification, see the editor's introduction to *Desert Islands and Other Texts* (DI: 292, n.1). My typology, somewhat by contrast, aligns Spinoza with Nietzsche (at least on the matter of *conatus/macht*), and separates this alignment from the treatment of force provided after *Anti-Oedipus*.

3. To quote Spinoza "to act absolutely in accordance with virtue is simply to act, live, and preserve one's being (these three mean the same) in accordance with the guidance of reason, and on the basis of looking for what is useful to oneself" (2000: 243).

4. To quote Spinoza, "The mind is averse to imagining those things which diminish or hinder its own power, and the power of the body" (2000: 175).

5. To quote Spinoza, "our salvation, i.e. our blessedness, i.e. our freedom, consists … in a constant and eternal love for God, or, in the love of God for human beings. This love, i.e. blessedness, is called 'glory' in the Scriptures … For whether this love is related to God or to the mind, it can rightly be called contentment of mind, which is not in fact distinguished from glory" (2000: 310).

6. It would, however, be a mistake to assume that Deleuze believes Nietzsche to have superseded or surpassed in whatever way the insights of Spinoza. To do this would be to controvert a fundamental Deleuzean principle regarding the relation between philosophers of different ages. Deleuze insists repeatedly that great philosophers are first and foremost creators of concepts, and that an adequate philosophy of history consequently takes the form of a genealogy of concepts

that positions concepts in terms of the ways in which they transform and "contaminate" each other, and not simply in terms of a chronology or dialectical succession (the latter being the *modus operandi* of a traditional, and for Deleuze unsatisfactory, philosophy of history). Thus it is possible for Nietzsche, or Deleuze for that matter, to employ a concept of Spinoza's in a rigorously Spinozist fashion, even though Spinoza himself would probably not have understood what Nietzsche and Deleuze were attempting to accomplish. For this principle, see the first paragraph of "Nomadic Thought" (DI: 252). Or, as Deleuze said about his own collaboration with Guattari, "When I work with Guattari each of us falsifies the other, which is to say that each of us understands in his own way notions put forward by the other" (N: 126).

7. See Deleuze, "On the Will to Power and the Eternal Return" (DI: 118, translation modified). On the "dogmatic image of thought", see *Nietzsche and Philosophy* (NP: 103–5).

8. Deleuze maintains that the key Nietzschean principle here is asserted in *The Will to Power*, where Nietzsche says that there are nothing but relations of force in mutual "relations of tension" (1968: 635).

9. Here the following passage from *Nietzsche and Philosophy* comes to mind: "Does the recuperation of religion stop us being religious? By turning theology into anthropology, by putting man in God's place, do we abolish the essential, that is to say, the place?' (NP: 88–9). In other words, a truly critical philosophy would not seek simply to reverse the fundamental oppositions God–Man, theology–anthropology, and so on, but it would, more radically, abolish the very place from which these reversals emerge and from which they derive their force. Deleuze consolidates this legacy of Nietzsche's.

10. See *Anti-Oedipus* and *A Thousand Plateaus*. Deleuze has always made it clear in his interviews that he prefers to characterize his intellectual itineraries and work in this "eventive" way rather than in terms of a more conventional approach that deals with a thinker's influences, formation, shifts of interest, trajectory of publication and so on. Besides Deleuze's *Negotiations*, see also Deleuze and Parnet's *Dialogues*.

11. This sketchy outline conforms to the narrative advanced in Deleuze and Guattari, *What is Philosophy?* Deleuze deals with structuralism in his "How Do We Recognize Structuralism?" (DI: 170–92). For a more general overview of structuralism's relation to philosophy, see Christian Delacampagne, *A History of Philosophy in the Twentieth Century* (1999).

12. For Deleuze's critique of psychoanalysis, see, in addition to *Anti-Oedipus*, the chapter "Dead Psychoanalysis: Analyse", in *Dialogues* (D: 77–123), and "Five Propositions on Psychoanalysis" (DI: 274–80). For works by other writers in this anti- or post-Freudian vein, see Jean-François Lyotard, *Économie libidinale* (1974) and Julia Kristeva, *La révolution du langage poétique* (1974). Also important for Deleuze and Guattari is the British "anti-psychiatric" school associated with R. D. Laing and David Cooper.

13. The Bandung Project got its name from the Indonesian city where the non-aligned movement, spearheaded by Indonesia, India, Egypt and Yugoslavia, held its first meeting. The aim of the movement was to form an international bloc that would not be subsumed by either the capitalist "West" or the Soviet-led "East".

14. An important retrospective analysis of this French social and political conjuncture is to be found in Kristin Ross, *May '68 and its Afterlives* (2002). See also Sunil Khilnani, *Arguing Revolution: The Intellectual Left in Postwar France* (1993), and Michael Kelly, *Modern French Marxism* (1983).

15. Paul Patton, in his excellent *Deleuze and the Political* (2000: 103–8), correctly points out that it is possible to extract "anti-political" propositions from nearly all of Deleuze's texts, and that these propositions show Deleuze (and Guattari) to be more concerned with generalized forms of social being rather than with capitalism *per se*. Patton, and I agree with him, insists however that it would be a mistake to take this for the whole story, since the *Capitalism and Schizophrenia* project also provides an "axiomatics" for constructing assemblages that are explicitly political.

16. This point is made in Brian Massumi's excellent analysis of Deleuze and Guattari's mode of production in his *A User's Guide to* Capitalism and Schizophrenia*: Deviations from Deleuze and Guattari* (1992: 194 n.51).

17. In the words of Deleuze and Guattari, it is the state that gives capital its "models of realization" (ATP: 428).

18. *Anti-Oedipus* is perhaps the *locus classicus* of this account of libidinal investment in the writings of Deleuze and Guattari.

TWO

Expression

Gregg Lambert

The concept of expression, or of "expressionism in philosophy", first appears and is fully developed in Deleuze's longer treatise on Spinoza published in 1968, the same year as the publication of his systematic study, *Difference and Repetition*. Thus, both major works can be understood together as two different approaches to the idea of difference in the history of philosophy. The problem of expression in Spinoza's philosophy concerns, first of all, the interplay between the internal thought and external bodies, and how ideas come to express this relation between inside and outside as being internal to the power of thought. The problem that Deleuze first sets out to resolve through his reading of Spinoza is precisely what is present in a true idea that makes it adequate to or "expressive" of the thing's nature "as it is in itself" (EPS: 15). The solution to the problem is found in Spinoza's radical principle of parallelism, in which the idea's expressive character is said to be immanent in things themselves, and it is the character of truth to express this immanence fully or perfectly. Although often ascribed to Spinoza's philosophy of parallelism, Deleuze derives a crucial part of this logic of expression from Stoic philosophy, and in particular, from the theory concerning the incorporeal nature of sense. However, the problem of expression is not restricted to Deleuze's commentaries on classical philosophers such as Spinoza, Leibniz, or Descartes. As I recount below, this problem also underlies Deleuze's works with Guattari on the nature of language understood as a set of "order-words" and "collective assemblages of enunciation", as well as his later meditations on the epistemological nature of power in the work of Foucault.

The mystery of parallelism

What does it mean to express an idea? In one sense, it means nothing less than the power of the understanding to express itself. The emphasis is on the power that is expressed by the act of understanding, not upon the particular attribute of the idea that is expressed; as Deleuze puts it, "the material of the idea is not sought in a representative content but in an expressive content . . . through which the idea refers to other ideas or to the idea of God" (SPP: 75). Here it is not the case, as it is with Descartes, that the property of an idea is "clear and distinct", but rather it is the capacity of the understanding to express its own substance adequately or inadequately. The famous subject–object dualism is subtracted from this exposition of the act of understanding, since the idea of understanding, its object and the power of the act are in fact identical. As Deleuze writes, "the traditional distinction between the sense expressed and the object designated (and expressing itself in this sense), thus finds in Spinozism direct application" (EPS: 105). Therefore, understanding understands itself and this expresses its essential property, which Spinoza calls its substance. *What* the understanding understands is defined as a mode, which is necessarily infinite. "The attributes turn about in their modes" is a phrase that Deleuze often employs to describe this new determination. "The attribute [of understanding] is expressed 'in a certain and determinate way,' or rather in an infinity of ways which amount to finite existing modes" (EPS: 105).

In Spinoza's philosophy of expression, moreover, to have an adequate idea does not mean a correspondence between an object and the idea that represents it, but rather refers to the power of the idea to "explicate" fully the essence of something, and for this, it must "involve" a knowledge of the cause and must "express" it (EPS: 133). If I have an idea of the illness that devastates my body, for this idea to be adequate it must fully express the cause of this illness, by the same manner in which a physician links or connects effects (symptoms) to one another in a chain, with one idea becoming a complete cause of another. Deleuze argues that "only adequate ideas, as expressive, give us knowledge through causes, or through a thing's essence" (EPS: 134). In a philosophy of expression the emphasis is placed on the creation of concepts that are fully expressive, and that completely explicate causes. "Real knowledge is discovered to be a *kind* of expression: which is to say that the representative content of ideas is left behind for an immanent one, which is truly expressive, and the form of psychological consciousness is left behind for an 'explicative' logical formalism" (EPS: 326, original emphasis). Consequently, for Spinoza as well as for Leibniz, a philosophy of expression first of all

32

concerns itself with a being determined as God, in so far as God expresses himself in the world; secondly, the philosophy of expression is concerned with ideas determined as true, in so far as only true ideas express both God and the world. As Deleuze shows, the concept of expression in this philosophy has two possible sources and areas of direct application: ontology, relating to the expression of God and the world; and logic, relating to "*what is expressed by propositions*" (EPS: 323, original emphasis).

In Spinoza's logic, however, attributes are names, but they are verbs rather than adjectives. Later in Deleuze's thought, this logic of expression explicitly informs the concept of "becoming" in such expressions as "becoming-woman", "becoming-animal" and "becoming-molecular". In each case, the name functions not as a noun, or proper name, but rather as a verb, or as a process of modification. As Deleuze shows, it was the Stoics who first showed the two different planes of sense by separating the sense that belongs to states of bodies from the sense of statements. They are independent of one another.[1] For example, "When the scalpel cuts through the flesh" (LS: 5), or when food or poison spreads through the body, there is an intermingling of two bodies, but the sense is different from the statement "the knife is cutting the flesh", which refers to an incorporeal transformation both on the level of the bodies and the level of the sense of the statement (ATP: 86). This third sense that lies between the two different senses, between the depth of the body and the surface of the proposition, is what Deleuze defines, following the Stoic theory of the incorporeal, as the event of sense itself. As Deleuze remarks,

> The question is as follows: is there something, *aliquid*, which merges neither with the proposition or the terms of the proposition, nor with the object or with the states of affairs that the proposition denotes, neither with the "lived," or representation or with the mental activity of the person who expresses herself in the proposition, nor even with concepts or signified essences?
>
> (LS: 19)

Sense would be irreducible to all these determinations, signalling an extra-being that belongs neither to the order of words nor to the order of things. This dimension is called expression.

On the one hand, therefore, sense does not exist outside the proposition that expresses it. *The expressed does not exist outside its expression.* On the other hand, sense cannot be completely reduced to the content of the proposition either, since there is an "objectity" (*objectité*) that is very distinct and does not resemble its expression. As an example of this paradox, in *The Logic of Sense*, Deleuze employs the phrase "the tree greens". What this phrase expresses is the sense of the "greening" of the tree, the sense of colour that is the pure event of its "arbrification". But here, the attribute of the thing (the tree) is the verb, "to green" or, moreover, the event that is expressed by this verb. But this attribute is not to be confused with the state of physical things, nor with a quality or property of things. As Deleuze argues, "the attribute is not a being", but an extra-being that is expressed by the proposition and this sense of "greening" does not exist outside the proposition that expresses it (LS: 21). Here, we can refer again to the two planes that are brought together in the expression, but which continue to remain distinct from one another, as two faces that coexist without becoming identical in their sense. Yet, as Deleuze remarks, this does not produce a circular reasoning or tautology, but rather an idea of difference that subsists or insists in the proposition and on the surface of things. *"The sense is both the expressible or the expressed of the proposition, and the attribute of the state of affairs"* (LS: 22, original emphasis), but what this sense expresses is the event of sense itself as a frontier that runs between propositions and things, statements and bodies, as the extra-being that first expresses their relation, a relation that does not exist outside the genesis of the expression. However, although the event of sense (or the "sense-event") is bound up with language, one must not conclude from this that its nature is purely linguistic in such a manner that language would function as its cause. The frontier does not pass between language and the event on one side, and the world or state of things on the other. Rather, this frontier occurs on both sides at once and, at the same time, distinguishes itself from the sense that occurs or manifests itself within each order, as if sense each time distinguishes itself from the sense of the proposition and the sense that belongs to the world of objects, causing a paradoxical difference to appear (see Zourabichvili 2003: 36). According to Deleuze, this difference would be the *sense* of sense itself.

Free indirect discourse and the collective assemblages of enunciation

What is the difference between a code and a language? As Benveniste recounts this distinction (1971: 53), a bee has a code and is capable of encoding signs that designate a message, but does not have a language. This distinction rests upon the fact that the bee cannot communicate to a second or third bee what it has not seen or perceived with its senses, while human beings are capable of what Deleuze defines as "free indirect discourse" (ATP: 77–80). As Deleuze and Guattari argue in *A Thousand Plateaus*, "the 'first' language, or the first determination of language is not the trope or the metaphor, but *indirect discourse*" (ATP: 76–7). We might ask why so much emphasis is placed on this distinction and on the determination of language as free indirect discourse. But, free from what if not from the subject as the first determination of language? As Humpty Dumpty says, "when *I* use a word, it means what *I* want it to, no more and no less … the question is which is to be master … and that's it" (LS: 18). Therefore, we might understand that Deleuze and Guattari's entire theory of language is made to answer this provocation, to prove that the subject is not master of the word it chooses to express its beliefs or its desires. As they argue:

> It is for this reason that indirect discourse, *especially "free" indirect discourse*, is of exemplary value: there are no clear, distinctive contours; what comes first is not an insertion of variously individuated statements, or an interlocking of different subjects of enunciation, but a collective assemblage resulting in the determination of relative subjectivation proceedings, or assignations of individuality and their shifting distribution within discourse.
>
> (ATP: 80, original emphasis)

Deleuze and Guattari go to great lengths to deny the existence of "individual enunciation". They write, "There is no individual enunciation. There is not even a subject of enunciation" (ATP: 79). Consequently, language is primarily social and is made up by statements and order-words. One does not speak as much as one repeats, the emphasis here being placed on the redundancy of statements as well as on the effect of the relative identity (or stability) that corresponds to the subjectivity of speech-acts. Thus, the subject (or "I") is actually the effect of redundancy that belongs to language and that determines the intersubjectivity of communication; then the collective assemblage of enunciation refers to the redundant complex of acts and the statements that accomplish this redundancy. Thus, the notion of the collective assemblage of enunciation takes on a primary importance in Deleuze and Guattari's theory of language and speech-acts because it will account for the social character of all language. The primary meaning of language is social and the so-called individual speech is only the effect of a more primary repetition at the level of statements and performatives (or order-words) that define a given social field. As they write, "The only possible definition of language is the set of all order-words, implicit presuppositions, or speech acts current in a language at a given moment" (ATP: 79).

In order to account for the real definition of the collective assemblage, that is, the causality that determines the redundancy in statements and the institution or order-words in language, Deleuze and Guattari return again to the Stoic theory of expression as the effect of incorporeal transformations both at the level of the sense of statements and at the level of bodies. We recall that the incorporeal was defined as an extra-being that occurs between the sense of the statement and the plane occupied by real bodies. It is the particular nature of this extra-being that will determine the event of transformation in sense on both planes instantaneously. What transforms the accused into the convict is the incorporeal attribute that is the expressed of the judge's sentence; again, the expressed cannot be separated from its expression, and neither can the attribute be located in the body of the convict to account for this transformation in sense. The logic of expression addresses precisely these transformative events both at the level of sense and at the level of bodies, or rather, the event that occurs at once both at the surface and in the depth. Thus, assemblages of enunciation do not speak "of" things, but rather speak at the same time on the level of things and on the level of contents.

For example, as Deleuze writes, bodies have age and mature according to a biological process, but the statement "you are no longer a child" transforms the expressed sense of the body as well as the meaning accorded to age into a moral category of subjection. By comparison, the statement "you are only a girl" expresses a similar transformation of the body's sense that is inserted into a set of other order-words that determine the social meaning of gender. Likewise, we might say that the colour of the body may *appear* as an attribute, but the inscription of race in the statement "you are a black man" or "you are a white male" introduces an incorporeal transformation that changes and determines the body's specific social meaning. It is only on the basis of the statement's enunciation that "black" or "white" *expresses* a meaning, the latter not able to be determined simply from the attributes of whiteness or blackness that belong to bodies. In both statements what each attribute expresses, although differently, is an incorporeal transformation that is applied directly to bodies and is inserted into the subject's actions and passions. In short, it subjects the body to an "order".

A society is composed of these order-words that pin meaning to bodies and cause them to be individuated or to correspond to their social meanings. As Deleuze and Guattari write, "There is no significance independent of dominant significations, nor is there subjectification independent of an established order of subjection. Both depend on the nature and transmission of order-words in a given social field" (ATP: 79). Society can thus be defined by the order-words that define the intermingling of bodies, actions and passions; collective assemblages of enunciation in a given society "designate this instantaneous relation between statements and the incorporeal transformations or non-corporeal attributes they express" (ATP: 81). It is in these moments that language becomes truly expressive, that is, when it becomes capable of expressing real attributes and applying these determinations directly to bodies and to states of affairs that compose the social field at any given moment.

As Deleuze and Guattari argue, although the above transformation applies directly to bodies, it is still incorporeal or internal to enunciation. For example, anyone can say "I declare war!" However, it is only a variable belonging to the situation that can cause the social field composed of bodies to enter into a general conflagration, thereby transforming the whole of society. "There are variables of expression *that establish a relation between language and an outside, but precisely because they are immanent to language*" (ATP: 82, original emphasis). This is why the incorporeal is sometimes defined as an extra-being that cannot be accounted for simply from the state of things (or bodies) or a non-linguistic being that does not originate from the sense of the statement (or language), but which first causes these two planes of being to become related and to express the event of their immanent joining. Thus, what causes the order-word (such as "you are sentenced to death", "I declare war!" or "I love you!") is "an extra something" that "remains outside the scope of linguistic categories and definitions", as Bahktin (as Volosinov) also argued (Volosinov 1986: 110), but which expresses the condition of the sense of the statement and, at the same time, expresses a real determination of the states of bodies and intervenes directly into the actions and passions that define them (ATP: 82). Thus, what Deleuze and Guattari define as the order-word cannot be equated with language in all its functions (description, designation, nomination, etc.); rather, it is what "effectuate[s] its conditions of possibility" (or what they call the "super-linearity of expression") (ATP: 85). In other words, it is what causes language to become expressive of the sense that is immanent to the plane of bodies. Without this variable, language itself would remain purely virtual, lifeless, and would not become a nominative order that refers to real transformative events on the plane of being.

Abstract machines

Finally, what is the relation of the problem of expression to the process of abstraction, which is proper to the power of philosophy, and refers to the plane on which concepts appear and are organized into complex diagrams of statements and visibilities that "explicate" the plane of being? Deleuze and Guattari define the relation of content and expression in a diagram that has four different levels, arranged both vertically and horizontally. First, on a horizontal axis, an assemblage comprises two segments, of content and expression. On the level of content, it is a machinic assemblage of bodies and states of bodies in various degrees of interaction; on the level of expression, it is an assemblage of enunciation, of acts and statements, and incorporeal transformations directly attributed to bodies. Then, on a vertical axis, the assemblage has what Deleuze and Guattari call "territorial sides", which stabilize it, as well as *cutting edges of deterritorialization* which carry it away" (ATP: 88, original emphasis). We can see how this diagram works by illustrating how both content and expression, bodies and statements, are "taken up" by a movement of either territorialization (which give an assemblage form, stability or relative fixity), or deterritorialization, in which case the formal property of the assemblage becomes an edge that is given motion and cuts through both bodies and statements. Only exceptional states of language cause language to enter into variation, or continuous variation, which is expressive of a state of the body as becoming.

As Deleuze and Guattari argue, language depends on its abstract machines and not the other way around. In *A Thousand Plateaus*, their overt polemic with the science of modern linguistics is an argument against an abstract machine that determines the representation of language without taking into account the specific causality of what they have defined as "non-linguistic factors" that are still internal to enunciation itself. By divorcing language from the social side of meaning, or by describing its categories as neutral and quasi-universal frameworks or structures, the abstract machine invented by modern linguistics only achieves an intermediate level of abstraction, allowing it to consider linguistic factors by themselves and in isolation from their social sense. By contrast, Deleuze and Guattari seek to re-invest their description of language with a pragmatic and political sense in order to correct the representation provided by the former. "From this standpoint," they write, "the interpenetration of language and the social field and political problems lies at the deepest level of the abstract machine, not at the surface" (ATP: 91). Thus, the question proposed in the beginning, "What does it mean to express an idea?", returns from this perspective as a problem of pragmatics.

What are the conditions necessary for the idea to become transformative both at the level of sense and at the same time a transformative event "intervening" into the states of affairs and of bodies (defined in the broadest sense)? What is the causality of the incorporeal transformation of sense both on the level of acts and statements and bodies? In other words, what is the origin and specific causality of new order-words? Recalling our discussion of the philosophy of expression in Spinoza, one can see here that the emphasis is placed again on the "cause" of this linking between statements and bodies, which it is the object of a pragmatics to fully "explicate". However, this explication is not restricted to speech-acts alone, but also to certain signs that circulate historically and determine or punctuate a duration of events, or which introduce a transformation before and after. In one sense, this accounts for their interest in certain dates that have become expressive, or which indicate the transformation of a nominative reality as well as the arrival of a new social order and a new collective assemblage of enunciation. Take "the night of 4 July 1917, or 20 November 1923," for example. The first date, of course, refers to the Russian Revolution; the second to the inflationary crisis and the collapse of the reichsmark that precedes the rise of National Socialism in Germany. But the real question, for them, is "What incorporeal transformation is expressed by these dates, incorporeal yet attributed to bodies, inserted into them?" (ATP: 86–7).

To further illustrate this problem of expression, we might consider a more recent date: 11 September 2001. What is the incorporeal transformation expressed by this date? What is the sense it expresses that is directly attributed to bodies, inserted into them? We cannot conclude that its meaning is limited to the chain of events that took place on the morning of 11 September, but rather to a transformation that continues to inform an interpenetration of new order-words and the intermingling of acts, bodies and statements. "A terrorist crashes an airliner", "an Arab is stopped at the border and questioned", "a prisoner of war is tortured for information", "a president declares war on terror", "a heightened state of alert is announced"; what these statements now express is a variability with regard to the former meaning of the signs expressed, which Deleuze and Guattari call "cutting edges of deterritorialization" (ATP: 88). Here, the sign that expresses the act of war becomes deterritorializing with regard to the former conflict between nation-states, just as the legal and juridical codes that define a state of war are placed in flux and can no longer determine the specific situations of the intermingling of bodies outside their former definitions (for example, the captive from Afghanistan is not entitled to the protections of the Geneva Convention, or the President's declaration of war is not obliged to adhere to international treaties concerning the treatment of prisoners). In just a few of these instances, we might perceive that the date, 11 September, expresses an incorporeal transformation that is directly applied to bodies, or as Deleuze and Guattari write, "intervene or insert themselves into contents" (ATP: 87), that is, into the framework of order-words that define the body as a site of individuation. Hence, the body of the prisoner or of the suspected terrorist corresponds to a new set of meanings that subject it to a new set of rights and procedures, and the new order-words that define these specific sites of individuation will produce unforeseen and transformative effects within other bodies and social subjectivities as well. This transformation would be the object of what Deleuze and Guattari define as political pragmatics, which concerns itself "with the variation of the order-words and non-corporeal attributes linked to social bodies and effectuating immanent acts" (ATP: 83). According to this transformational research, a statement of the kind "The president declares war on terror" must be analysed "only as a function of its pragmatic implications, in other words, in relation to the implicit presuppositions, immanent acts, or incorporeal transformations it expresses and which introduce new configurations of bodies" (ATP: 83).

Deleuze often cites the phrase "There will be a naval battle tomorrow" in order to pose the question of the internal factor that would cause this sentence to express the sense of a date or an order-word (ATP: 86). Nevertheless, Deleuze also cautions, we are never presented with an interlinkage of order-words and the causality of specific contents (or events), but, instead, seem to constantly pass from order-words to the "silent order of things" (Foucault, cited in ATP: 87). Consequently, in *Foucault*, Deleuze shows that power relations designate "that other thing" that passes between discursive statements and non-discursive visibilities (FCLT: 83). In other words, "power" today assumes the name of that extra-being that runs between two different orders and yet expresses their relation, or that causes their relation to come into view as a problem of knowledge. However, if earlier in Spinoza power was unified by the idea of one substance expressing itself, today power can only be determined as an encompassing field of forces, or as a multiplicity of "nomadically distributed differential elements" (Canning 2001: 311–13). The question, here again, is how these elements combine to give rise to each other mutually, which is a question of their "virtuality", as well as of the immanence of power relations to the terms that express these relations at any given moment. As Deleuze writes,

> If power is not simply violence, this is not only because it passes in itself through categories that express the relation between two forces (inciting, inducing, producing a useful effect, etc.) but also

because, in relation to knowledge, it produces truth, in so far as it makes us see and speak. (FCLT: 83)

With this final statement, we can perceive the relation of the concept of power to the problem of expression, since it is identified as that extra-being that lies at the frontier of both propositions and bodies and that first produces a relation to truth: "It produces truth as a problem" (*ibid*.: 83).

Note

1. For a complete account of the Stoic theory of incorporeals, see "The Third Series of the Proposition" in Deleuze, *The Logic of Sense* (LS: 12–22). Deleuze's own source for this theory, however, is primarily drawn from Bréhier (1928).

THREE

Difference, repetition

Melissa McMahon

Introduction

Deleuze's notions of difference and repetition are developed within a project that has both a negative and a positive component. The negative or "critical" aspect is the argument that philosophy, in its very conception, has laboured under a "transcendental illusion", which systematically subordinates the concepts of difference and repetition to that of identity, mostly within what Deleuze calls the "regime of representation". The illusion is "transcendental" (the term comes from Kant) in so far as it is not simply an historical accident that can be corrected with the right information, but forms a necessary and inevitable part of the operation of thought, and thus requires a perpetual work of critique. Part of Deleuze's project consists in diagnosing this illusion, and showing how it falsifies the "true" movement of thought. In this movement, difference and repetition, in and for themselves, would be appreciated as the ultimate elements and agents of a thought "of the future": not a historical future, but the future as the essential object of a vital and liberated philosophy, implicit even in philosophies of the past.

The positive component of Deleuze's project can already be glimpsed here, if only by default. We find a more direct expression in Deleuze's essay on Bergson's concept of difference, where the stakes of a philosophy of difference are firmly tied to a definite vision of the true goal of philosophy: "If philosophy is to have a positive and direct relation with things, it is only to the extent that it claims to grasp the thing itself in what it is, in its difference from all that is not it" (DI: 32). It is the goal of *precision* that Deleuze assigns to philosophy here: that of grasping things in their utter "thisness", a motif that recurs throughout Deleuze's work on this subject. Thus, in *Difference and Repetition*, Deleuze asks whether the concept of difference, rather than being an intermediary notion, is not "the only moment of presence and precision" (DR: 28). And in the same book, when introducing his notion of repetition, he contends that repetition is a "necessary and justified conduct" only in relation to what is singular and irreplaceable (DR: 1): precisely the thing in its difference from all that is not it.

The goal of "grasping things in their being" is an ancient and even defining task of philosophy. Plato's dialogues are commonly understood as engaged in the task of identifying an essence corresponding to the question "What is *x*?" (the Good, the Just, the Beautiful, and so on), and Aristotle defined metaphysics as the discipline that addresses the problem of the essential attributes of things, or "that which is *qua* thing-that-is".[1] But in both cases this activity seems to turn on a conceptual notion of essence as simple identity. And, returning to the critical part of Deleuze's project, it is the concept of identity – and the concepts of difference and repetition that make them a function of identity – that on Deleuze's account is especially inadequate for accounting for the singular object of thought.

The regime of identity: re-presentation

The function of the concept of identity, as Deleuze presents it in *Difference and Repetition*, is essentially that of "managing" difference. Thus, for example, a concept subordinates differences by picking out qualities or things as "the same" or identical across (and despite) different cases; such are our general concepts of, for example, "redness" or "dogs". In another way, difference is made relative to the concept of identity as a mode of its "division" or "specification". The classical model here is the Aristotelian one of genera and species, where a concept-genus is divided according to the difference of contrasting attributes; the difference of being "rational", for example, divides the genus "animal" into "human" and "non-human" species. The explicit or implicit assumption is that whatever differences may *exist* outside the concept, these cannot be *thought* without being referred to a concept of identity, and, "ceasing to be thought, difference dissipates into non-being" (DR: 262). The problem here is not only that the notion of difference is understood only as a function of a concept of identity, and thus not "in itself"; it is also a certain *kind* of difference that is excluded on this model. The conceptual method defines an essence or *nature*, and thus differences that are "accidental" or "contingent" – those belonging to space and time, to what "happens" or the individual case – fall outside the general purview of the concept or the limits of its division.

There have been attempts in philosophy, to which Deleuze refers, to extend the limits of the concept so that, in principle at least, it includes even the most contingent details of an individual thing. Thus Leibniz maintained that all differences, including ones of space, time and accident, were included within the concept of a thing. This thesis – the "principle of sufficient reason" – meant that there was, in principle, only one thing that corresponded to a given concept, properly comprehended, and vice versa. The ultimate identity of concept and thing, however, is only able to be grasped by the infinite mind of God; we use it in order to assume the rationality of all existence for the purpose of scientific study, but our notions of things are always incomplete. The case of Leibniz nevertheless raises a series of important questions bearing on Deleuze's project, which also gives an initial indication of how the notion of repetition is intimately entwined with the problem of difference.

The first question is whether a concept that applies only to one thing, being wholly individual, is still in fact a concept. In other words, our concepts seem to exist precisely in order to designate a *set* of things with common characteristics, to abstract from the particular case in order to form general – that is, *repeatable* – statements. What is the use of a concept that only applies to "this"? How is such an individual thought *communicable* (again, *repeatable*), and is there thought without communicability? In what sense is a grasp of the thing *precise* if it cannot be formulated in recognizable concepts? These are issues raised in one of the most famous modern objections to the desire of philosophers to capture the singularity that pertains to a contingent moment in space and time: Hegel's critique of the alleged "richness" of "sense-certainty" at the beginning of his *Phenomenology of Spirit* (1977).[2] He takes the example of the immediate sense-data of our consciousness, which, as a concrete case of "thisness", appears to be the most authentic and real form of knowledge. When it comes to formulating this knowledge in concepts, however, we are reduced to the most empty and abstract terms: simply an "I", "this", "here", "now", which could apply to any experience and thus say precisely nothing of "this" one.

From Deleuze's perspective, the problem with the case of Leibniz and with Hegel's example is that the identity of the concept is still retained as the central reference point for thought, according to the model of thought as *representation*. The "regime of representation" is the system whereby the concept of identity – whether general or individual – forms the meeting point between a *nature of things* and a *nature of thought*. In challenging this conception, Deleuze is not only challenging the idea that (on the objective side) there is a "nature of things", expressed in an ordering of essential properties, and that (on the subjective side) the concept forms the basic unit of intelligibility; he is also contesting the notion of identity in its role as the ideal or intended relationship between thought and its object. That is, he challenges the notion that the aim of thought is to re-present, to make explicit or conceptualize what already exists in a non-conceptual form. Deleuze does not challenge this notion from a position of "fact": that "in fact" our representations do not coincide with a nature of things, being inadequate or unsuitable for such a purpose. Rather, he challenges the notion on the level of the very conception it presents of the goal and function of thought; from the standpoint of "right". For Deleuze, representation, as well as related ideals such as "reflection" or "communication", present a false "image" of the purpose and activity of philosophy.

It is not that the representation and identification of objects through concepts have no currency in the world. On the contrary, this defines the main sphere of everyday experience – what Deleuze calls the realm of "common sense" – where we recognize and order objects in relation to ourselves according to the requirements of habit. But for this very reason Deleuze finds this "commonsensical" notion inadequate as an image of *thought*, which would rather imply a disruption or exception to the regular course of affairs. In the same way, on the level of society as a whole, philosophy implies a *challenge* to the established order of things, which in any case has no need of philosophy in order to function: "if philosophy refers to a common sense as its implicit assumption, what need has common sense of philosophy, given that it shows, alas, every day that it is capable of forming one of its own?" (DR: 134–5, translation modified). Deleuze is not only making a political argument here. He is also making the claim that if representation works within a given order, or within a given consciousness, as its habitual mode of operating, it does not account for how that order comes about, nor for how it evolves. When common sense and the system of representation posit an underlying order of things and a natural direction of thought whose work is simply to make this implicit arrangement explicit, it simply presupposes *itself*, in another form, as its own condition of possibility, and gives no account of its actual process:

> if it is a question of rediscovering at the end what was there in the beginning, if it is a question of recognising, of bringing to light or into the conceptual or the explicit, what was simply known

implicitly without concepts . . . the fact remains that all this is still too simple, and that this circle is truly not tortuous enough. The circle image would reveal instead that philosophy is powerless truly to begin, or indeed authentically to repeat.   (DR: 129)

For Deleuze, thought occurs at the "edges" of a given system as the principle of its initiation and revolution: thought occurs not "naturally", but when we are *forced to think*. We could also say, putting it another way, that whereas the image of thought as re-presentation assigns a passive or speculative role to the thinker as *spectator*, for Deleuze the thinker is an *actor*, with all that this implies of being at the juncture of an *event* and being engaged in a *drama*.

The order of the Idea: dramatization

"Dramatization" is, in fact, the name that Deleuze gives to the model of thought that he presents as an alternative to the system of representation through the concept. Rather than ask the question "What . . .?" in order to grasp the essence of a thing, we should rather ask the questions: "Who . . .?", "How . . .?", "When . . .?" and "Where . . .?"[3] In philosophy, such questions tend to be denigrated as indicating only the empirical examples or circumstantial manifestations of an essence, rather than "the thing itself", and thus miss the point of the philosophical enterprise. For Deleuze, however, this objection again maintains the concept of identity as the sole principle of essential unity, which places the "one-ness" of the conceptual essence on one side, and its multiple manifestations on the other. In contrast, Deleuze posits his notion of the *Idea* or *problem* as the fundamental element of thought that integrates these coordinates and gives them a scope beyond the empirical in its ordinary sense. Deleuze's notion of the Idea owes something to Plato, whose dialogues, Deleuze argues, function more effectively if we understand them as "dramatizations" of a central problem rather than simply an incidental detour to answering the question "What is . . .?". More narrowly, the distinction that Deleuze draws between the concept and the Idea can be traced to Kant. Kant distinguishes concepts, which combine with sensible experience to form the basic elements of our *knowledge* and the general unity of our objective representations, and Ideas, which form a horizon of unity and principle for our *actions*, and which cannot be *known*, but only *thought*. While concepts define the domain of possible experience, the proper tendency of Ideas is to exceed the bounds of possible experience, hence their special role in Kant's philosophy as an index of our freedom. The distinction between *knowledge* and *thought* is one carried by Deleuze into his own development of the opposition between concept and Idea. In *Difference and Repetition*, for example, Deleuze maintains that *learning*, rather than knowledge, is the ultimate and self-sufficient goal of thought, pertaining not to a preparatory stage in a process that would be fulfilled by knowledge, but to a different order altogether (DR: 164).

Deleuze builds on Kant's description of the Idea as "problematic" (because unknowable) in order to develop his thesis of the Idea as itself a "problem" (DR: 168–70). We are awakened to the problem by an encounter with a "problematic object" or event, which exceeds our representative capacities, but for the same reason provokes the exercise of all our powers, creating a relay between sense, memory, imagination and thought. This object or "sign", on the one hand, serves as the index of a virtual horizon for thought: "objective" (in the sense of "coming from outside") but "indeterminate". On the other hand, it presents a set of singularities that form the coordinates or "constructive template" for an actual case of resolution.[4] What Deleuze here calls the "singularities" of a problem are precisely those coordinates suggested by the questions "Who ...?", "How ...?", "Where ...?" and "When ...?". These questions, however, now form the conditions of actuality of a problem rather than the sensible manifestation of a concept. Thus Deleuze's ultimate response to Hegel's argument against the "richness" of immediacy is that the significance of the singular – "this", "here", "now" – is only grasped within the context of a problem, a "drama" of thought that gives it sense, in the absence of which it is effectively impoverished.

> Hegel substitutes the abstract relation of the particular to the concept in general for the true relation of the singular and the universal in the Idea. He thus remains in the reflected element of 'representation', within simple generality. He represents concepts, instead of dramatizing Ideas: he creates a false theatre, a false drama, a false movement. (DR: 10)

What it means for the singular to be "thought" here is not to be represented or comprehended through a concept, but to be aligned along the trajectory of an action or event.[5] There is no identity or resemblance that underlies the passage from the unthought to the thought (any more than a solution resembles its problem): thought is both a response to the absolutely new and itself creates something new.

It is this *difference made by* thought as a response to – *repetition of* – a unique or singular event that is at the core of Deleuze's understanding of these notions. Deleuze presents this activity of thought as the *determination of the indeterminate*. The "object" or "horizon" of thought is indeterminate in two senses. In the first place, the horizon of thought is indeterminate "by default", because thought does not presuppose any determined or determining "nature of things" as its foundation. In the second place, it is the positive apparition of indeterminacy in the world, in the form of the problematic object or sign, that provokes thought into action. This dual indeterminacy contrasts with the system of representation, which is based on the concept serving as a meeting point or "happy medium" between a pre-determined thought and being. For Deleuze, however, thought marks a disjunction and a struggle between itself and *what* is thought. Thought emerges in the confrontation with its "outside", which grips and spurs on its response, but there is precisely no common measure or mediation between the two. Confronted with this absolute difference – what Deleuze calls the "transcendental Difference between the Determination as such and what it determines" (DR: 86) – thought *cannot but make* a difference. Thought is thus always shadowed by the unthinkable as both its *raison d'être* and its impossibility, its grounds (*fond*) and its "ungrounding" (*éffondement*). This unthinkable difference, that is, the non-identity of the unthought and thought, is in effect the highest object of thought for Deleuze:

> How could thought avoid going that far, how could it avoid thinking that which is most opposed to thought? With the identical, we think with all our force, but without producing the least thought: with the different, by contrast, do we not have the highest thought, but also that which cannot be thought? (DR: 266)

We mentioned above the tendency of the Idea in Kant to always "go beyond" limits, and in Deleuze this is the maintenance or "insistence" of the Idea-problem beyond any actual case of resolution. This maintenance of indeterminacy on the "objective" side of thought is matched, on the "subjective" side, by the fact that the act of determination is subject to certain conditions, and in particular *time* as thought's "form of determinability". Just as, in the system of representation, the concept of identity served as the pivot for a mediation between the subject and object of thought, the "pure and empty" form of time serves here as the place in which the conditions of thought and the "excess" of the Idea meet, in their *disparity*, however, rather than their identity.

Deleuze's ideas here are complex, and are again based on a "dramatic" or even "tragic" conception of thought whereby the two "halves" of an action – its conditions and its effects – are unable to be reconciled: they do not "match up" or "rhyme", but reveal a "sublime" force that trans-forms and goes beyond the actor (DR: 87). The pure and empty form of time is the marker of the *future* in the event of thought, or what Deleuze calls, after Nietzsche, the "untimely". Despite Deleuze's dramatic imagery, however, events in thought are not to be gauged according to the standard historical criteria of scale and significance. Events belong equally to a "micro" regime of "imperceptible" happenings (to use the later language of Deleuze and Guattari): "Underneath the large noisy events lie the small events of silence, just as under the natural light there are the little glimmers of the Idea" (DR: 163).

Repetition in difference: the community and communication of thought

Deleuze's model of thought rejects all notion of a common ground – in the form of a general concept, a shared reality and even between thought and its object – that would normally form the conditions of thought and its communicability. In one sense, this means thought is a necessarily solitary activity; in *Difference and Repetition*, Deleuze presents the voice of thought as the emergence of "isolated and passionate cries" (DR: 130), and later says, "When you work, you are necessarily in absolute solitude" (D: 6). On the other hand, Deleuze also promotes the collec-tive aspects of thought in his work – which he put into practice in his coauthored books with Guattari – and throughout his philosophy he emphasizes the importance of the process of teaching and learning, some of which is indicated above and is reaffirmed in *What Is Philosophy?*, where he assigns philosophy the task of a *"pedagogy* of the concept" (WIP: 12).[6] It is thus not a romantic or esoteric model of thought that Deleuze produces, which would disregard the problem of its transmis-sibility or restrict its scope. There is nothing "exclusive" about the solitary nature of thought for Deleuze; as he himself adds, this solitude is "extremely crowded", populated as it is by multiple "encounters", a merging of "movements, ideas, events, entities" (D: 6, translation modified).

In fact, the conditions of thought as Deleuze presents them already contain the principle of its perpetuation, in the sense that they comprise elements that necessarily go beyond the individual thought. In affirm-ing this, we dedicate our thought to an ideal of its repetition, which, in the absence of an underlying or ideal of identity, can only be its differ-entiation. The relationship of one thinker to another, of one thought to another, as Deleuze presents it, reproduces the configuration involved in the initial event of thought. Indeed, "reproduces" is redundant here, as there is nothing "secondary" about a philosophy, a person or a book serving as the "problematic object" or event, a complex set of singularities that sets off a chain of thought. Thought is transmitted through a form of relay where the injunction is to repeat what cannot be represented, and (thus) repeat as different. There is a tangential relationship between thoughts, where the component of one problem becomes a component of a new, and necessarily different, problem. Each instance is animated by the "spirit" of the first, from a wholly different position, and at the same time refers to a future from which another will arise. It is this "disjointed" temporality, which is neither eternal nor historical, that expresses the aforementioned sense of the "untimely", following Nietzsche's imperative to "act in an untimely manner, thus against the time, and in this way on the time, in favour (I hope) of a time to come" (quoted in NP: 107, translation modified).

This form of communication (or "transmission" if we want to avoid the connotations of "commonality" in the former term) is what Deleuze and Guattari later expressed as "rhizomatic". This is opposed to the "arboreal" (tree-like) form, where parts are related to each other only through their relationship to a common root, and whose importance is measured according to their distance from the root. In contrast, the rhizome spreads horizontally through leaps where each germination marks a new root system and one cannot assign an origin or end-point. The rhizome is a term taken from botany (grass is an example of a rhizome), but is no less a philosophical concept in Deleuze and Guattari's hands than the "tree-system". For this latter concept has a long pedigree in the history of philosophy, whether explicitly in Aristotle's model of conceptual division (represented in "Porphyry's Tree"), or implicitly in any philosophy that assigns a central principle (even "being" itself) in order to organize around it a series of secondary orders, tertiary orders and so on. As with most of Deleuze's notions, there is a political resonance here as well as a philosophical one, pertaining to the institutional hierarchy of philosophy. In so far as each act of thought is a new beginning, emerging from the set of contingencies that make up our problem, we think *with* the thinkers of the past (not "after" or "like"), as our contemporaries and companions, and look ahead as they did.

Conclusion

In his essay on difference in Bergson, Deleuze states that the problem of difference is both "methodological and ontological" (DI: 32): we cannot separate the being of difference from the mode of its pursuit and development – its differentiation. Thus difference is defined as both the "particularity that is" and an "indetermination, newness which creates itself" (DI: 48), and this double aspect of difference is what we understand as its repetition. It is for this reason that the question of precision in philosophy does not consist in the isolation of a conceptual essence, but incorporates the coordinates of a problematic apparatus. In response to the question "What is ...?", we must "determine its moment, an occasion and circumstances, its landscapes and personae, its conditions and unknowns" (WIP: 2). These factors, unique in any given case, are unlimited in scope, as they are the conditions of a creative thought animated by a will to transform, whose product goes beyond the thinker.

The critique of the Western philosophical *logos* is a project shared by many twentieth-century European philosophers. But Deleuze's determination to produce a constructive model of thought in the face of declarations of philosophy's "end" – what he himself called his "naiveté" (N: 89) – is perhaps what most distinguishes him among his contemporaries and what constitutes his most original contribution to philosophy. While Deleuze recognized the existence of threats to thought in his time, from both inside and out, there is an insistent tone of optimism in his work, in virtue of his commitment to the "micro" realm of the contingent as the site of production and revolution; that "most difficult thing ... to make chance an object of *affirmation*" (DR: 198).

Notes

1. See Deleuze's analysis of Plato (NP: 75–6; DR: 188) and Aristotle's *Metaphysics* (1998: Book G, Ch. 1, p. 1).
2. G. W. F. Hegel, *Phenomenology of Spirit* (1977: §A, I. "Sense-certainty: or the 'this' and 'meaning'").
3. Deleuze introduces this notion of a "method of dramatization" in his book on Nietzsche (NP: 75–9), and it forms the topic of his paper "Method of Dramatization" (DI: 94–116). The series of questions Deleuze proposes resembles the Latin hexameter once used as a tool for instructing students of criminology: *quis, quid, ubi, quibus auxiliis, cur, quomodo, quando* (who, what, where, by what means, why, how, when). They summarized what were called in rhetoric "the circumstances": the person, the fact, the place, the means, the motives, the manner and the time. In the Preface to *Difference and Repetition*, Deleuze compares works of philosophy to "a very particular species of detective novel", thus emphasizing the way thought forms a response to an indeterminate "happening", and develops its concepts in order to intervene and "resolve local situations" (DR: xx).
4. In this context, Deleuze speaks of the *differentiation/differenciation* of the Idea-problem. The *differentiation* of the Idea-problem refers to the complex of

singularities it presents in its virtual or potential state. The *differenciation* of the Idea-problem is its dramatization or resolution in an actual state of affairs (see DR: 206–10).

5. There is a mathematical sense to the "singular" here, as also to the terms "integration" and "differential" used by Deleuze, from the language of the calculus, invented by the philosopher Leibniz (at the same time as Newton).

6. What Deleuze calls a "concept" here is not the concept of identity in representation but more a reformulation of his previous notion of the Idea.

FOUR

Desire

Eugene W. Holland

The aim of this essay is not to explain what desire means, but to show how the concept gets constructed and how it works. Creating concepts is the principal task of philosophy, and part of what this entails is extracting elements or dynamics from the works of other philosophers and combining them in new and productive ways. Perhaps surprisingly, but in fact like much in his work, Deleuze's concept of desire has its source in Kantian philosophy. But its construction draws on elements from Bataille, Marx, Nietzsche, Spinoza and, of course, Freud and Lacan. Moreover, Deleuze historicizes the concept of desire in a manner that is crucial to the way it works.

Kant defines desire as "the faculty which by means of its representations is the cause of the actuality of the objects of those representations" (1911: 16). Whereas pure reason is concerned with how we can know objects, practical reason, Kant says in the second critique, "is concerned not with objects in order to know them, but with its own capacity to make them real" (2002: 14). At first glance, this is a bizarre claim for Kant to advance. How could practical reason alone possibly involve turning mental representations into reality? In what he calls its "pathological" mode, he acknowledges that it really can't; all it can do is produce a hallucinatory or delirious impression of reality. But transmuted into a higher form, which Kant calls the will, desire can intervene in reality; and in fact, it is the concept of will that enables Kant to posit the rational individual as a free causal agent in the real world. Desire gets transformed into "a will which is a causal agent so far as reason contains its determining ground" (Kant 2002: 114). In order to convert desire into a will that has rational causal agency in the real world, however,

Kant must invoke three transcendent Ideas (God, the Soul, and the World), and this is where Deleuze parts company with Kant.

How does Deleuze maintain a causal relation between desire and reality without ending up with either unreal, pathological delirium or a reality guaranteed only by transcendent ideas? Part of a solution is derived from Spinoza and Nietzsche. Spinoza's concept of *conatus* entails a will that strives to realize itself immanently rather that in obedience to transcendent law. Meanwhile, Nietzsche's concept of will to power effectively erases the Kantian distinction between desire and will, freeing desire as incarnated in the artist or noble superman to become a creative legislator of reality, rather than a legislator subject to a transcendent reality principle (first critique) and an equally transcendent moral law (second critique). Another part of a solution is derived from Marx: his concept of species-being highlights the ability of human beings to picture objects in the mind before producing them in reality, rather than producing them instinctually (as bees and spiders do). Drawing on Kant, Marx and Nietzsche, then, Deleuze defines desire simply as the production of reality: "desire produces, [and] its product is real" (AO: 26). And where Kant subjected the desire–reality relation to a categorical and hierarchical distinction between the pathological–delusional and the moral–rational, Deleuze invents a concept of desire that includes both the creative and the productive, before any socially defined "reality principle" supervenes to draw the distinction between them. Nature, as Marx put it, is first and foremost the "inorganic body" of humankind (1975: 328). But the function of social representation is precisely to separate desire from reality (to separate a body from what it can do, as Spinoza characterizes the effect of superstition), to retrospectively inject so-called "needs" and scarcity and lack into a desire–reality relation that is immediate and full on the unconscious, species-being level. The result is that individuals and groups come to believe consciously that they lack or need something: a something that had in fact been produced by desire itself, but that subsequently gets taken from them by social order. As Deleuze and Guattari explain in *Anti-Oedipus*, "Marx notes [that] what exists in fact is not lack but passion, as a 'natural and sensuous object.' Desire is not bolstered by needs, but rather the contrary; needs are derived from desire: they are counterproducts within the real that desire produces" (AO: 27). As Georges Bataille had also argued in *The Accursed Share* (1988), need and utility get introduced into an economy that is itself characterized by super-abundance. For Deleuze, then, desire produces reality, even though social representation and belief deprive us of much of that reality *ex post facto*.

The relation between desire and social order is not, however, unchanging. In *Anti-Oedipus*, Deleuze and Guattari introduce a conceptual distinction between desiring-production and social production in order to take the historical variability of this relation into account. They are two sides of the same coin. Arguing once again with Kant, they insist that:

> there is no such thing as the social production of reality on the one hand, and a desiring-production that is mere fantasy on the other … The truth of the matter is that *social production is purely and simply desiring-production itself under determinate conditions*.
>
> (AO: 29, original emphasis)

But even though they are identical in nature, they always operate under different regimes. And it is under capitalism that this identity in nature but difference of regime becomes the most pronounced and visible.

Under capitalism, desiring-production and social production get categorized as libido and labour-power respectively. This categorization is both true and false: it is on the order of an objective illusion. Marx had already explained that labour-power appears for the first time under capitalism as the abstract subjective essence of wealth, as the activity of production in general, because capital strips labour of any previous determinations in putting it to work on privately owned means of production, which impose their own determination on it; as a commodity, labour-power takes the form of an abstract quantitative exchange-value, before being endowed with qualitative use-value and particular determinations (such as skills, discipline and so on). Wealth is henceforth understood not in terms of qualities of objects produced, but in terms of quantities of labour-power invested in them. Deleuze and Guattari argue that the exact same thing is true of the concept of libido in Freud: "His greatness lies in having determined the essence or nature of desire, no longer in relation to objects, aims, or even sources (territories), but as an abstract subjective essence – libido or sexuality [in general]" (AO: 270). And just as labour-power as the "abstract subjective essence" of economic value appears as the result of the privatization of production, libido as the abstract subjective essence of erotic value appears as the result of the privatization of reproduction: the result of the isolation of reproduction from society at large in the institution of the "private sphere" of the nuclear family. This is one of the reasons why Deleuze and Guattari argue that psychoanalysis is a strictly capitalist institution: capital privatizes reproduction in the private sphere at the same time that it privatizes ownership of the means of production in the economic sphere. And each sphere develops a corresponding discourse or mode of representation: psychoanalysis, political economy. So the two spheres don't just *appear* separate; under capitalism, they *are* in fact separate. The difference of regime between desiring-production and social production is so great because of the privatization and segregation of production and reproduction into two separate spheres.

Even though capitalism segregates reproduction from social life, it nevertheless delegates to the nuclear family the task of forming subjectivity in its own image. Because of its isolation from society at large, the nuclear family traps desire in a very restricted system of representation, which psychoanalysis will then reproduce in its theory of the Oedipus complex. For children growing up within the confines of the nuclear family, the objects closest to them – other family members – are precisely the ones that the incest taboo forbids them to desire. Social forms where relations of reproduction are imbricated with relations of production and with social relations in general don't trap desire in this kind of straitjacket. The nuclear family thus appears as a perfect training ground for asceticism, by denying desire the objects nearest and dearest to it. So when Deleuze and Guattari echo Spinoza and Reich in asking how it is that people can desire their own repression, the answer is, for capitalism anyway, that the capitalist mode of reproduction breeds asceticism into its subjects literally from birth.

The determinate conditions under which capitalist social production shapes desiring-production also help explain why desire becomes so abstract under capitalism. Not only is it denied its closest objects, but these objects no longer represent concrete social functions, but merely abtract familial ones. Social life outside the family is rife with variegated social roles, which the nuclear family reduces to just three: child, mother and father; subject of desire, object of desire and castrating mediator of desire. This structure of Oedipal desiring-production, it turns out, mirrors term for term the structure of capitalist social production: the workers as subject of labour, the commodities they produce as the object of labour and capital itself as the prohibitive mediation between the one and the other. The nuclear family thus programs its members to submit, as good docile subjects, to prohibitive authority – the father, the boss, capital in general – and to relinquish until later, as good ascetic subjects, their access to the objects of desire and to what Marx calls their "objective being" – the mother, the goods they produce, the natural environment as a whole. No specific social roles or functions need be passed from one generation to the next; indeed, the concrete requirements of social production change too fast for the family to play much of a role in job-training, just as fashion and lifestyle fads change too fast for parents to play an adequate role in consumer training. What the Oedipal nuclear family produces is quite abstract, but perfectly sufficient as such: obedient ascetic subjects programmed to accept the mediation of capital between their productive life-activity and their own enjoyment of it, who will work for an internalized prohibitive authority, no matter what the specific job or field, and defer gratification until the day they die. The Oedipus complex of the nuclear family thus appears as though it had been "fabricated to meet the requirements of ... [the capitalist] social formation" (AO: 101), even though – or perhaps precisely because – those requirements are purely abstract.

And so it is the very isolation of both production and reproduction from the nexus of social relations that makes labour-power and libido so radically indeterminate and abstract, revealing their identity in nature as productive activity in general, before being assigned distinct objects, spheres and modes of representation. Deleuze and Guattari thus liken Freud's position in the history of theories of desire with the position of Adam Smith and David Ricardo in the history of theories of labour: each discovered the indeterminacy of productive activity, but then re-alienated that activity onto a private territory and mode of representation – the nuclear family and capital. Marx transformed bourgeois political economy into a revolutionary materialism by refusing the subordination of labour to determination by capital; in the same way, Deleuze and Guattari transform bourgeois psychoanalysis into a revolutionary materialism by refusing the subordination of libido to determination by the nuclear family and the Oedipus complex. Just as the aim of universal history in Marx is to free labour-power from the last and most abstract of its external determinations, its alienation by capital, the aim of universal history for Deleuze and Guattari is to free libido from the last and most abstract of its external determinations, its alienation by the Oedipus complex. And for Deleuze and Guattari, these are one and the same project, although it gets represented in two separate spheres due to the dual privatizing operations of capital, segregating production and reproduction.

The radical indeterminacy of desire, then, is the key to the concept of universal history propounded by Deleuze and Guattari in *Anti-Oedipus*. Schizophrenia is the name they assign to desiring-production in its absolutely indeterminate, free state, even though desiring-production always takes place under determinate conditions where social order constrains desire by prescribing certain objects and aims, and proscribing many others. These prescriptions and proscriptions are carried out by processes of coding and overcoding that assign qualitative value (desirable/undesirable) to various objects and behaviours. Capitalism, however, is unlike previous social forms in that its basic institution – the market – is inimical to coding of any kind. The abstract calculus of the "cash nexus" instead decodes by assigning only quantitative (cash) value to objects and behaviours. Capitalism thus fosters schizophrenia as the free form of desire not only by segregating production and reproduction from society at large, but also by subjecting social life itself to the abstract quantification of the market, thereby freeing desiring-production from social coding. Of course, capitalist society also must and does recode as best it can, so as to prevent capitalist social life from becoming completely meaningless (decoded); the nuclear family, state schooling, job training and consumer training (advertising) all serve this purpose. Indeed, the struggle between decoding and recoding can be considered the central drama of capitalism, according to Deleuze and Guattari, even though they suggest that the basic historical tendency of capitalism is to decode and free desiring-production from social order. It is on the side of decoding, in other words, that capitalism puts the realization of schizophrenia as the free form of desire on the agenda of universal history.

The drama between decoding and recoding takes place on what Deleuze and Guattari call (borrowing from Antonin Artaud) the Body without Organs (BwO). As we have said, desiring-production is by nature indeterminate, but at the same time subject to determination by social institutions and representations, which impose order, objects and aims on it. The BwO stages the struggle of desire to escape determination – whether instinctual, habitual or social; it thus designates the human potential for freedom. True, the BwO is the locus of coding, where social representations capture desire and assign it determinate aims and goals; but it is also the locus of decoding, where desire exceeds or subverts any and all socially imposed representations. Whereas previous social forms used the BwO to impose codes and overcodes on desire, capitalism tends instead to unleash free-form desire on the BwO and thus foster widespread schizophrenia: hence the subtitle of *Anti-Oedipus*: *Capitalism and Schizophrenia*. The BwO appears as such and in its potential for freedom, Deleuze and Guattari therefore insist, only with capitalism toward the end of universal history, opening the prospect of a post-capitalist market finally subordinating social production to desiring-production, rather than the other way around. Indeed, the relation between desiring-production and social production is crucial to the way the concept of desire works here: for *desiring-production provides immanent criteria by which to judge the adequacy or inadequacy of various historical forms of social production*.

Here again we must return to Kant, although to a Kant corrected, as it were, by Marx and Artaud. For here, too, Deleuze and Guattari take

Kant's critique of metaphysics as a starting-point for their own critique of capitalist society and of the role of psychoanalysis within it. Speaking in the name of reason, Kant had asserted that the conscious mind utilizes a set of processes (called syntheses) to arrive at knowledge, and insisted that whatever did not conform to those processes would be condemned as metaphysical. Of crucial importance to Kant (and thence to Deleuze) was the idea that, since these processes were constitutive of conscious thought, they provided immanent criteria for judging something to be either knowledge or metaphysics, depending on whether it was based on legitimate or illegitimate use of the syntheses. In a similar way, but speaking not in the name of reason but in the name of desire and especially of schizophrenic desire, Deleuze and Guattari insist that the unconscious, too, operates according to a set of constitutive syntheses in order to process or constitute experience in such a way as to guarantee the free play of desire; and they insist that psychoanalysis must either be shown to conform to these processes or else be condemned as metaphysical.

Moreover, in as much as psychoanalysis is a strictly capitalist institution, its system of representation is understood as merely an expression and reinforcement of the capitalist social order. Hence, the Oedipus complex expresses, first, the privatization of reproduction in the nuclear family in a decoded social order and, secondly, the delegation to the family of certain recoding functions. These functions are necessary to, but excluded from, the wider social field by the privatization of production and the rampant decoding of social relations by the market. Deleuze and Guattari will therefore call not just for psychoanalysis, but even more so for the capitalist social relations of which it is an expression to conform to the syntheses of the unconscious. Their concept of desiring-production thus serves as a revolutionary fulcrum for social critique as well as for the critique and transformation of psychoanalysis into what Deleuze and Guattari call schizoanalysis. Society itself must conform to the "logic" of the syntheses of the unconscious, or else be condemned as repressive. Universal history, in fact, depends on the prospect that legitimate uses of the unconscious syntheses will prevail over illegitimate uses on the BwO, that schizophrenic desiring-production will determine the conditions of social production, instead of being determined by them.

This version of universal history, it must be said, gets subjected to considerable irony in the second volume of the *Capitalism and Schizophrenia* project, *A Thousand Plateaus*. Here, the apparently random and certainly achronological dating of the plateaus appears to poke fun at the one-dimensional linearity of the universal history propounded in the first volume. By this time, no doubt, the problem confronting Deleuze and Guattari had changed. Perhaps "universal history" had already accomplished its work, but in any case the new problems were "geographical" rather than historical in conception; "globalization" and lateral differences are henceforth what matter, rather than linear "progress" surmounting "underdevelopment". Not that the problem of underdevelopment has actually been solved, but it now gets conceptualized in a different way, as actively produced contemporaneously by advanced capitalism, rather than as some kind of temporal "holdover from the past". In brief, for what Deleuze and Guattari in their last collaboration (*What is Philosophy?*) call "geophilosophy", universality pertains to the capitalist world market as a multiple network of simultaneous (although uneven) relations rather than to capitalist history as a single line of temporal development. The concept of the BwO, however, continues to serve as a focal point for Deleuze and Guattari's reflections on desire, and in fact occupies an entire plateau in *A Thousand Plateaus* ("Plateau 6: November 28, 1847: How do you make yourself a Body without Organs?").

In the context of the later collaborations (*A Thousand Plateaus* and *What is Philosophy?*), the BwO – now called a "plane of consistency" – appears as one plane among several, including the plane of immanence of philosophy, the plane of reference of science, the plane of composition of painting, and so on. Each plane is characterized by a specific type of activity (thought takes place on the plane of immanence, knowledge on the plane of reference, affects and percepts on the plane of composition), and desire is what takes place on the BwO: "The BwO is desire; it is that which one desires and by which one desires" (ATP: 165). In *A Thousand Plateaus*, the BwO becomes a matter of technique rather than of diagnosis or therapy, as the very title of the plateau suggests. And at the same time, the historical optimism of *Anti-Oedipus* gives way to considerable caution about the relation of desire to the BwO in *A Thousand Plateaus*. Earlier, the BwO staged the struggle between decoding and recoding, between schizophrenia and paranoia (the ascription of fixed meaning under conditions – notably capitalist decoding – where meaning no longer applies). Now the battle is couched in terms of the plane of consistency versus stratification on the plane of organ-ization, and the dangers confronting desire are more numerous. Desire can over-proliferate like a cancer, or it can break loose and plunge into the void. Utmost care is required for desire to occupy the BwO freely, without over-coagulating and becoming fixed, on one hand, and without becoming wildly chaotic, on the other. Under pressure from physiologically based instinct and socially induced habit, the BwO can succumb to organ-ization: instincts and habits bind perception and action to the recognition and accomplishment of pre-assigned objects and tasks in order to satisfy "needs" and "duties" as defined by social order. But desire is inimical to any and all organ-ization of this kind: it seeks always to disorganize and free itself from instincts and habits so as to experiment with new modes of perception and action, new modes of existence.

That is why Deleuze and Guattari insist, somewhat surprisingly, that desire is opposed as much to gratification as it is to repression. Fixation on some poor-substitute symptom arising from repression is little better or worse from this perspective than fixation on "true" objects of gratification: both shut down desire (whether by blockage or evacuation), instead of giving desire free reign to fully invest the BwO and explore its plane of consistency. The examples Deleuze and Guattari propose of such desire on the BwO – masochism, courtly love, and so on – show that, unlike pleasure and need, the aim of desire is to maintain and pursue investment of the BwO indefinitely. Comparison with Lacan's concept of the "metonymy of desire" is instructive here (although the comparison actually gets made in *Anti-Oedipus*). For Deleuze and Guattari, the loss of the "object a" is not a tragedy precipitating human beings into a vain attempt to restore a former fullness of being; it is rather joyful deliverance from fixation on any "naturally", socially or neurotically imposed object or activity. It is this deliverance that enables desire instead to remain invested in the BwO and explore a constantly renewed open set of trajectories upon it. So the play of desire on the BwO, as long as it doesn't fixate on codes or spin off in the void, operates as a *difference-engine*, continually forming, deforming and reforming modes of passionate attachment to reality.

As such, it takes its place alongside a number of other difference-engines highlighted by Deleuze and Guattari, most notably capitalism, which itself promotes differentiation by subordinating qualitative codes to the quantitative calculus of the cash nexus, as we have seen. Capitalism is not the only difference-engine, however: evolution is another, and expression is yet another. In all these cases, there exists (what can loosely be called) a "dialectic" of differentiation and capture. In the capitalist economy, the market differentiates both production (through the division of labour) and consumption (through consumerism), from which surplus-value is captured. In the case of life, random genetic mutation multiplies differences, from which natural selection then consolidates (or "contracts") organs and species. In the case of expression, what Peirce calls "infinite semiosis" generates differential relations among signifiers and signifieds, which are then consolidated or captured in the sign-function by sedimented habit, codification, and representation. In all three arenas, desire on the BwO favours the moment of differentiation over the moment of contraction: as an expression of life, free-form desire dis-organizes the organ-ization of the organism; in alliance with market decoding, schizophrenic desire frees productive activity from external determination; in the domain of expression, desire decodes representation and puts the process of semiosis into continual variation.

Deleuze constructs a concept of desire, then, so as to combine the notions of free will operating immanently, will to power operating creatively, and species-being operating productively in the real world.

PART II

Encounters

FIVE

Sense, series

Judith L. Poxon and Charles J. Stivale

At the end of the 1960s, Gilles Deleuze found himself in at once troubled and exhilarating circumstances. The trouble came from an illness to which he had fallen victim, tuberculosis, the effects of which he would suffer for the rest of his life. However, at the same time, in 1968–69, he had completed the work required within the French university system at the time to defend his dissertation, consisting of a "secondary thesis", his 1968 book on Spinoza translated as *Expressionism in Philosophy: Spinoza*, and his "principal thesis", also published in 1968, *Difference and Repetition*.[1] At the same time, however, Deleuze was developing yet another study, *The Logic of Sense* (1969), related to these contemporary texts in its continued examination of the concepts of expression, affect, difference and repetition. Yet, this study moved beyond these important works through Deleuze's careful probing and gradual extension of the key term in the title, sense, and through his articulation of an alternative logic by which this key term might be understood, through a play of series. In this essay, we explore this conceptual extension and articulation.

We can begin to approach Deleuze's concept of sense by contrasting it with the "common sense" and "good sense" of the philosophical tradition. For Deleuze, common sense and good sense are complementary aspects of the fundamental *doxa* of representation. That is, they constitute two essential yet unexamined presuppositions of Western thought. Common sense, expressed in the formulation "Everybody knows", assumes the existence of a universal *cogito*: a knowing subject whose rational thought displays a natural affinity for truth. According to this understanding, all of the human faculties are brought together under the banner of a transcendental identity patterned on the identity of God and mirroring the identity of the objects of knowledge.[2] Within the domain of common sense, then, knowledge is reduced to recognition; we know that the dog we see is a dog because we recognize it as the same dog we have already perceived, imagined or remembered it to be. Clearly, recognition and common sense function to domesticate difference by dismissing as inconsequential all of the details about this particular dog, at this particular moment, that might prompt us not to recognize it as a dog. We miss an encounter with this particular dog, and settle for a dog that represents our pre-existing Idea of dog-ness (DR: 131–7).

Good sense, too, functions for Deleuze to contain difference within a predictable pattern of unity and identity. Good sense affirms that time unfolds in one direction only, from the past to the future, and that logical thought proceeds from the most to the least differentiated, that is, from the particular case to the universal concept. In the domain of good sense, it is the present moment that bears the responsibility of ordering the flow of time; for this reason, then, the essential function of good sense is to foresee what is to come. Thus good sense, like common sense, traps us in an image of thought based on recognition and representation: we shall know that we are seeing a dog tomorrow because we shall recognize it as the dog we foresaw today (LS: 75–8). In contrast, as we shall see, the sense of which Deleuze writes is a sense that emerges as pure event, and as such as affirmation of difference-in-itself.

Deleuze opens *The Logic of Sense* by reviewing the Platonic dualism that underlies conventional understandings of sense. This is not the dualism of body and mind (or soul) that we have come to expect from Western thought, but rather a dualism within bodies; for Plato, Deleuze argues, there exists a fundamental dualism between bodies that receive the action of an Idea (Plato's *copies*) and bodies that fail to receive this action (Plato's *simulacra*). That is, there are bodies that "represent" the eternal essence of the pure forms by participating in that essence – and are thus legitimate copies of those forms – and there are bodies that are merely copies of copies (of copies …), or simulacra, and are thus illegitimate. For Plato, the realm of copies is the realm of Being, while simulacra are characterized by unlimited becoming (LS: 1–2).

In place of this Platonic dualism, Deleuze offers a quite different dualism that emerges from the thought of the Stoics, who distinguish not between copies and simulacra but between actually existing bodies – "with their tensions, physical qualities, actions and passions, and the corresponding 'states of affairs'" (LS: 4) – and incorporeal effects, or events, that are generated by the interactions or mixtures of bodies. For Deleuze, as for the Stoics, only bodies (understood in the broadest possible sense, and including all living and non-living things) have depth and real existence, while events float on the surface of bodies and cannot be said to *ex*-ist, but rather to *sub*-sist or *per*-sist in the relations between bodies (LS: 4–7). Bodies are dynamic and self-causing, while events, including Ideas, are caused by bodies. Linguistically, bodies are associated with nouns, while events are verbs, in particular infinitive forms of verbs. Bodies exist in the pure present, in being, while events subsist in both the past and the future, in becoming. The value of this Stoic dualism over the Platonic one is that it allows Deleuze to assert the primacy of bodies over the Idea; as he puts it, "bodies with their states, qualities, and quantities, assume all the characteristics of substance and cause [and] conversely, the characteristics of the Idea are relegated to the other side . . .: *the ideational or the incorporeal can no longer be anything other than an 'effect'*" (LS: 7, original emphasis). In this way, bodies no longer represent disembodied Ideas, and difference – previously understood as a mere side effect of identity – is now freed from its constriction within the Same, that is, within common sense or representation.

But what do these competing dualisms have to do with sense? Deleuze lays the groundwork for his concept of sense by considering a prevailing understanding of the relations between language, as instantiated in the proposition, and events. Noting that it is "the characteristic of events to be expressed or expressible, uttered or utterable, in propositions which are at least possible", Deleuze turns to what he describes as "three distinct relations within the proposition" in order to find the condition(s) of possibility according to which propositions might express events (LS: 12). The first of these relations is denotation, which relates the proposition to a given external state of affairs. That is, denotation is that property of a proposition that allows it to communicate something about the world. The second, manifestation, relates the proposition to the speaker who utters it, expressing her desires and beliefs. The third, signification, relates the proposition to universal or general concepts, and establishes a web of connections with other propositions in a kind of relay; that is, the signifying term serves as premise for some propositions while others also function as its premise. Considered on this model, the basic function of the proposition is predication: "That dog is black and white." What this means is that propositions, understood as limited to denotation, manifestation, and signification, rely on common sense; we are able to utter this statement by virtue of recognizing "dog", "black" and "white" as static ideas that "everyone knows". Clearly, then, if Deleuze is to free language and thought from representation, he must articulate a fourth dimension of propositions.

Moreover, the problem with this schema is that each of these relations – of denotation, manifestation and signification – presupposes the other two in an endless circle of self-reference. What Deleuze is after, then, is a dimension of the proposition that can function as the ground for these other three, a dimension that in and of itself accounts for the possibility that propositions can express events. That dimension is sense, "*the expressed of the proposition*, ... a pure event which inheres or subsists in the proposition" (LS: 19, original emphasis). Sense, for Deleuze, is not identical to either the proposition itself or to that which is denoted, manifested or signified by the proposition. Rather, sense is a surface along which the proposition comes into contact with that which it denotes, manifests and signifies, a surface that likewise brings together the realm of actual bodies and virtual Ideas. Ironically, perhaps, the nature of sense emerges most clearly in an examination of nonsense, absurdity and paradox, because it is there that language is most obviously freed from its referential function. Nonsense words, exemplified in the work of Lewis Carroll, have no existence apart from language; they do not denote real objects, manifest the beliefs and desires of real persons, or signify meaningful concepts. Nevertheless, they still convey sense, and in so doing affirm the immanence of sense to language itself. So if denotation, manifestation and signification can account for the possibility that language expresses something about the world only by relating language to something external to it, Deleuze's concept of sense needs no external referent to stand as the condition of possibility of expression.

This is where the related concept of the series emerges as essential to our understanding of Deleuze's sense. We have seen that sense is the surface that both joins and separates the actual realm of bodies and the virtual realm of events, but we now need to understand why both actual and virtual realms are organized as series. The series is important to Deleuze because it instantiates a mode of organization of difference that avoids the pitfalls of representation, within which difference is tamed by the mechanisms of resemblance, identity, analogy and opposition. Series avoid these traps, first, because "*the serial form is necessarily realized in the simultaneity of at least two series*" (LS: 36, original emphasis).[3] Secondly, in any series, the terms of that series differ from one another (even if they are apparently "repetitions"). Thirdly, the system, or structure, that is produced by the juxtaposition or contact of two or more series necessarily retains this difference within itself. Moreover, the relations between and among the terms of a series are "multi-serial" in nature (LS: 37): they permit an infinite number of connections, and those connections cannot be made to conform to a centralized organization. Examples of pairs of heterogeneous series cited by Deleuze include: a series of events and a series of things; a series of propositions and a series of states of affairs; and a series of verbs and a series of adjectives. In all cases, says Deleuze, what is essential is:

> that [the two series] are never equal. One represents the signifier, the other the signified. But thanks to our terminology, these two terms acquire a particular meaning. We call "signifier" any sign that presents itself in an aspect of sense; we call "signified," on the contrary, that which serves as the correlative to this aspect of sense, that is, that which is defined in a duality relative to this aspect.
>
> (LS: 37)

Here Deleuze is hijacking the then well-accepted structuralist terms "signifier" and "signified" in order to redefine the centralized understanding of signification in terms of "the relation and distribution of series in general" (LS: 39). To do so, he goes one better than Lacan in adapting the Edgar Allan Poe story, "The Purloined Letter" (deployed by Lacan in his "Seminar on 'The Purloined Letter'" (1966: 11–61)). Deleuze's purpose is to reveal that the place of the minister within the tale's shifting series creates "a paradoxical case, which ensures the relative displacement of the two series, the excess of one over the other, without being reducible to any of the terms of the series or to any relation between these terms" (LS: 40). The nature of this paradoxical case is that it should, by occupying a place within both series, guarantee that they remain in communication with each other, while nevertheless keeping them endlessly diverging. Deleuze here locates an "extremely mobile *empty place*", or "an *occupant without a place*", always generating dislocation of sense between and through series (LS: 41, original emphasis).

One might well ask how such a mechanism of dislocation would work, and Deleuze returns to his reference of choice in *The Logic of Sense*, Lewis Carroll's deployment of "the esoteric word" (e.g. the portmanteau word "'frumious' = fuming + furious" (LS: 44)), which functions, says Deleuze, "not only to connote or to coordinate two heterogeneous series but to introduce disjunctions in the series", a variable movement (depending on the type of esoteric word employed) of "connection", of "conjunction" and of "disjunction" between series (LS: 47). This alternate mode of conceptualizing the signifying function flies entirely in the face of the contemporary understanding (in the late 1960s) of the production of meaning, that is, the relation of signifier to signified. In *The Logic of Sense* as well as in his 1967 essay (only published in 1972) "How Do We Recognize Structuralism?" (DI: 170–92),

Deleuze draws from the authors most associated with the structuralist movement (notably Louis Althusser, Foucault, Roman Jakobson, Lacan and Claude Lévi-Strauss) to appropriate their *examples* and recast these in support of a newly defined concept of "structure". However, as Dorothy confided to Toto, with this serially conceptualized structure, "we're not in Kansas any more".

For Deleuze, that is, structure is constituted by the relations between two heterogeneous series, one signified and one signifying (as articulated above), the terms of which exist only in relation to each other. As Deleuze succinctly puts it, "A structure includes two distributions of singular points corresponding to the base series. And for this reason, it is imprecise to oppose structure and event: the structure includes a register of ideal *events*, that is, an entire *history* internal to it" (LS: 50). But this distributive structure relies on the paradoxical element that serves as "the principle of the emission of singularities", belonging to no series, or to both, but keeping them in circulation and circulating through them. For, as Deleuze concludes, this element above all assures "the bestowal of sense in both signifying and signified series", with sense being "what is attributed in such a way that it determines both the signifier and signified as such" (LS: 51). Hence, no structure exists "without series, without relations between the terms of each series, or without singular points corresponding to these relations. But above all, we can conclude that there is no structure without the empty square, which makes everything function" (LS: 51). In other words, events, especially including the sense-event, are immanent to structure; structure cannot exist without the event of sense.

In this essay, we do not mean to provide a reading of *The Logic of Sense* in its entirety (even were we capable of doing so): although to this point we have attended closely to the text corresponding to the end of the "Eighth Series of Structure". What we now propose is to suggest ways in which Deleuze's concepts of sense and series operate elsewhere in his work, even in texts in which the terminology of *The Logic of Sense* has shifted into different registers. We can explore only two such registers, one in the domain of theology, the other in the domain of rhizomatics.

A first question that arises for us is this: If the concepts of sense and series undo the representational thinking denoted by the proposition, and inaugurates a new understanding of structure, how does that concept resonate in the domain of theology? We have shown above that the propositional model of language beyond which Deleuze wants to move is implicated in an idealist logic where difference is subordinated to identity or to the Same, and bodies are subordinated to Ideas. Moreover, Deleuze asserts that good sense and common sense – twin underpinnings of that propositional model of language – join forces to ground the "alliance" of self, world and God, because, according to the *doxa* of representation, God is "the final outcome of all directions [good sense] and the supreme principle of identities [common sense]" (LS: 78). Elsewhere he writes of what he calls the "order of God", noting that this order is constituted by:

> the identity of God as the ultimate foundation; the identity of the world as the ambient environment; the identity of the person as a well-founded agency; the identities of bodies as the base; and finally, *the identity of language as the power of denoting everything else*.[4] (LS: 292, emphasis added)

The ability of a unified language-system to denote "everything else" is an integral part of this system of interlocking identities, all of which are erected on the foundation of divine identity. So what happens to that system when language becomes non-representational? What effect does Deleuze's logic of sense have on God?

One answer to this question emerges in Deleuze's essay "To Have Done with Judgment", in *Essays Critical and Clinical*. Although there is no explicit discussion of sense or series in this essay, the concepts lurk beneath the surface in ways that function to undo what Deleuze calls "the doctrine of judgment" (ECC: 126). According to this doctrine, man is defined by his condition of infinite indebtedness to God, an indebtedness that in turn guarantees the immortality of his soul. And it is not just an overtly theological concept of judgement that concerns Deleuze here; rather, even "the judgment of knowledge . . . implies a prior moral and theological form" that is based on this indebtedness (ECC: 127). The problem with judgement, says Deleuze, is that it is opposed to the creative force of existence; "Judgment prevents the emergence of any new mode of existence" (ECC: 135).

To undo the doctrine of judgement, then, Deleuze proposes an ethic of combat. He insists that while this combat might at first present itself as combat against judgement, such combat against the Other – even the judging Other – always succumbs to the system of judgement it attempts to undo. Instead, combat must emerge as the struggle within oneself by which a "force enriches itself by seizing hold of other forces and join-ing itself to them in a new ensemble: a becoming" (ECC: 132). In other words, what Deleuze is envisaging is the opening up of the combatant to the becomings that are produced in the coming together of hetero-geneous forces; combat "is a powerful, nonorganic vitality that supple-ments force with force, and enriches whatever it takes hold of" (ECC:

133). Most important for our purposes here, the outcome of combat is "an idiosyncrasy of forces" best expressed in what Deleuze, following D. H. Lawrence, calls a symbol, which he describes in terms that clearly resonate with those he uses to articulate the concepts of sense and series:

> [A symbol is] an intensive compound that vibrates and expands, that has no meaning, but makes us whirl about until we harness the maximum of possible forces in every direction, each of which receives a new meaning by entering into relation with others.
>
> (ECC: 134)

In expressing the power of combat to overturn the system of judgement, symbols express a *sense* that is generated by the endless interplay of the heterogeneous *series* of forces that give rise to it. Symbols, expressing sense, reveal the power of combat as "the way to have done with God and with judgment" (ECC: 134). In other words, Deleuze's concepts of sense and series undermine the possibility of theology as it is traditionally understood in the Western tradition.[5]

How, then, might these forces of combat function in our lived critical activity, alongside the spiritual and also *vital* work of combating the judgement of God? In our view, a possible answer emerges from observing closely how Deleuze undertook his different creative collaborations within and beyond philosophy. The most celebrated of these collaborations, of course, was with Guattari – in *Anti-Oedipus*, *A Thousand Plateaus*, and *What Is Philosophy?* as well as in numerous interviews and occasional essays – but one must not forget his important interview text, *Dialogues*, and the 1988–89 video interview, *L'Abécédaire de Gilles Deleuze*, both with Parnet. Although space considerations prevent a detailed review of these texts, we can nonetheless reflect succinctly on the ways in which they extend and transform the sense–series pair.

In the opening lines of "Introduction: Rhizome" in *A Thousand Plateaus*, Deleuze and Guattari reflect on their having written *Anti-Oedipus* together and immediately confront the multiplicity inherent to sense-making in series, "Since each of us was several, there was already quite a crowd. Here [in *A Thousand Plateaus*] we have made use of everything that came within range, what was closest as well as farthest away" (ATP: 3). They keep their own names in this project so as better to disfigure themselves:

> To make ourselves unrecognizable in turn. To render imperceptible, not ourselves, but what makes us act, feel, and think … To reach, not the point where one no longer says I, but the point

where it is no longer of any importance whether one says I. We are
no longer ourselves. Each will know his own. We have been aided,
inspired, multiplied.   (ATP: 3)

Just as the opening lines of *Anti-Oedipus* were deliberately meant to
shock and disconcert,[6] so, too, *A Thousand Plateaus* turns on its ear any
common-sense conception of collaborative reflection and critical sense-
making.

To understand better how these collaborative projects correspond to
the Deleuzian dynamism underlying the sense–series pair, we can refer
to Deleuze's response, seven years before *A Thousand Plateaus*, to a
letter from Cressole. Deleuze explains in patient and indeed moving
detail the operation of sense-making inherent to possible readings of
Anti-Oedipus, practices that extend to *A Thousand Plateaus* as well:

> You either see it as a box with something inside and start looking
> for what it signifies, and then if you're even more perverse and
> depraved you set off after signifiers. And you treat the next book
> like a box contained in the first or containing it. And you anno-
> tate and interpret and question, and write a book about the book,
> and so on and on. Or there's another way: you see the book as a
> little non-signifying machine, and the only question is "Does it
> work, and how does it work?" How does it work for you? . . . This
> second way of reading's intensive: something comes through or
> it doesn't. There's nothing to explain, nothing to understand,
> nothing to interpret. It's like plugging in to an electric circuit . . .
> It relates a book directly to what's Outside . . . one flow among
> others, with no special place in relation to the others, that comes
> into relations of current, countercurrent, and eddy with other
> flows – flows of shit, sperm, words, action, eroticism, money,
> politics, and so on.   (P: 7–8)

In quoting this passage at length, we emphasize the means by which
sense-making functions along the *milieu*, the in-between of a paradoxical element that incessantly flows between series, for example, Deleuze-
series and Guattari-series (and their respective crowds) to inspire a
sense-flow between and beyond the "two". Or in the book-series and
reader-series, the "two" can work as a force not of closed signification
nor of signifier and signified captured, but rather of active production,
of following the flows in order to open onto new series and flows. This
is what Deleuze and Guattari describe, in "Introduction: Rhizome", as
the "principle of rhizomatic multiplicity" in contrast to arborescent

pseudomultiplicities: "Puppet strings, as a rhizome or multiplicity, are tied not to the supposed will of an artist or puppeteer but to a multiplicity of nerve fibers, which form another puppet in other dimensions connected to the first" (ATP: 8). In this way, the rhizome as a radical mode of sense-making in series "connects any point to any other point" and even "brings into play very different regimes of signs, and even nonsign states", without beginning nor end, "but always a middle (*milieu*) from which it grows and which it overspills" (ATP: 21).

One might well ask if there are more practical or immediate ways to conceptualize these flows of signifying (and asignifying), and to respond, we consider how Deleuze and Parnet addressed the question of how to undertake dialogue otherwise, explicitly in the 1977 *Dialogues* and implicitly in *L'Abécédaire*. In *Dialogues*, Deleuze extols encounters (*rencontres*), particularly a "pick-up method", in his intellectual work (D: 7–10) because through encounters with friends (he names his friend Jean-Pierre, his wife Fanny, Foucault and Guattari), one reaches "the desert, experimentation on oneself, [which] is our only identity, our single chance for all combinations which inhabit us", an experimentation that is too often stifled by "ordering these tribes [that populate the desert] ... getting rid of some and encouraging others to prosper" (D: 11). From her side, Parnet questions whether Deleuze (with Guattari) has adequately worked to break down dualisms and, in contrast, she proposes to seek escape in the multiplicity inherent to the "AND, as something which has its place between the elements or between the sets. AND, AND, AND – stammering" (D: 34). Through a constant proliferation of AND, one could "undo dualisms from the inside, by tracing the line of flight which passes between the two terms or the two sets ... draw[ing] both into a non-parallel evolution, a heterochronous becoming" (D: 35). Although this method still seems peculiarly binary, Deleuze's perspective encompasses the stammerings that Parnet extols within their variable, in-between modes of collective enunciation in the subsequent chapters of *Dialogues*. Deleuze and Parnet proceed by a constant and deliberate displacement of the writers' identities (with some exceptions in Chapter 3), and as a result of this overlap and folding of thoughts and concepts shared by two interlocutors who are in fact a crowd, an in-between of thought comes to the fore through the folds of friendship, that is, through the resonances, differences and repetitions available only within the intimacy of mediation.[7]

In contrast, the movement of *L'Abécédaire*, by dint of its structural unfolding as an ABC primer ("A as in Animal", "B as in *Boire*" [drinking], "C as in Culture", etc.), allows for some weaving around and through subjects, but not the kind of in-between that Deleuze and Parnet sought a decade earlier. Indeed at one point (in "C as in Culture"), when Deleuze brings up how he seeks the impact of the Ideas through encounters (*rencontres*) with film-makers, Parnet almost panics and stops him abruptly, saying, "You're starting in on my [letter] 'I'! Stop right away! You're starting in on my [letter] 'I'!" Despite the richness of this 8½-hour video interview, it is clear that Parnet subsequently became aware of such dialogic limitations through the necessarily linear unfolding of the exchange. So on the DVD version of *L'Abécédaire* released in 2004, Parnet and director-producer Pierre-André Boutang sought a solution by offering a new mode of access, "par le milieu" (through the middle/ *milieu*), that is, providing links on each of the three separate discs to key thematic points, rather than to the start of each letter (also available, of course). Parnet even explains this apparatus in the box set with an excerpt from (yes) *Dialogues*:

> To flee from the arbitrariness of alphabetical letters. Enter and leave through the middle, Gilles Deleuze had suggested: that's what this DVD now offers us today, other accents, tiny and infinite variations, for movements of a musical thought. "The *milieu* has nothing to do with an average, it is not a centrism or a form of moderation. On the contrary, it is a matter of absolute speed. Whatever grows from the middle [*milieu*] is endowed with such a speed" [D: 30]. (*L'Abécédaire* DVD)

Although this apparatus is not seamless – for example, it is limited to the links available on each particular disc (six on disc 1 (A–F), nine on disc 2 (G–M) and seven on disc 3 (N–Z)) – a skilled DVD surfer could learn to access rapidly the different series or *milieus* in-between the discs and thereby create fruitful jumps and produce variations of sense and expression that open Deleuze's thought anew.

As Deleuze mentions elsewhere in "C as in Culture", it is precisely by living in the fold of the wave as surfers do that one not only maximizes the benefits of *rencontres*, that is, passages of new sense-making between series, through the *milieu*, but also achieves the Deleuzian ideal of getting out of philosophy through philosophy. Such juxtapositions of sense-making through, between and beyond specific series are precisely what Deleuze undertakes, alone and with Guattari, in the various works of the 1970s and 1980s: the variety of plateaus that open transversal relations and micropolitics of signifying and asignifying assemblages, implicating strange modes of desire and affect, and creating new relations and unheard-of becomings; the movements beyond philosophy through painting, cinema and literature, with their logic of sensation, crystalline moments, and stylistic becoming-minor; and the movement in the final years to articulate the fold as well as the critical and clinical as ways of comprehending the *milieu* of a philosophy always in search of senses and series conceptualized otherwise.

Notes

1. Deleuze's biographical information is available in the brochure on Deleuze prepared for a display by the French Ministère des Affaires Etrangères, available at www.adpf.asso.fr/adpf-publi/folio/deleuze/ (accessed Dec. 2004).
2. Deleuze explores this ordering of identities, which he calls the "order of God", in "Klossowski or Bodies-Language", included as Appendix 3 in *The Logic of Sense* (LS: 280–301).
3. The Knight's Song, in Carroll's *Through the Looking Glass and What Alice Found There*, serves as a paradigmatic case for Deleuze (see LS: 29–30).
4. In the aforementioned Appendix 3 on Pierre Klossowski (see n.2), Deleuze develops his critique of the order of God.
5. A question for another essay would be: do the concepts of sense and series clear the way for *another* theology? For reflections on Deleuze, anti-theology and the judgement of God, see Poxon (2001) in Mary Bryden's volume, *Deleuze and Religion* (2001).
6. "It is at work everywhere, functioning smoothly at times, at other time in fits and starts. It breathes, it heats, it eats. It shits and fucks. What a mistake to have ever said *the* id. Everywhere *it* is machines – real ones, not figurative ones: machines driving other machines, machines being driven by other machines, with all the necessary couplings and connections. An organ-machine is plugged into an energy-source-machine: the one produces a flow that the other interrupts. The breast is a machine that produces milk, and the mouth a machine coupled to it . . . Hence we are all handymen: each with his little machines. For every organ-machine, an energy-machine: all the time, flows and interruptions. Judge Schreber has sunbeams in his ass. *A solar anus*" (AO: 1–2).
7. These resonances and overlaps are, in many ways, a practical extension of Deleuze's *Difference and Repetition*. On the experimentation in *Dialogues* and its limitations, see Stivale (2003a).

SIX

Assemblage

J. Macgregor Wise

Assemblage

Assemblage, as it is used in Deleuze and Guattari's work, is a concept dealing with the play of contingency and structure, organization and change, however, we should also keep in mind that these pairs of terms are false alternatives (D: 99). The term in French is *agencement*, usually translated as "putting together", "arrangement", "laying out", "layout" or "fitting' (Cousin *et al.* 1990: 9–10). It is important that *agencement* is not a static term; it is not *the arrangement* or *organization* but the *process* of arranging, organizing, fitting together. The term as it is used in Deleuze and Guattari's work is commonly translated as *assemblage*: that which is being assembled. An assemblage is not a set of predetermined parts (such as the pieces of a plastic model aeroplane) that are then put together in order or into an already-conceived structure (the model aeroplane). Nor is an assemblage a random collection of things, since there is a sense that an assemblage is a whole of some sort that expresses some identity and claims a territory.

We can get a sense of the term assemblage by seeing how it is used in different contexts. In the field of geology it refers to "a group of fossils that, appearing together, characterize a particular stratum" ("Assemblage" n.d.). There is a contingency to the elements in that the fossils present are somewhat random depending on what poor creature perished how, when, at what particular time and in what place and manner to be preserved here. Of course it is not completely random because only certain animals existed in that form at that time in that location. There is also a contingency to the arrangement itself for the same reasons. But these fossils do not just appear together in strata; they constitute a *group* and they express a particular *character*. The term is used in a similar sense in archaeology, palaeontology and ecology ("a group of organisms sharing a common habitat by chance") ("Assemblage" n.d.).

These examples illustrate that an assemblage is a collection of heterogeneous elements. These elements could be diverse *things* brought together in particular relations, such as the detritus of everyday life unearthed in an archaeological dig: bowls, cups, bones, tile, figurines and so on. This collection of things and their relations express something, a particular character: Etruscanness, for example. But the elements that make up an assemblage also include the *qualities* present (large, poisonous, fine, blinding, etc.) and the affects and effectivity of the assemblage: that is, not just what it *is*, but what it *can do*. To paraphrase Deleuze and Guattari, we do not know what an assemblage *is* until we find out what it *can do* (ATP: 257), that is, how it functions. Assemblages select elements from the *milieus* (the surroundings, the context, the mediums in which the assemblages work) and bring them together in a particular way. "We will call an assemblage every constellation of singularities and traits deducted from the flow – selected, organized, stratified – in such a way as to converge (consistency) artificially and naturally; an assemblage, in this sense, is a veritable invention" (ATP: 406). The elements of an assemblage to which Deleuze and Guattari refer are not just things because things themselves are qualities, speeds and lines.

An example from Deleuze and Guattari may help illustrate this point. Re-reading a case of Freud's, they describe a child moved by the sight through his window of a horse pulling an omnibus. The horse has collapsed in the street and is being whipped by the driver. Most probably, this horse is about to die. Deleuze and Guattari describe this scene as an assemblage. On the one hand, the assemblage is horse–omnibus–street (a collection of objects in a particular relation), but it is also

> a list of active and passive affects in the context of the individuated assemblage it is part of: having eyes blocked by blinders, having a bit and a bridle, being proud, having a big peepee-maker, pulling heavy loads, being whipped, falling, making a din with its legs, biting, etc. These affects circulate and are transformed within the assemblage: what a horse "can do." (ATP: 257)

Assemblages create *territories*. Territories are more than just spaces: they have a stake, a claim, they express (my house, their ranch, his bench, her friends). The dying horse claims a territory, it does not simply occupy space. Territories are not fixed for all time, but are always being made and unmade, reterritorializing and deterritorializing. This constant making and unmaking process is the same with assemblages: they are always coming together and moving apart. Assemblages face the strata, where they come into being and become organized (literally: this assemblage of artifacts is found in a particular stratum, a particular layer of a particular type of soil or rock). But Deleuze and Guattari write that assemblages also face the Body without Organs – the unfixed, shifting mass of movement, speed and flows – where they become dismantled and their elements circulate.

Let us take an example of a particular type of territory or territorial assemblage: home. "Discover the territorial assemblages of someone, human or animal: home" (ATP: 503–4). Home is how we make a place our own, how we arrange artifacts, qualities and affect to express us.[1] I do not mean this in the bourgeois "I-am-my-home-décor" way, but rather how to express a space of comfort for ourselves. Deleuze and Guattari describe a child, alone and afraid in the dark (ATP: 311). The child hums or sings a little tune, a little refrain to comfort itself. That singing of a tune creates a space of comfort: home. And one need not be fixed in one's dwelling to create home: an airline seat, a stroll in the neighbourhood, a car for daily commuting, a space on a lawn at a picnic or on a beach. Home is thus not a pre-existing space; it is not the house. It is the continual attempt to create a space of comfort for oneself, through the arrangement of objects, practices, feelings and affects (see Wise 2003).

Let us consider another example. Recently I flew to an academic conference where I was to meet up with a good friend of mine and one of her colleagues at the airport. Since my friend's colleague had never met me, she gave him a brief description to recognize me: black cowboy boots, black raincoat, small leather purse, glasses, goatee. The traits in this partial description constitute an assemblage, a set of somewhat random elements, which collectively and yet partially make me up, express qualities or in this case a form of identity. The point here is that this assemblage does not have to consist of these particular elements, or even similar ones – it turns out that of that apparel I had only the raincoat with me on that trip (and had grown a full beard). Rather, despite the absence of these specifically assembled elements, the colleague found other traits – movement, demeanour – to reassemble into the same sort of thing: me (or an iteration of me).

Assemblages (and homes and what we take for identities) are less objects and qualities than lines and speeds. My identity-assemblage is a collection of slowness, viscosity, acceleration and rupture (ATP: 4), gaits, patterns, tics, habits, rhythms (the tapping foot, the slow stare, the pacing of the pace – and the pace of pacing).

But there is another dimension to assemblages. In addition to the systems of things, actions and passions that we have been discussing (which Deleuze and Guattari refer to as *machinic assemblages)*, assemblages are also systems of signs, semiotic systems (ATP: 504). That is, assemblage elements include discourses, words, "meanings" and non-corporeal relations that link signifiers with effects. Deleuze and Guattari call this a *collective assemblage of enunciation*. Archaeological assemblages are not just the things that are dug up and their qualities and relations, but the discursive assemblages through which the things, qualities and relations are expressed through nomenclature, jargon and the semiotics of the dig: the semiotic system that transforms a cup into a particular type of cup.[2] Home-assemblages, then, are not just collections of objects, practices, feelings and affects, but also take up particular languages, words and meanings. The earlier description of my self consisted also of patterns of speech, vocal tics, collections of words, expressions and meanings: in short, signifiers.

We can enter into an assemblage through a process of taking up or taking on the particular relation of speed, slowness, effectivity and language which makes it up. Thus one could enter into another's sense of home, or identity (which is quite different from either walking into someone's house or imitating their mannerisms). It is not a process of imitating but of *becoming*. Little Hans, the child watching the dying horse, wishes to enter that assemblage. For Deleuze and Guattari, "The question is whether Little Hans can endow his own elements with the relations of movement and rest, the affects, that would make it become horse, forms and subjects aside" (ATP: 258).

To summarize, Deleuze and Guattari write that assemblages have two axes. One axis is the creation of territory, on strata, thus moving between making (territorialization) and unmaking (deterritorialization) on the Body without Organs. The other axis is the enunciation of signifiers, collectively, moving between technology (content, material) and language (expression, non-corporeal effects). Assemblages are made and unmade along each of these dimensions.

Technological assemblages

In this second part of the essay, I wish to show how the concept of assemblage can help us better understand a particular issue in technology studies: the relation between the technological and the human (see

Slack & Wise 2002; Slack & Wise forthcoming). Since the ways that this relation has traditionally been posed are not productive, and indeed are overly simple, the concept of assemblage presents a more emergent way of thinking about the complexity of human–technology relationships. In this section of the essay I shall delineate and critique three common approaches to the human–technology relation (the received view, the contextual view and the view of articulation), using the example of the mobile telephone to illustrate each perspective. By reviewing this human–technology issue, we shall see how assemblage can animate thinking about this problem and make new connections.

The most common formulation of the relation of human and technology, which Slack and Wise (forthcoming) have called "the received view of culture and technology", posits the human and the technological as specific things that are completely different and that could act on one another. According to this view, I may be surrounded by technologies (phones, calculators, spreadsheets) but they are external to myself: mere tools. Technologies are not human and human beings are not technologies. Those who hold this view, then, get rather uneasy when technologies and human beings begin to merge: either human beings becoming more like technologies or technologies becoming more human, or technologies becoming a part of human beings through implants. This received view leads to seemingly endless debates about whether technologies are controlling human beings (technological determinism) or whether human beings completely control technologies (social determinism). Either way, technologies and human beings are seen as being discrete entities (to be studied separately or in relation).

For example, if one were to study mobile telephones from this perspective, one would study the development of the technology itself, and how today's mobile phones have transformed in function, power and size (and one might even find oneself saying that mobile phones have "evolved" in certain ways). One would also study the effects of the technology on human beings or society, usually posed in terms of "impact" as in *the impact of mobile phones on notions of public and private*, or how these phones have imposed an imperative on users to be accessible at all times, or how they have increased feelings of safety or danger. Or one could study the effects of society and social needs on the technology of the phone (for example, noting how the mobile phone viewed as a business technology emphasizes particular functions and features, whereas the mobile phone viewed as a personal technology emphasizes others). Either way, this perspective views mobile phones as discrete objects with identities of their own, which can be studied by themselves in isolation.

The second perspective on the human–technology relation argues that we need to examine these technologies in context. Technologies are not separate from their context, and nor are human beings. We cannot, then, consider a technology in isolation; it is always in use in context somewhere. A recent study by Philip Howard of Internet use takes up this perspective, which he refers to as an *embedded media perspective*, arguing that "new media mechanisms are also culturally laden tools for communication grounded in social contexts" (2004: 22). Howard argues:

> Communication technologies became deeply embedded in personal lives very quickly, mediating our interactions with other people and the way in which we learn about our world. Understanding society online requires that we study media embeddedness – how communication tools are embedded in our lives and how our lives are embedded in new media. (Howard 2004: 2)

The two advantages of this approach for research, says Howard, are that such study is of the "local and immediate" rather than the abstract, and that human beings and technologies constrain each other: "Communication tools provide both capacities and constraints for human action and . . . individual users are responsible for taking advantage of capacities and overcoming constraints in daily use" (*ibid.*: 24–5). Note that this approach sees social determinism or technological determinism as contextual rather than absolute. However, if something is said to be "embedded" in something else, can it not also be "disembedded"? If so, then this approach still posits human beings and technologies as separate and unique.

To return to our example of the mobile phone, the embedded perspective would focus more on everyday uses of the technologies: who uses the technology, when, and for what purposes? These are questions not to be answered in the abstract or as a generality, but through attention paid to actual everyday uses (*these* people in *this* context use *these* features of mobile telephony). For example, recent research has focused on how teenagers in Japan, Scandinavia, Korea and elsewhere use the text messaging features of mobile phones to keep in contact with peers throughout the day, to keep parents updated of their whereabouts and activities, to monitor and control communication and establish "face", to flirt and to play games, and there are other uses (see Katz & Aakhus 2002; Rheingold 2003; Yoon 2003). Taking this perspective, one can see the phone as simply one aspect of the rhythms of a teenager's everyday life, and see how these users have exploited certain features of the phones and carefully crafted communication patterns and language to cope with the limitations on message length. But although the mobile phone is something that gets used in certain ways, and has become at times an essential part of everyday sociability and cultural practice for these groups, this perspective still treats the mobile phone as a singular entity, something that was not a part of the context, that was introduced to the context, and is now used in the context. In other words, the mobile phone is something that can be disembedded.

A third approach to the human–technology relation is that of articulation. The concept of articulation is the idea that different elements can be connected (articulated) or disconnected in order to create unities or identities. Stuart Hall (1986) uses the image of an articulated lorry (a semi-truck in which the cab and trailer are separable). Different cabs can be articulated with different trailers. Each combination results in a particular unity: a truck, but a different truck each time. In response, in part, to the contextual view outlined above, Jennifer Slack argues that the concept of context is, in her words, "a substantial theoretical problem" (1989: 329) since multiple researchers would probably define the relevant context quite differently. In contrast, Slack presents a model of articulation that sees the context as being *constitutive* of the technology and vice versa. Technologies cannot be disembedded. In terms of a broader theory of articulation, Slack argues:

> The unities forged and broken in this expanded universe are not simply physical objects, such as trucks, but complex connections of elements that are themselves articulations. These elements or identities might be social practices, discursive statements, ideological positions, social forces, or social groups ... The unities they form can be made up of any combination of elements.
>
> (1989: 331)

Any articulation is historically contingent. Articulations must be made, sustained, transformed and unmade in particular concrete practices. Thus, to articulate, to make or break connections between objects, between ideas, between objects and ideas, takes power: "Power not only draws and redraws the connections among the disparate elements within which identities are designated, but in the process, power designates certain of these articulations as dominant and others as subordinate" (*ibid.*: 333). Technology, too, can be viewed as an ongoing series of articulations, as can being human.

If we look at the study of mobile phones from the context of articulation, we get a very different set of questions from those posed in the examples above. How has mobile phone technology been articulated to particular functions and uses (text as well as voice, plus a calculator, web browser, videogame, stopwatch, and other features)? How has the mobile phone been articulated to discourses of progress, convenience, efficiency, and style? How has the mobile phone been articulated to particular populations (youth, businesses)? How does the mobile phone articulate to discourses and policies of neoliberalism (stressing individual self-expression)? How has the mobile phone been articulated to discourses and practices of gender and to gendered bodies? What are the mobile phone's articulations to the economy? Of what articulations does the mobile phone itself consist (as a unity it must be the result of particular articulations)?

The discussion of articulation gets us part way back to assemblage; perhaps assemblage is a more complex model of articulation. It, too, involves combinations of heterogeneous parts into provisional, contingent wholes. However, assemblage differs from articulation in a number of ways. First, assemblages are not just things, practices and signs articulated into a formation, but also qualities, affects, speeds and densities. Secondly, assemblages work through flows of agency rather than specific practices of power. And thirdly, whereas articulation emphasizes the contingent connections and relations among and between elements, assemblage is also about their territorialization and expression as well as their elements and relations.

So, to continue with the mobile phone example, and in contrast with the other approaches to this technology that we have covered, from the perspective of assemblage, we would talk about the thumb-key-software-transmission assemblage. This is more than just saying that the hand and the phone are articulated in particular ways, but that the hand is becoming phone and the phone is becoming hand on the way to create this assemblage. The texting teenagers of Japan are called the *oyayubi-soku*, the Thumb Tribe, and in Finland mobile phones are referred to as *känny*, a diminutive form of the Finnish word for hand (Rheingold 2003: 4, 12). But this assemblage also includes being present elsewhere, phatic communication (i.e. texting for its own sake, to maintain an affective bridge), becoming private publicly, grasping, having an expensive phone, and what the assemblage does: how it shapes space, transforms behaviour, rings, bothers, emotes. Assemblages are particular arrangements of elements, organized, which have their own patterns of movement and rest; picture the person with the mobile phone on the sidewalk, walking and talking in a particular way. Assemblages also disperse, with elements moving into different relations and configurations (phone in pocket, changes in movement and regard relative to those around one). Then the phone rings and one enters the assemblage again, reterritorializing, but in a different way.

Abstract machine

Although these examples have been fairly local and specific, with assemblages appearing relatively personal (my assemblage, your assemblage, and so forth), it is important to focus at once on the specificities and contingencies of an assemblage, and also on large-scale assemblages and the ways that assemblages work across multiple sites. "Assemblages may group themselves into extremely vast constellations constituting 'cultures' or even 'ages'," say Deleuze and Guattari (ATP: 406), and they use the example of Foucault's (1977) work on discipline and the prison. If we focus just on one specific facet, namely the disciplinary functioning of the prison assemblage, we miss the larger connections, the crisscross of links between it and other assemblages, for example, the system of education, the workplace and the hospital, to name but three (see e.g. ATP: 67).

To return again to the mobile phone example, focusing on just one person or group's use of phones obstructs the ways those particular assemblages may express a broader set of functions or principles. Deleuze and Guattari refer to such functions or principles as the *abstract machine*. In the mobile phone example we can point to an abstract machine that we might call, borrowing from Raymond Williams's (1975) discussion of television, a regime of *mobile privatization*. That is, television developed, according to Williams, within a social complex that emphasized the private sphere of the home, but also the mobility of the new suburbs of the 1950s. We might identify an abstract machine similar to mobile privatization that emphasizes mobility, autonomy, privatization, and individual empowerment through neoliberalism (see Rose 1999; Hay 2000). That abstract machine composes itself and then informs assemblages: "within the dimensions of the assemblage, the abstract machine, or machines, is effectuated in forms and substances" (ATP: 511). And so we are not just dealing with an assemblage, but a regime of assemblages, which, in the case of the new form of mobile privatization, includes not only the mobile phone but also the array of self-service or self-check assemblages and many others.[3] But each assemblage is entered into locally: I pick up the mobile phone and flip it open; my body changes speed, path and consistency; I enter into an assemblage of language, a collective assemblage of enunciation – acts, statements, "incorporeal transformations attributed to bodies" (ATP: 88) – which makes some statements possible and others not. That collective assemblage of enunciation is brought into a particular relation with "bodies, actions, passions" (ATP: 88), that is, the machinic assemblage. By entering into this assemblage (but never arriving, always in process), I am enacting the abstract machine of mobile privatization, and it is enacting me.

The concept of assemblage shows us how institutions, organizations, bodies, practices and habits make and unmake each other, intersecting and transforming: creating territories and then unmaking them, deterritorializing, opening lines of flight as a possibility of any assemblage, but also shutting them down. I swipe a card through one slot and I am admitted to (or excluded from) entry or access, and at the same time, my location may be mapped, unless I am deliberately unmaking the process by switching cards, falsifying the process. In one of his final essays, Deleuze writes, "we're at the beginning of something new" (N: 182), a new regime of assemblages, which he refers to as a control society. "We're moving toward control societies that no longer operate by confining people but through continuous control and instant communication" (N: 174): continuous education, flexible and mobile workspaces always in touch with the office, continuous remote monitoring of parolees, constant accumulation of purchasing habits and preferences. We should not get distracted by the technologies themselves, the machines such as the mobile phone and the self-service kiosk: "the machines don't explain anything, you have to analyze the collective apparatuses of which the machines are just one component" (N: 174). That is, you have to analyse the assemblages we enter into and create. We need to be able to hear "the sound of a contiguous future, the murmur (*rumeur*) of new assemblages of desire, of machines, and of statements, that insert themselves into the old assemblages and break with them" (K: 83). Resistance to control-assemblages needs "to be assessed at the level of our every move" (N: 176).

Acknowledgement

I should like to thank Charles Stivale and Gordon Coonfield for their comments on previous drafts of this essay; it is much richer for their contributions. I should also like to thank Jennifer Slack, who pushed me to develop this concept of assemblage fully in my work.

Notes

1. For the specificity of Deleuze's use of "affect", see Gregory J. Seigworth's contribution to this volume (Ch. 13).
2. See, for example, Bruno Latour's (1999) description of how soil and vegetation samples are articulated to scientific apparatuses and naming systems. Although "assemblage" is not a term Latour uses, the Amazonian forest and savannah and the scientists studying them consist of a number of assemblages.
3. Self-service assemblages are the machines that allow you to check out library books, scan and pay for groceries and check in for a flight without having to deal with actual people. The ATM is a forerunner of such machines, as are machines that dispense drinks and snacks.

SEVEN

Micropolitics

Karen Houle

But where do doctrines come from, if not from wounds and vital
aphorisms which, with their charge of exemplary provocation, are
so many speculative anecdotes?   (LS: 148)

Exemplary provocation

Tuesday morning. My "Introduction to Women's Studies" class. A
perpetually politicized space. Roughly 100 blank or hostile faces. Mostly
white, mostly women, mostly middle-class. This week's topic: "Gender-
based Violence". After reading the article "Keeping Women in Our Place:
Violence at Canadian Universities" (Harris 1999), students must complete an anonymous assignment: "Honestly and thoroughly describe the
ways in which gender-based harassment has affected your life". Each of
them will put their typed report in an envelope, and take another's out.
And read it. And "respond" to it, even if just to sign their name.

Thursday morning. Completed assignments go into an envelope,
including my own. I have told the class that I will do this exercise too,
since gender-violence carves itself into my life, and the lives of people I
know and love. And that the work that I do which I call feminism is not
incidentally related to that carving. Each of us draws out an innocent
enough looking sheet to respond to.

Thursday, late afternoon. Today, I have seen ten students. Not a blank
face among them. Nine females. One male. Each one eventually got
around to telling me about having been sexually assaulted. How they had

tried not to think about it, it was, after all, a thing of the past, until now. Each now takes time. A whole day. Ten bodies. The burgundy-haired woman skewers me: "Well, what am I supposed to do now?!" She leaves, overwhelmed and furious with the exercise, and with me. In my head, I hear Joseph Conrad: "We could not stand women speaking the truth. We could not bear it. It would cause infinite misery and bring about the most awful disturbances in this rather mediocre, but still idealistic fool's paradise in which each of us lives his own little life" (Conrad 1984: 131). In activating, I yank my students out of their fool's paradises, their moderately functional lives, and I abandon them, like Hansel and Gretel, in their respective creepy forests with no breadcrumb trail ... *How can I justify my actions, my so-called politicized pedagogical practices?*

A whole ecology of loss: local gynomiseries. Their extended family of global misery: coral reefs withering; sub-Saharan Africa riddled with AIDS; the widening gap between the grossly rich and the totally fucked; child prostitution, and/or blow jobs offered by 12-year-old girls to sports stars in Anne of Green Gables land; wonky climates caused by (among other things) jet vapour contrails (a causal correlation confirmed, courtesy of the 24-hour no-fly period after 9/11); fewer birds calling everywhere everymorning; teratogenic chemicals divvied up into breast milk and narwhale blubber, and so on. "Loss. Loss and losing. Grief, failure, brokenness, numbness, uncertainty, fear, the death of feeling, the death of dreaming. The absolute relentless, endless, habitual, unfairness of the world" (Foucault 1983: xiv); a corresponding loss of "belief in the world" (Rajchman 2000: 25). What does such loss mean to individuals? What does it mean to whole cultures, whole people who have learned to live with the "tyrannical bitterness of our everyday lives" (Foucault 1983: xiv) as "a constant companion"? (See Roy 2002). How can we conceive of, let alone dare to actualize, a politics that is *responsive* to the imperative of this immeasurable, yet perpetually immanent loss? According to what story, what compulsions, could we even imagine, let alone bring about a better future? An immeasurable future.

> ...You have not grown old and it is not too late
> to dive into your increasing depths
> > Rainier Maria Rilke, "You See, I Want a Lot" (1981: 27)

The micropolitical and the macropolitical

To respond adequately to the provocation that is the state of affairs in which we find ourselves – that is, a response that "disrupts" in order to create change, rather than to extend that state, or to flee from it – we do not need a theory of politics, we need an "analytics" (Foucault 1978: 82). Deleuze and Guattari give us one in their distinctions between the micropolitical and the macropolitical. In *A Thousand Plateaus*, the "Micropolitics and Segmentation" plateau lays out this "analytics" in the form of an ontology, an account of the components and nature of the parts of the Real and their relations. For Deleuze and Guattari, the Real, which includes the social, the individual ("the actual") and the virtual, is composed entirely of lines or "segments". Ontology is cartography, the study of those lines, but also a politics, "the study of the dangers of each line" (ATP: 227). This "study" is itself, or at least is intended to provoke, *intervention* in the present, coincident with grasping the nature of those lines and their dangers, and how those are functioning in any given domain. "Micropolitics", then, I take to refer to three possible things: (i) the scrutiny of the lines and the systems of reference that can then be applied as hermeneutic to a field of enquiry and action; (ii) a focus upon the rupturing practices that *one* kind of line or segmentation – the molecular – and *one* kind of assemblage – the abstract machine of mutation – are peculiarly capable of; and (iii) a style of intervention that Deleuze and Guattari consider to be distinct from, and more adequate than, what is called the "macropolitical". A liberal democratic project of reform, such as "democratizing" Iraq, is a good example of the latter. Moreover, micropolitical intervention is not limited to the operational theatre of what is normally considered "the political" (voting and Constitution drafting, for instance), but is a virtual possibility attending the total domain of the Real. To practise a micropolitics, practices of counter-actualization, might involve any or all of these three things. The "Micropolitics and Segmentation" plateau involves all three.

Distinguishing lines: size doesn't matter

Everything is lines and all lines are segmented. To the "arborified", tree-structured segmentation, Deleuze and Guattari oppose "rhizomatic" segmentarity. Those things or states of affairs made up of the former are called "molar assemblages" while those primarily composed of, or dominated by the latter are called "molecular assemblages". "The two forms are not simply distinguished by size", as the terms seem to suggest, "as [if] a small form and a large form; although it is true that the molecular works in detail and operates in small groups, this does not mean that it is any less coextensive with the entire social field than molar organization" (ATP: 215).

Deleuze and Guattari's political ontology does not set out an opposition between the individual and the State but an opposition between the kinds of lines and functions that appear in, and cut across, the individual and the social:

> Every society, and every individual, are thus plied by both segmentarities simultaneously: one molar, the other *molecular*. If they are distinct, it is because they do not have the same terms or the same relations or the same nature or even the same type of multiplicity. If they are inseparable, it is because they coexist and cross over into each other. The configurations differ ... but the two segmentarities are always in presupposition. In short everything is political, but every politics is simultaneously a *macropolitics* and a *micropolitics*.   (ATP: 213, original emphasis)

This ontology is indeed more complex than the ones that classic political ontologies have tended to operate with. "Class" or "gender" are molar (binary) categories, which do not lend themselves well to fully identifying multiple nodes of provocation and intervention, nor to explaining how we can "desire the very thing that dominates and exploits us" (Foucault 1983: xiii). Deleuze and Guattari's version tells us that each of these molar classes contains not-yet-specified "masses":

> that do not have the same kind of movement, distribution, or objectives [as the molar class], and do not wage the same kind of struggle ... *mass is a molecular notion* operating according to a type of segmentation irreducible to the molar segmentarity of class.   (ATP: 213, original emphasis)

What this ontology offers, at a minimum, is a more *complete* model for reading the political than the discourses of liberalism and radical politics. The political does not begin with, or come to a full stop at the edge of, the human world, but weaves the entire register (social, mental, natural–material) into the political. In this, a micropolitical model does not underdescribe the Real. It does not limit the loci of "political intervention" to a set number of already identified coordinates, nor the loci of possible "successful interventions" to a set number of already prescribed and measured outcomes; nor does it identify "politicians" as those who have a certain measure or hold a certain office (N: 170–71). Thus, micropolitics is a more flexible, adequate tool to take to conundrums such as "multiculturalism", "pollution" and "gender violence".

Each of these issues is a variation on the continuous, compelling question, "How might I live?". Deleuze and Guattari's answer, that there are *two* kinds of living to do or to be, already seems a turn for the better. One involves attending to the possibilities inherent in the microfabric of a life, and the other attending to the possibilities inherent in the macrofabric. What seems impossible on one register can have vital force on another. Isaac Stern, the great violinist, who died in September 2001 at the age of 81, said that the playing of music made him "the eternal optimist" (Kozinn 2001). That optimism didn't come from the achievement of perfection in any given piece of music but, rather, in what seems almost paradoxical, from having lived a lifetime in the constant company of the impossibility of duplicating a single performance. Stern's perpetual attending-to the vital fact of a tentative outcome – the thing never fully given in advance but that must be risked each time and fully – turns out to have been not a source of weariness and discouragement, but the very thing that allowed him perpetually to believe that the next time he performed a piece it might be a little better. His was a "belief" *towards* the better, but not *in* the better;[1] a direction and a kind of "connection of desire to reality . . . [which] possesses revolutionary force" (Foucault 1983: xiv).

The quality of possibility

This division, between the molar and the molecular, "is not just meant to indicate two states of a single process, but also to isolate two different processes" (ATP: 212). Those different processes are, on the one hand, a tendency to introduce and/or preserve homogeneous space (resemblance), to inhibit "resonance" (macropolitical), and on the other hand, a tendency to introduce or preserve heterogeneous space, to organize resonance (micropolitical). Micropolitical assemblages are "defined . . . by the nature of 'mass' – the quantum flow as opposed to the molar segmented line" (ATP: 217). Flows: something stirring and escaping, eluding the guard, trickling out from under the door, processes enabled by and defining the micropolitical. Arborescent lines, like families and religion, are machined by the abstract machine of overcoding. They tend to eat up the "budgets of flexibility" available within the imaginary, within the body, within the social, and convert these to rigid binaries, dichotomous segments, hierarchies. Random bits enter a line-up, stand in reference to, and "vibrate" only in relation to a centralized external axiom, a power centre that governs the whole as an ordered series. Predictable functions can then be extracted from this alignment. This is the basic process of the macropolitical, whether it occurs in an electron-spin tube (where electrons of all degrees of spin are converted into, strictly, clockwise and anticlockwise spins, and from which current can be generated), or whether it occurs via a legal document. The "Universal Declaration of Human Rights", for instance, defines what it is to be human (although it describes no actual person), and in this *it speaks to us*, equally. Our group-being is constituted in and through these external, equal-segmenting foci. Yet, the axiomatic itself does not prevent human rights abuses from taking place between us. It is only what we can increasingly appeal to, to speak for us, in the event of such abuse: a complex form of not speaking for ourselves (see Foucault & Deleuze 1977: 211).

Changes lobbied for, and introduced into macropolitical systems, whether massive or slight, tend to create changes in quantity, but not quality. Gay rights activists' mounting of Charter challenges in order to win the right to marry will result in more married people but no fundamental challenge to the institution and "qualities" of marriage. What get "emitted" by such systems are rigid "segments that are determinate as to their substance, form and relations" (ATP: 212). There is "a tendency to recognize and evaluate difference only from the standpoint of an implicit standard or prior identity" (Patton 2000: 47). On the contrary, what gets "emitted" by micropolitical assemblages are "existential mutations". The kind of difference unique to these "qualitative multiplicities" is not *secondary or derivative*. It is "difference as such": a joining, a neighbouring, a break or a rupture that does not define or extend a continuum; rather, it incites a heterogeneity, a shift in kind or register or a third thing altogether, a singularity, a plane of consistency, a residuum not "contained" in the prior series.[2] As we saw with the example of Stern, the infinite range of capacities that a given body contains are expressed when the impossible is involved, when we are open to truly creative additions not envisaged, yet nonetheless contained as a potentiality in and foretold by everything that led up to them (AO: 42–3). Existential mutations do not involve particular pre-fitted solutions "taken up"; rather, they contain or enable the genuine possibility of experimentation by the members, to "internally generate and direct their own projects" (Guattari 2000: 141) in direct and immediate relation to the pace and shape of their own specific problematics: "a reinvention of the ways in which we live as couples or in the family ... or as bodies" (*ibid.*: 34). What is emitted from the micropolitical is a "different logic" (*ibid.*: 44): the capacity to aim towards change that is not directed towards any goal that as yet can be conceived. Successful outcomes of the micropolitical are thus not merely the less false and more true but *the more interesting*.

A peculiar affectivity accompanies the micropolitical: the affective coefficient of knowing that things could be otherwise. One is exactly, yet temporarily, in that very place, where what that is, is as yet undetermined.[3] John Rajchman says of this "feeling" and "the political" dimension of that affectivity that,

> it is not so much a matter of being optimistic or pessimistic as of being realistic about the new forces not already contained in our projects and programs and the ways of thinking that accompany them . . . to make connections one needs not knowledge, certainty or even ontology, but rather a trust that something may come out, though one is not yet completely sure what. (2000: 7)

It is in virtue of its simultaneous "ramping up" of disruptive possibility and "(re)-trusting" in "outcomeness" that the micropolitical could be said to constitute a more adequate response to the increasing depths of the present, the "imperatives of the immeasurable" (Negri 2003: 182).

Losing time properly

The capacity inherent in the micropolitical must be understood as intimately related to Deleuze and Guattari's ontology of time, which I shall only gesture towards here. "All great results produced by human endeavour depend upon taking advantage of singular points when they occur" (Guattari 2000: 11). The becoming of the present is entangled in the becoming of the past,[4] and in the becomings of those for whom our present constitutes the conditions of their own unfolding. Events can be variably hospitable to the "to come" (Rajchman 2000: 12; Negri 2003: 258). The micropolitical, in contrast to the macropolitical intervention, is or enables "a firstness, a kind of power or chance, a freshness of what has not yet been made definite by habit or law" (Rajchman 2000: 55). One of those habits not yet made definite is the habit of time moving in one direction, and cause dutifully aligning with it. In responding adequately to the present, we can, according to Deleuze and Guattari's account of time, "go back into the event, to take one's place in it as a becoming, to grow both old and young in it at once" (N: 170). Lars von Trier quipped, "The good thing is that you never know how it would have been, you only know how it turns out" (Feinstein 2004: 11). This coming to know how it turns out does not at all annul the chief site of pragmatic intervention into a life (Guattari 2000: 8); such an intervention is always now, and the intervention's outcome is entangled in one's quality of engagement with that now, in one's openness to firstness, a quality that Deleuze himself attempted to model in a daily and lived manner. To act now, to respond adequately now, involves double vision:

"a backward-looking interpretation of the symptoms of pre-existing latent material to the forward-looking, pragmatic application of singularities toward the construction of new universes of reference for subjectification" (Guattari 2000: 150).

Each moment's unfolding involves massive loss and its losses are uniquely immeasurable: loss of the possibilities that are not themselves actualized by this now, and loss of the territories of possibilities that are foreclosed, for future beings, by this same now. While the fact of this loss, the loss that perpetually subtends the present, is unavoidable, the concept of the micropolitical tells us that *those losses are not, and need not be equal*. Consider this: in *A Thousand Plateaus* Deleuze and Guattari write, "the question . . . is not whether the status of women, or those on the bottom, is better or worse, but the type of organization *from which that status results*" (ATP: 210, emphasis added). This is a startling remark. It shifts the fulcrum of action and evaluation (thus culpability, ethical or political) from the outcomes of an action to the nature of the grounds upon which an outcome was enabled. It says that the worthiness of a thing or a state of affairs lies in the conditions of its becoming. The conditions of molecular-becoming are qualitatively distinct from the conditions of molar-becoming. The losses that attend the present in which we act, while unavoidable, can be fewer and less violent precisely to the degree that we intervene micropolitically to enable the "firstness" to come.

Return to provocations

Deleuze wrote, "Either ethics makes no sense at all, or this is what it means and has nothing else to say: not to be unworthy of what happens to us" (LS: 149). That little phrase never fails to move me. Worthiness is perhaps nothing more than the coefficient of those "better losses" and "fewer violences" in my nows. If nothing else, it is a register of the capacity to move and to be moved. This worthiness makes present and effective a *vital trust*: the "trust that something may come out, though one is not yet completely sure what" (Rajchman 2000: 7).

When I teach, I play two registers. The molar, to which the assignment "Honestly and thoroughly describe the ways in which gender-based harassment has affected your life" is directed, and the molecular, towards which the implosion of an adequate response lies. The former asks about the patterns that tend to reproduce themselves in relation to these quite stable things or states of affairs called "man" and "woman". With just a little excavation, whole series (man–woman) can be discerned that really do resonate with alarming regularity, and very painfully in too many instances "inside" the first series, the "human" one. But when the burgundy-haired woman stormed out of my office I like to imagine it was because in a very short time she had had a run-in with, and was animated by, a multiplicity of, not a poverty of registers.

First, being confronted on all flanks (classmates, instructor, memories) by creepy gender patterns broke the tyranny of the single story as it had habitually appeared in her thinking. This "breaking" almost always occurs by virtue of the anger provoked when one cannot make oneself heard over the monotonous, claustrophobic story being told about oneself. Including what one is about to become. Resistances to the reinstallation of rigid binaries (male–female after human–non-human has buckled) can be brought into play while working from and with these molar categories:

> If we consider the great binary aggregates, such as the sexes or classes, it is evident that they also cross over into molecular assemblages of a different nature ... For the two sexes [molar organizations] imply a multiplicity of molecular combinations bringing into play not only the man in the woman, and the woman in the man, but the relation of each to the animal, the plant, etc.: a thousand tiny sexes. (ATP: 213)

The "task" of getting the students to write and read immeasurable (yet expressible) personal experiences through the bifocal lenses of gender, and "requiring" them at the same time to attempt an adequate response on those same terms, had as its aim precisely to bring those tiny segmentations into view, to provoke their appearance even while I was apparently inviting a limited differentiation (man–woman). This is a task of putting students up against impossibility in order to make it vital, rather than of a piece with the losses it described.

To answer the question "What is 'micropolitical'?", one can adapt Deleuze and Guattari's answer to the question "What is philosophy?": the greatness of a politics is measured by the nature of the events to which its force summons us or that it enables (us) to release in responsiveness (WIP: 34). The political is non-stupid, non-automatic, non-habitual response (Rajchman 2000: 11). Every response shapes and reshapes an event's becoming. Micropolitics entails responsiveness in the direction of an expanded, multiplied capacity to be summoned, and an expanded capacity to respond. Micropolitics is the most viable candidate at the present time, for countering the seductive fascisms of "one size fits all" and its evil sidekick, the "single story told as though it's the only one" (John Berger, quoted by Roy 2002). If this is indeed what it is and what it does, then micropolitics is the kind and spirit of "the political" that activists and intellectuals alike ought to be thinking and (en)acting, now.

Notes

1. I am reminded of Althusser's remark on the significance of discourse that "tries to break with ideology, in order to dare to be the beginning" (1971: 162).
2. These three kinds of breaks correspond to the three forms of synthesis discussed by Deleuze and Guattari (AO: 42–84).
3. Brian Massumi (2002a) similarly describes the relation between a body and its own indeterminacy, in motion, in variation.
4. "Entanglement" is a term that refers, in quantum physics, to "a strange state of two particles so deeply connected that they share the same existence ... With entanglement, a little goes a long way. Entangle 250 quantum bits and you can simultaneously hold more numbers than there are atoms in the Universe" (www.newscientist.com/hottopics/quantum/quantum.jsp?id=22444700 (accessed Dec. 2004)).

EIGHT

Becoming-woman

Patty Sotirin

The concept of becoming-woman is both intriguing and controversial. While becoming-woman exemplifies the radical contribution and creativity of Deleuze's (and Guattari's) thought, it has provoked harsh criticism, particularly from feminist scholars. I preface my discussion of becoming-woman with a brief introduction to the concept of becoming. Then I address becoming-woman in two contexts, both described in *A Thousand Plateaus*: becoming-woman in the context of feminism and becoming-woman in the context of the girl.

Becoming

With the concept of becoming, Deleuze counters our fascination with being and power. Being is about those questions that have engaged philosophers, scientists and theologians alike for centuries: what is the essence of life, especially human life, and who are we, biologically, culturally, historically and spiritually? What does it mean to exist? Our fascination with power engages us in questions of control, possession and order: how is life, organic and inorganic, but especially human life, ordered, classified, distributed and managed? How ought we reproduce ourselves to preserve the essence of who we are and who and what hinders us from being all we can be or helps us so that we can be all that and more? Running behind these questions are becomings that do not stop to participate in the organized forms we can recognize as men and women, human beings and animals, children and adults, families and organizations. In *A Thousand Plateaus,* Deleuze and Guattari posit a line of becomings that begins with becoming-woman: "on the near side, we encounter becomings-woman, becomings-child (becoming-woman, more than any other becoming, possesses a special introductory power . . .). On the far side, we find becomings-elementary, -cellular, -molecular, and even becomings-imperceptible" (ATP: 248). These becomings animate the possibilities of life, constantly moving through what we know to be real or true and running beyond the limits, boundaries and constraints that make those realities and truths what they seem to be.

Becoming explodes the ideas about what we are and what we can be beyond the categories that seem to contain us: beyond the boundaries separating human being from animal, man from woman, child from adult, micro from macro, and even perceptible and understandable from imperceptible and incomprehensible. Becoming moves beyond our need to know (the truth, what is real, what makes us human); beyond our determination to control (life, nature, the universe); and beyond our desire to consume or possess (pleasure, beauty, goodness, innocence). So becoming offers a radical conception of what a life does. For Deleuze, becomings are about passages, propagations and expansions. I illustrate the conceptual creativity of becomings by attending to five animating dynamics: becomings as elements of Deleuze's "positive ontology"; the "block of becoming"; the importance of thresholds; immanence; and becomings as non-representational.

"Positive ontology"

Deleuze's work is often applauded for the "positive ontology" it pursues. By this, scholars acknowledge that Deleuze is concerned with unfettering possibility to experiment with what a life can do and where a life might go. In other words, Deleuze affirms the possibilities of becoming something else, beyond the avenues, relations, values and meanings that seem to be laid out for us by our biological make-up, our evolutionary heritages, our historical/political/familial allegiances, and the social and cultural structures of civilized living. There is in this a radical affirmation of the sort of possibilities for becoming that we cannot think of in logical or moralistic terms: becomings that can only be felt or sensed or conjured, that require us to take risks and experiment in ways that affirm the vitality, the energies and the creative animations of existence.

The block of becoming

The block of becoming diverts attention from becoming as a transformation from one identity to another and attends instead to what

Deleuze and Guattari call "multiplicities" composed of heterogeneous singularities in dynamic compositions. Becoming is "always in the middle" and in-between (ATP: 293). We might be tempted to think of becoming in terms of where or who we were when we started and where or who we are when we end up. But becoming is not about origins, progressions and ends; rather, it is about lines and intensities, "modes of expansion, propagation, occupation, contagion, peopling" (ATP: 239). To put this another way, Deleuze and Guattari have described the movement of becoming as "rhizomatic", a term that refers to underground root growth, the rampant, dense propagation of roots that characterizes such plants as mint or crabgrass. Each rhizomatic root may take off in its own singular direction and make its own connections with other roots, with worms, insects, rocks or whatever, forming a dynamic composition of "interkingdoms [and] unnatural participations" (ATP: 242) that has no prescribed form or end. It is important to note here that roots, rocks and insects each have their own "molar" or insular configuration, their own distinctiveness that sets them off and apart from each other. But such "molar" configurations are composed of an infinity of particles; lines of becoming may break off particles, recomposing them, deterritorializing them from their proper place in a molar configuration. For example, the rhizomatic roots of mint plants may break through a seemingly impenetrable concrete retaining wall, one molecule at a time; the detachment of each concrete particle by the collocation of a plant particle has its own singularity. The molar configurations of plant and wall are multiplicities that the molecular lines of becoming may move through and beyond, recomposing each into a plant-wall.

The importance of thresholds

Thresholds are zones "in-between" two multiplicities, what Deleuze and Guattari refer to as "zones of proximity", where the elements of multiplicities enter into, and pass through and between each other. Thresholds precede the bifurcations and distinctions that separate one multiplicity from another. As Deleuze and Guattari observe, "the self is only a threshold, a door, a becoming between two multiplicities" (ATP: 249). While we might think of the self as that which is ours, the site of our uniqueness and that which most distinguishes us from others, in this observation Deleuze and Guattari cast the self as preceding these forms and functions of self-organization. So the importance of thresholds is that these "in-betweens" are becomings. When we are "in-between", on the threshold, what keeps us distinct from this or that can become indiscernible or indistinct or imperceptible.

One such threshold that has gained considerable notoriety is the cyborg, an "in-between" human and machine, organic and inorganic, biological and technological, natural and unnatural, real and artificial, fact and fiction, reality and fantasy, power and desire. The cyborg is a threshold at which the possibilities we have hoped for in the past and those we seek in the future become indistinct; we are all now becoming "hybridized", "biomatic" and "technocorporeal". The rhizomatic spread of cybernetic systems has rendered contemporary life a cyborgian threshold for the initiatory journeys into becoming, a threshold that, to paraphrase Deleuze and Guattari, is "where becoming itself becomes" (ATP: 249). As several feminist theorists have pointed out, the cyborg is a threshold for feminist theoretical–political interventions; an "in-between" that participates in both molar struggles over the embodied identities, institutionalized orders and material conditions of women's lives and the wild imaginings and radical practices that strive toward transgressive, creative and indeterminate possibilities for living differently (see Balsamo 1996; Braidotti 2002; Grosz 1994; Haraway 1991). Once again, we find here a radical affirmation of possibilities that cannot be predetermined, "where one changes becoming depending on the 'hour' of the world, the circles of hell, or the stages of a journey that sets scales, forms, and cries in variation" (ATP: 249).

Immanence

Thus far, I have emphasized the radical creativity and dynamic vitality of becoming. But it is the immanence of becoming that is the most critical aspect of becomings. Deleuze's philosophy is often called a philosophy of immanence because it is concerned with what a life can do, what a body can do when we think in terms of becomings, multiplicities, lines and intensities rather than essential forms, predetermined subjects, structured functions or transcendent values. Such forms, subjects, functions and values constitute planes of organization, hidden structures that can be known only through their effects, for example, the "nuclear family" with its underlying patriarchal structure, heteronormative subjects, reproductive functions and Judeo-Christian values. In contrast, a plane of immanence has no structure and does not produce predetermined forms or subjects; instead, there are "relations of movement and rest, speed and slowness ... molecules and particles of all kinds" (ATP: 266). Deleuze and Guattari refer to this plane as a Body without Organs, a BwO: a body that is not organized in accord with biological functions, organic forms, or cultural–historical values. Rather, a BwO deconstructs these seemingly inviolable arrangements, deterritorializing particles, intensities, energies in molecular lines of flows, thresholds and becomings.

Deleuze and Parnet explain the movement of a plane of immanence as "proceeding by thresholds, constituting becomings, blocs of becoming, marking continuums of intensity, combinations of fluxes" (D: 130). Multiplicities, thresholds, becomings are intersected, traversed and brought into coexistence, like the vibrations of different sounds, the sound of a bird, a rainstorm, a thunderbolt, a child's cry, that are brought together in the immanence of a moment, becoming a single sound, so that the singularity of each vibration becomes imperceptible even as this imperceptibility is just what is heard. This is a description of a life: multiplicities, thresholds, lines and intensities come into coexistence in "the indefinite and virtual time of the pure event" (Smith 1997: xxxv). This simultaneous collapse and expansion of spatiotemporal dimensions into pure events and individuations or "haecceities" comprise the "thisness" that is our immanent existence.

Becoming as non-representational

Finally, becoming is non-representational:

> Becoming is certainly not imitating, or identifying with something; neither is it regressing-progressing; neither is it corresponding, . . . [nor] producing . . . Becoming is a verb with a consistency all its own; it does not reduce to, or lead back to, "appearing," "being," "equalling" or "producing".　　　　　　(ATP: 239)

For Deleuze and Guattari, becomings are processes of desire. When they talk about becoming-woman, they are adamant about this non-representational process of movement, proximity and desire:

> What we term a molar entity is, for example, the woman as defined by her form, endowed with organs and functions and assigned as a subject . . . [Becoming-woman is] not imitating or assuming the female form, but emitting particles that enter the relation of movement and rest, or the zone of proximity, of a microfemininity, in other words, that produce in us a molecular woman, create the molecular woman.　　　　　　(ATP: 275)

Becoming-woman does not have to do with being a woman, being like a woman or standing in for a woman. Rather, Deleuze and Guattari offer becoming-woman as a key threshold for a line of flight that passes through and beyond the binary distinctions that define and confine our lives. Becoming-woman is the first threshold because becomings are always molecular deterritorializations, that is, effects destabilizing dominant molar forms and relations. The "molar entity par excellence" is man, the rational, white, adult male (ATP: 292). Hence, there can be no "becoming-man" because becomings resonate to the subordinate figure in the dualisms constituted around man as the dominant figure: male/female, adult/child, white/non-white, rational/emotional and so on. As Claire Colebrook puts it, becoming-woman is "a privileged becoming in so far as she short-circuits the self-evident identity of man" (2000: 12). Becoming-woman disrupts the rigid hierarchies of sexual binaries such as male/female, heterosexuality/homosexuality, masculinity/femininity that organize our bodies, our experiences, our institutions and our histories. Both men and women must become-woman, Deleuze and Guattari argue, in order to deterritorialize the binary organization of sexuality; sexuality then becomes "the production of a thousand sexes, which are so many uncontrollable becomings" (ATP: 278). This is the unleashing of desire, the opening of a life, and the threshold to imperceptibility.

Becoming-woman: feminist politics and women's talk

Becoming-woman offers a critical alternative to a feminist politics that continually hangs itself up on binary oppositions such as woman/man, female/male, feminine/masculine, mother/father, nature/culture and emotion/reason. While women's struggles for definition and control over their own bodies, histories and subjectivities are certainly necessary, Deleuze and Guattari warn that continually confronting "the great dualism machines" of history, society, philosophy and science will only emphasize and reinforce binary relations rather than liberating women from them. Instead, they urge women to conceive of a molecular political movement that "slips into molar confrontations, and passes under or through them" (ATP: 276). In other words, a vital feminist politics must become rhizomatic rather than confrontative and must make of itself a BwO, a Body without Organs, so that feminism is no longer confined to the subject of women's rights, bodies, histories and oppressions, to an identity-based, representational mode of politics. By becoming rhizomatic, feminist politics can engage in a "contagious" micropolitical movement "capable of crossing and impregnating an entire social field" (ATP: 276). And yet, if a molecular women's politics is rhizomatic, a rampant process of desire without plan or logic that "slips into and through" confrontations between molar identities, then what becomes of feminism as a political force?

This is the concern of the "third-wave" feminist scholars participating in discussions on the NextGENDERation e-network over the mercurial and ephemeral political alliances and demonstrations that have materialized through web-based connections. In these exchanges, the question raised is:

> What happens to knowledges coming out of the struggles of multiple, but differentiated, subject positions related to sexual differences, ethnicities, and sexualities as we know them today, when they are collapsed in an undifferentiated concept of "the multitude"? A movement that all too easily forgets which embodied struggles generated crucial tools such as "the personal is the political", the politics of everyday life and the politics of desire.
>
> (Andrijasevic & Bracke 2003)

Other feminist scholars warn that by casting "becoming-woman" as a privileged and undifferentiated phase of becomings, Deleuze and Guattari enervate the political force of feminism and deny the sexual specificities of becoming. For example, Patricia MacCormack points out that becoming-woman is, after all, the creation of woman by men, in the service of "a male project toward alterity. Women remain, in this project, the first marker of difference and of marginality" (2001). These are serious concerns.

At the same time, becoming-woman has energized feminist thinking and activism in the work of Rosi Braidotti, Claire Colebrook, Moira Gatens, Camilla Griggers, Elizabeth Grosz, Tamsin Lorraine, Dorothea Olkowski and others. For example, Grosz (1994: 174) argues that the BwO offers feminism a volatile body, one that resists traditional hierarchies, oppressions and dualisms to enter into micro-struggles, micro-particularities in wild, unpredictable trajectories and relations. Colebrook extols the "spirit of positive becoming" for feminist thought: "This might provide a way of thinking new modes of becoming – not as the becoming of some subject, but a becoming towards others, a becoming towards difference, and a becoming through new questions" (2000: 12). Such becomings, she suggests, resonate to:

> the peculiar modality of feminist questions and the active nature of feminist struggle. When confronted with a theory or body of thought feminism has tended to ask an intensely active question, not "What does it mean?", but "How does it work?" What can this

concept or theory do? How can such a theory exist or be lived? What are its forces? (*Ibid.*: 8)

Let us consider the case of women's small talk: chatter, gossip, girl-talk, bitching. The labels belong to a molar identity: feminine, feminized and feminizing; signified as denigrated and denigrating (see Bergmann 1993). The intensities of such talk – the pettiness, nastiness, nosiness, cattiness – are often ascribed to aspects of women's embodied, essential nature: menstruation, hormones, monthly irritabilities, and perpetual insecurities, jealousies and resentments (Pringle 1988: 238). Further, the careful focus on mundane details and relationships is often attributed to women's biologically and sociohistorically ascribed responsibilities for taking care of the minutiae of our familial, domestic and emotional lives. Finally, the pleasures of small talk are bound to patterns of women's sociality and oral culture: intimate conversations, friendship pacts, secret alliances and petty victories (see Jones 1990). It is little wonder that such talk is often seen as a performance of innate femaleness (see Ashcraft & Pacanowsky 1996).

I contend, however, that women's small talk – gossip, bitching, girl-talk, chatter – does not "represent" women, either as an expression of women's essential biochemical, psychic or sociocultural nature or as a mode of capitulation or resistance to their gendered subordination. Hence, feminism need not recuperate, reclaim nor apologize for women's small talk (see Sotirin & Gottfried 1999). I suggest, rather, that the concept of becoming-woman allows us to think about such talk differently, in terms of how it works and what its forces are. The becoming-woman of women's small talk opens possibilities for a "contagious microfemininsm" that does not "take a stand" on any particular identity or issue so much as open radical alternatives for living a "political" life by creating wild lines of resonance and intensity through and beyond the binary relations of domination and oppression that structure the molar positions of conventional gender politics.

In Deleuze–Guattarian terms, small talk is a threshold, a becoming-woman that articulates the singularities of mundane events and asserts the immanence of everyday life: in the speed and linkages that transport opinions, confidences, insults and judgements; in the affective flows that deterritorialize conventional relations of propriety, hierarchy and reason; in impulsive, often illogical, sometimes destructive energies; in the coexistence of intense affects – dissatisfactions, pettinesses, trivialities; and in the heterogeneity of all such microlevel impulses that threaten to overrun the quietude of everyday life. To paraphrase Deleuze and Guattari, we can be "thrown into becoming" by the "most insignificant of things", including the trivialities and pettinesses of small talk. Further, there is no deviation from the majority without "a little detail that starts to swell and carries you off" (ATP: 292) such as a hormonal shift, a snide comment, or a pang of resentment: little details that create rhizomatic lines of becomings. For example, the sounds of women's chatter offer a threshold to a line of becomings-animal, linking women to hens – clucking, scolding, ganging up to "hen-peck" the weaker members of the flock – and to cats – fighting, hissing, scratching, yowling. The clucking of the hens and the hissing of the cats can be thought of as particular particles of affective intensity and sound vibrations that move with considerable speed through women's social networks and pass under and through the nature–culture binary that undergirds these stereotypes of women's talk.

The core of small talk, especially of gossip, bitching and girl-talk, is the secret: having secrets, telling secrets, keeping secrets, but mostly passing secrets along. Deleuze and Guattari seem to be describing women's small talk as they describe the secret:

> Men alternately fault [women] for their indiscretion, their gossiping, and for their solidarity, their betrayal. Yet it is curious how a woman can be secretive while at the same time hiding nothing, by virtue of transparency, innocence, and speed . . . There are women . . . who tell everything, sometimes in appalling technical detail, but one knows no more at the end than at the beginning; they have hidden everything by celerity, by limpidity.   (ATP: 289)

According to Deleuze and Guattari, there are three becomings of the secret: a becoming-child in having a secret (as in the playground taunt, "I have a secret"), whereby it loses its content; a becoming-feminine as the secret becomes transparent, a secret everyone knows, whereby it loses its form as a secret; and a becoming-molecular as the content is molecularized and the form becomes a "pure moving line" (ATP: 290). The becoming-molecular of the secret is a composition of sound and vibration. In the becomings of the secret, women's small talk articulates the petty, the mundane, the everyday, the here-and-now with an immanent plane of affects, intensities, sounds and vibrations. At the same time, small talk is forever recuperated or reterritorialized; as common wisdom would have it, small talk keeps women in their (molar) places.

Perhaps the most poignant example of the work of the secret is in what popular treatises such as *Odd Girl Out* (Simmons 2002), *Reviving Ophelia* (Pipher 1994), *Schoolgirls* (Orenstein 1995) and *Queen Bees and Wannabes* (Wiseman 2003) have dubbed "the secret culture of adolescent girls": a web of intense affects and energies, where small talk, especially secrets, moves through dense packs of schoolgirls, creating and destroying popularity, friendship and self-worth. Secrets, innuendos, and lies move contagiously through such packs, becoming publicly transparent, becoming molecular particles of betrayal, aggression, loyalty and affection, becoming pure moving lines, thresholds between isolation and inclusion, self-coherence and dissolution. These are lines that spin off into the black holes of depression, fear, anxiety and self-destruction; they carry as well the risk of "turning into lines of abolition, of destruction, of others and of oneself" (D: 140), saturating the event of girlhood. Such is the risk of becomings.

Becoming-woman: the girl

It is not casually that I introduce the figure of the girl. Deleuze and Guattari's descriptions of becoming-woman highlight the girl and both the reasons for this emphasis and the concerns that have been raised about it are important to appreciate. The girl is a becoming, say Deleuze and Guattari; she is a becoming-molecular, a line of flight, "the block of becoming that remains contemporaneous to each opposable term, man, woman, child, adult" (ATP: 277). There is, in the girl, an "in-between" to all of the most pernicious dualisms that constitute us as subjects and that give significance to our most fundamental relationships. Becoming-woman is the introductory segment of becomings because the girl is the autopoetic force of becoming: "Girls do not belong to an age group, sex, order, or kingdom: they slip in everywhere, between orders, acts, ages, sexes; they produce n molecular sexes on the line of flight in relation to the dualism machines they cross right through" (ATP: 277). The girl is an experiment, constantly traversing borderlines of childhood and adulthood, innocence and disenchantment, naiveté and wisdom. She is not becoming a woman; she is always a becoming-woman.

However, there are aspects of the girl–becoming-woman that feminists have rightly decried. First, although Deleuze and Guattari object to the fact that the girl's body is "taken from her" in that she too often becomes the object of masculine desire and the property of a patriarchal economy, the notion that the girl is a becoming seems also to "take away" her body. Secondly, the necessity for both women and men to become-woman denies any gender specificity to the girl. By rendering the specificities of the girl's sexuality moot, becoming-woman denudes a feminist perspective of a standpoint for critique and intervention. Thirdly, since becoming-imperceptible is the immanent end of becoming-woman, the girl seems to replicate unwittingly the subordination and suppression of girls culturally and historically. Consider the American Association of University Women's report on girls in the classroom (Wellesley College & AAUW 1992), which found that the talents and capacities of girls for mathematics and science become less perceptible to teachers and others within academic institutions as girls move into the higher grades (as they become women). More seriously, the reductions and suppressions of the girl in becoming-woman resonate to cultural–historical devaluations of women, their imperceptibility within a patriarchal economy that denies or justifies women's oppression, and the most egregious practices of sexual discrimination and oppression (infanticide, genital mutilation, child molestation). Girls too often slip imperceptibly under the radar of public policies, institutional safeguards, community concerns and familial priorities. These are indeed serious concerns.

At the same time, the girl offers intriguing opportunities for feminist theory and politics. The girl is neither a representation nor the starting-point for becoming-(a-)woman. Rather, the girl is the force of desire that breaks off particles from the molar compositions that constitute us as women and men, young and old, heterosexual, homosexual or bisexual, creating lines of rampant propagation and contagion and a "diversity of conjugated becomings" (ATP: 278). In short, the girl knows how to love: "Knowing how to love does not mean remaining a man or a woman; it means extracting from one's sex the particles, the speeds and slownesses, the flows, the n sexes that constitute the girl of *that* sexuality" (ATP: 277, original emphasis). The vision of love in this description is not about carnal lust, Oedipalized desire, or misogynist romance. "Knowing how to love" is not about being in love, being loved or making love between sexed beings. Rather, the flows and conjugations of the girl constitute a dynamic affective composition that runs imperceptibly but with great force through everybody and everything. Thus, "knowing how to love" is the "immanent end of becoming". And since everybody and everything is the aggregate of molar entities, becoming everybody and everything, that is, becoming-imperceptible and indiscernibly in-between, is to make a different world (ATP: 280). The girl is the rhizomatic line and the threshold into this alternative world. This is a compelling conception of love, life and what might become of the world.

Conclusion

Becoming-woman and the girl are creative and exciting Deleuzian concepts. And yet, there is need to attend to the serious concerns that feminists and others have raised over the masculinist bias of becoming-woman, notably the dissipation of feminist political force that it portends and the lived dangers of slippage into black holes and imperceptibility that Deleuze and Guattari seem to ignore in conceptualizing the girl as the threshold for becoming-woman. Still, to give over the concept of becoming-woman to these concerns would be to reterritorialize the possibilities that it offers and domesticate the animating potential of becoming. I have argued that becoming-woman opens creative possibilities, provides a powerful alternative to feminist molar politics, and engages with theoretical feminism's most vital impulses and sensibilities. As philosophical concepts, becoming-woman and the girl allow us to think differently, imagine new modes of becomings, animate forces of desire, and open doors and thresholds into new worlds.

NINE

The Minor

Ronald Bogue

In a lengthy diary entry dated 25 December 1911, Kafka outlines the
characteristics of small literary communities, such as those of East
European Yiddish writers or the Czech authors of his native Prague
(Kafka 1977: 191–5).[1] In such minor literatures, Kafka observes, there
are no towering figures, like Shakespeare in English or Goethe in German, who dominate the landscape and thereby discourage innovation
or invite sycophantic emulation. Literary discussions are intense in a
minor literature, political and personal issues interpenetrate, and the
formation of a literary tradition is of direct concern to the people. In
Kafka: Toward a Minor Literature, Deleuze and Guattari argue that
Kafka's diary entry is less a sociological sketch of particular artistic
milieus than a description of the ideal community within which he
would like to write. Despite his adoption of German as his medium, they
claim, Kafka's aspiration is to create within the major tradition of German letters a minor literature, one that experiments with language,
ignores canonical models, fosters collective action and treats the
personal as something immediately social and political. What Kafka's
example ultimately discloses for Deleuze and Guattari is an approach
to writing that may be extended to literature as a whole.

Deleuze and Guattari argue that in a minor literature "language is
affected with a high coefficient of deterritorialization" (K: 16), everything "is political", and "everything takes on a collective value" (K: 17);
hence, they conclude, "the three characteristics of minor literature are
the deterritorialization of language, the connection of the individual to
a political immediacy, and the collective assemblage of enunciation" (K:
18). That minor literature connects the individual and the political is a

110

relatively clear point, but what Deleuze and Guattari mean by the deterritorialization of language and the collective assemblage of enunciation requires some elucidation.

Minor literature's deterritorialization of language must be understood within Deleuze and Guattari's general theory of language, which they articulate most clearly in sections four and five of *A Thousand Plateaus*. Language, for Deleuze and Guattari, is a mode of action, a way of doing things with words. Just as the jury transforms the defendant into a felon upon the declaration of a guilty verdict, so all language instigates "incorporeal transformations" (ATP: 86) of bodies (bodies construed in the broadest sense to include not simply solid physical objects but also images, sounds, hallucinations – the gamut of the non-discursive). Language's primary function is not to communicate neutral information but to enforce a social order by categorizing, organizing, structuring and coding the world. Every language presupposes two strata of relations of power: a discursive "collective assemblage of enunciation" and a non-discursive "machinic assemblage of bodies" (ATP: 88). These discursive and non-discursive assemblages are regulated patterns of social action, one shaping words, the other shaping things, and the two interacting as words intervene in things by producing incorporeal transformations of bodies.

Linguists traditionally characterize a language in terms of constants and invariables, treating variations in the actual use of a language as either meaningless phenomena or as deviations from a norm. Hence, the standard pronunciation of a given word determines the range of its acceptable enunciations (insignificant variants) and unacceptable enunciations (deviations). Dialects, sociolects and idiolects are regarded as departures from the standard tongue, ungrammatical sentences as violations of standard syntax, malapropisms as deviations from standard usage, and so on. Deleuze and Guattari counter, however, that variables are primary in a language and that constants, norms and rules are secondary enforcements of power relations. The world of language usage, of linguistic *action*, is one of perpetual variation, interaction, negotiation and contestation, in which language users shape and mould words as elements within shifting contexts, now playing with phrases, altering patterns, and inventing meanings, now restricting linguistic variation and thereby enforcing distinctions of class, privilege, sophistication, gender and social role (most notably through schools, but also through courts, professions, diverse media and so on).

When language users subvert standard pronunciations, syntactic structures or meanings, they "deterritorialize" the language, in that they detach it from its clearly delineated, regularly gridded territory of conventions, codes, labels and markers. Conversely, when users reinforce linguistic norms, they "territorialize" and "reterritorialize" the language. The processes of deterritorialization and reterritorialization go on perpetually within every language, as standard linguistic practices are either transformed and set in disequilibrium or repeated and perpetuated. Hence, one may speak of a language's relative "coefficient of deterritorialization", some language communities restricting the play of their linguistic lines of continuous variation more than others. Deleuze and Guattari state that in a minor literature "language is affected with a high coefficient of deterritorialization" (K: 16), and in their study of Kafka they argue that Prague German in Kafka's day had a high level of deterritorialization, in that it was a governmental "paper language" detached from an indigenous tradition of usage and affected in various ways through its appropriation by Czech speakers. Kafka exploited Prague German's various zones of deterritorialization in his works, they claim, exacerbating its tendencies toward disequilibrium and creating within the major language of German a minor, foreign tongue. But Deleuze and Guattari's argument, finally, is not that some languages are major and others minor, or that a minor literature is possible only within a major language, for major and minor "do not qualify two different languages but rather two usages or functions of language" (ATP: 104).[2] Their point is that every language, no matter how large or small its population of users, is open to a major or a minor usage, to a reterritorialization or deterritorialization of its components and practices, and minor writers make a minor usage of their linguistic medium when they create minor literature.

For Deleuze and Guattari, there is no strict separation of form and content in the minor usage of a language, and hence no marked differentiation between stylistic experimentation and political critique. Language is a mode of action, an ongoing implementation of relations of power, and all linguistic elements – phonemic, morphemic, syntactic and semantic – are involved in the generation of power relations via discursive practices. In this regard, language usage as a whole is immediately and thoroughly political. Minor writers deterritorialize linguistically enacted relations of power, and hence what might seem, for example, a mere stylistic experimentation with syntax (such as one finds in e e cummings's poetry) in fact is a linguistic practice with an inextricably political dimension. Conversely, what might seem a commentary on the content of linguistic representations – say, a framing of a son's confrontation with his father as a meeting between defendant and judge – is actually an experimentation with semantics (in this case, perhaps the activation of the line of continuous variation of "I'm innocent!" that passes through a familial and a judicial context). Minor writers make language stammer; they deform and transform its regular patterns in such a way that the language itself stutters, as the language's virtual lines of continuous variation are actualized in new and unpredictable combinations. And in the process, minor writers contest and undo the power relations immanent within the dominant, major usage patterns of a language.

Minor literature is a literature of "minorities", yet not in the usual sense of that word. Majorities and minorities are not determined by sheer numbers. The group of Western white male adults may represent a relatively small sample of the world's population; nevertheless, that group functions as the majority, and those outside that group are members of various minorities. Nor are minorities defined by fixed identities or characteristics. Instead, majorities and minorities are mutually determined through their positions in power relations, and thus through their function rather than their possession of some defining trait, whether statistical, religious, ethnic, racial or biological. Minor literature seeks to subvert dominant power relations, and in that sense its orientation is in support of the struggles of minorities. Yet not all works written by minorities are instances of minor literature, for minorities may perpetuate binary power relations if they do not themselves become other and deterritorialize the codes that determine their position as minorities. Conversely, Western white male adults may produce minor literature, but only if they engage in a becoming-other that undermines their own position of privilege.

Minor literature's first two characteristics, then, are that it deterritorializes language, and in so doing it "connects the individual to a political immediacy" (K: 18). Its third characteristic is that it engages a "collective assemblage of enunciation" (K: 18) and thereby opens up new possibilities for political action. Deleuze and Guattari label the discursive relations of power that underlie the usage of a given language a "collective assemblage of enunciation", primarily to make the simple point that no individual user invents a language. Rather, language is collectively produced and reproduced through social interaction. In this regard, all literature, whether major or minor, engages a collective assemblage of enunciation. In a major literature, however, authors seek to develop a unique voice and express themselves as individuals, whereas in a minor literature writers try to efface themselves and articulate collective voices, specifically, those of the minorities whose identities are determined through asymmetrical power relations. Yet minor writers face a difficult problem; they cannot simply speak in the name of a given minority, for that minority is defined, structured and regulated by the dominant powers it seeks to resist. Thus, minor writers necessarily must attempt to articulate the voice of a collectivity that does not yet exist. Their task, then, is to help invent a "people to come" (ECC: 90), or at least promote new possibilities for the future formation of an active, self-determining collectivity. They do so not by promoting specific political action or by protesting oppression (although such actions do have their own value), but by inducing processes of becoming-other, by undermining stable power relations and thereby activating lines of continuous variation in ways that have previously been restricted and blocked.

If we rephrase Deleuze and Guattari's tripartite definition, then, we may say that minor literature: (i) experiments with language; (ii) treats the world as a network of power relations; and (iii) opens possibilities for a people to come. What this means in concrete terms may perhaps best be approached by considering a bit further Deleuze and Guattari's handling of Kafka, the minor writer they examine most closely. They see Kafka's experimentation with language as arising from his situation as a Prague Jew speaking a deracinated, formal German that has been given a regional flavour through its contact with Czech speakers. Kafka's knowledge of Czech, as well as his later exposure to Yiddish literature and Hebrew texts, helps to distance him even further from his native tongue, eventually leading him to discover a subtly unsettling way of using German. Although Kafka observes the stylistic proprieties of standard German, he does so with a detached fastidiousness and an ascetic impoverishment of materials that render the language uncannily foreign while remaining technically correct. Deleuze and Guattari provide no specific examples of Kafka's stylistic innovations, citing instead the experimental practices of such writers as e e cummings, Louis-Ferdinand Céline and Samuel Beckett as instances of a minor deterritorialization of language. Yet their point is clear: what e e cummings, Céline and Beckett do overtly, Kafka does in a covert fashion: he makes language strange.

"The Metamorphosis" provides Deleuze and Guattari with an apt illustration of the interpenetration of the personal and the social in minor literature, as well as an example of becoming-other as a means of attempting change. Often this story is read as a fable of modern despair or a symptom of Oedipal anxiety, but Deleuze and Guattari insist that its subject is thoroughly political. Although Gregor's insect transformation takes place within the confines of the family household, the relations of power that affect him extend well beyond its walls. Gregor is enslaved to his job because of his father's debts to the company. The boss's representative, the boot-clad manager, enters the Samsa apartment and chastises Gregor, in the name of his parents, for neglecting his business duties; once the manager leaves, Gregor's father picks up the manager's cane to drive Gregor back into his room. When Gregor's father is later transformed into a vigorous authority figure, he is clad in a bank messenger's uniform and his voice seems to Gregor to be that of several fathers. And when the Samsas eventually decline into shabby resignation before their fate, their positions at the dining table are usurped by the three anonymous lodgers, representatives of some unnamed bureaucratic or commercial organization. Far from expressing a neurotic's obsession with fathers, "The Metamorphosis" presents relations of power that render the family members mere connecting points in a network of socioeconomic, gender-coded forces. Gregor's father is a mere relay in circuits of bosses, sub-bosses, agents and representatives whose influence saturates the household. In response to his imprisonment within this network of forces, Gregor becomes other, becomes-animal in an effort to alter his situation. Gregor's becoming-insect, like the many other animal becomings in Kafka's stories, is not symbolic or metaphoric, but metamorphic, a simple process of undoing codes and deterritorializing coordinates in order to open a line of flight. Unfortunately, Gregor's efforts fail. His father repeatedly blocks his escape, and his sister, who had initially encouraged Gregor in his becoming-animal, abandons him when he continues to cling to his human identity.

Deleuze and Guattari may seem to be offering a mere allegorical reading of Kafka's tale, but they insist that Kafka is not just talking about power; rather, he is engaged in an experimentation on the real. The relations of power immanent within the world are enmeshed in linguistic codes and representations, and Kafka's story actualizes those relations of power in such a way that they are modified and reconfigured. This somewhat elusive point is most clearly developed in Deleuze and Guattari's discussion of *The Trial*. Kafka's novel presents the Law as a complex machine, whose parts are heterogeneous objects, spaces, vehicles, institutions and people. Everyone is connected with the Law – K, K's uncle, Leni, the artist Titorelli, the little girls outside Titorelli's studio – and every place is a legal site. The tenement contains a courtroom, the bank storage room is a penal chamber, the cathedral is staffed by a prison chaplain, and Titorelli's studio adjoins the law court offices. The Law machine's final purpose is not to judge right and wrong or assign guilt and innocence, but simply to function: to generate, shape, situate and regulate its own components in perpetually moving circuits. This Law machine is a kind of caricature of the power mechanisms Kafka saw at work in the Austro-Hungarian Empire, but also a prescient blueprint of disciplinary regimes to come.

In *The Trial*, then, Kafka engages in sociopolitical critique, but not by overt commentary or explicit analysis. Nor does his critique promote a

specific programme of action or alternative model for social organization. K initially wants to learn the facts of his case and put an end to his
involvement with the Law, but eventually he discovers that outright
acquittal is impossible and that his best strategy is one of indefinitely
prolonging and postponing his case. There is no way of stepping outside the Law entirely; there is no alternative order beyond and separate
from the circuits of power within which he must operate. Indefinite
prolongation and postponement are means of functioning within the
Law machine but in such a way that its mechanisms slip, short circuit
and break down. K's movements from site to site, from person to person, follow the connections of the network of power, yet, as he proceeds, he and his surroundings mutually modify one another. His
relations with women initiate him into a becoming-woman, his contacts
with children into a becoming-child, but finally K's metamorphic becoming is that of a becoming-imperceptible, as he attains the status of
an anonymous locus of concurrent functioning and dysfunctioning of
the machine. It is this conjunction of functioning and dysfunctioning,
of a simultaneous assembling and dismantling of the law machine, that
constitutes Kafka's critique of power, and that critique is also the vehi-
cle of possible social change.

What *The Trial* does, we might say, is identify and extract configurations of power relations immanent within the representations and codes
of Kafka's world, and then modify, mutate and transform them in such
a way that they disclose "the diabolical powers of the future that are
already knocking at the door – capitalism, Stalinism, fascism" (K: 83).
Kafka's novel is an experimental deformation of the institutions, codes,
mechanisms and practices around him that discloses their tendencies
toward future configurations and uses. Virtual lines of continuous variation that might eventuate in the diverse state forms of bureaucratic
capitalism, totalitarian Stalinism or absolutist fascism are immanent
within Kafka's world, and his novel discloses those lines of variation
through its experimental mutation of present relations, forms and
conditions.

These lines of continuous variation are vectors of potential development of actual power relations in Kafka's world, vectors that may reinforce and intensify oppressive codes and practices, or perhaps open up
something new. Minor literature's third characteristic is that it gives
voice to collective assemblages of enunciation "insofar as they're not
imposed from without and insofar as they exist only as diabolical powers to come or revolutionary forces to be constructed" (K: 18). In *The
Trial* Kafka reveals potential vectors for the emergence of a "coming
collectivity" but "without our knowing yet what this assemblage will be:

fascist? revolutionary? socialist? capitalist? Or even all of these at the same time, connected in the most repugnant or diabolical way? We don't know" (K: 85). What Kafka's example finally indicates, then, is that although minor literature furthers the invention of a people to come, it cannot do so through the delineation of some utopian social order, but only through the risk-laden instigation of a movement toward an unknowable future.

In *Kafka*, Deleuze and Guattari largely restrict their discussion of minor literature to prose fiction, but elsewhere Deleuze suggests some ways in which the notion of the minor might be extended to the theatre and cinema as well. In "One Less Manifesto",[3] a lengthy essay on the contemporary Italian playwright Carmelo Bene, Deleuze outlines the features of a minor theatre via an analysis of Bene's *Richard III*, a reworking of Shakespeare's history play in which the characters' lines are Shakespeare's (via a loose Italian translation) but their actions are new (Deleuze 1993b). Bene excises half Shakespeare's text and all the male characters except Richard, and in the process he scrambles Shakespeare's plot of state power and uncovers a latent tale of Richard's obsession with the women of the play. As Richard and the women characters recite Shakespeare's lines, the women engage in various seductive actions while Richard straps diverse prostheses to his body and lurches in increasingly bizarre movements. This action, in Deleuze's analysis, is a staging of Richard's becoming-woman, a process whereby Richard departs from his official state identity not by imitating the women but by becoming unnatural, non-human, eccentrically "other" via his interaction with them, by passing between the poles of male and female. But besides modifying and deforming Shakespeare's text, Bene also sets assorted components of the drama in disequilibrium, directing his actors to vary their vocal inflections, gestures and movements in strange patterns, electronically altering stage sounds, putting costumes to unconventional uses, and disposing props and settings in configurations that impede the actors and interfere with the audience's perception of the action. Bene's minor theatre, then, like minor literature in general, critiques power relations (political, social, gender, etc.) by undoing them, and opens new possibilities through a process of becoming-other. What is noteworthy about minor theatre, however, is that it experiments not simply with language, but with all the dimensions of drama – voice, gesture, movement, sound, costume, setting and stage – and that such experimentation highlights the inextricable relationship between language and action.[4]

The concept of the minor is not of central concern in Deleuze's cinema studies, but in *Cinema 2: The Time-Image* he does invoke Kafka, minorities and the minor use of language when discussing the *cinéma vérité* of Pierre Perrault and Jean Rouch and the political cinema of such directors as Brazil's Glauber Rocha, Senegal's Sembene Ousmane, the Philippines's Lino Brocka and Egypt's Youssef Chahine. Here, Deleuze's focus is on the cinematic equivalent of minor literature's invention of a people to come. In Rouch's "ethnofictions" of West African villagers and urban workers, for example, Rouch documents actual ways of life, but in each film he invites his actor-subjects to invent the specifics of the plot and develop their own personas as the film is constructed. The actors speak from their actual situation, but in participating with Rouch in the creation of the film, they also fabricate new voices and identities that point toward the formation of future collectivities. And as they do so, Rouch tries to lose his own Western gaze and enter a "cine-trance" in which his camera moves freely around his subjects and improvises with them in the discovery of new ways of seeing. Deleuze finds a similar invitation to self-invention in Perrault's documentaries of French-Canadian folkways, as well as a parallel subversion of the standard technical practices of film reportage. And in the films of Brocka, Chahine, Ousmane and Rocha, Deleuze sees the same combination of formal innovation and collective self-invention. Hence, he argues, however programmatic the political aims of these directors might seem, their ultimate political goal as film-makers is to go beyond current identities and create the images and voices of a people to come.[5]

What is common to minor literature, minor theatre and minor cinema is a minor usage of language, an experimental deterritorialization of the power relations immanent within words. In minor theatre, experimentation extends from words to the contextual constituents of speech action: voice, gesture, movement and setting. In minor cinema, experimentation embraces all the elements of speech action while extending as well as to ways of seeing. But what is central to the concept of the minor, whether it be applied to fiction, theatre or cinema, is that in artistic experimentation the formal and the political are inseparable. In concentrating on Kafka as an exemplar of minor literature, Deleuze and Guattari counter the common assumption that the great works of European modernism are largely apolitical, and in tying Kafka's innovations to the linguistic experimentations of such writers as cummings, Céline and Beckett, they suggest that a broadly conceived political dimension permeates many supposedly formal modernist tendencies. Their insistence on the centrality of Kafka's ethnicity calls into question presuppositions of the homogeneity of European culture while at the same time inviting comparisons of Kafka's practices to those of minority writers in general.

If minor literature is the literature of minorities, and if minorities are defined by their position of subordination in power relations, it would seem that non-Western, non-white, colonial, postcolonial, women, and gay and lesbian writers could all be approached as practitioners of minor literature. The challenges posed by this proposition, which Deleuze and Guattari do not pursue in detail, are twofold. First is the implication that the often overtly political dimension of minority literatures has, or should have, an aesthetic dimension as well; in other words, that litera-ture's political deterritorialization necessarily involves the deterri-torialization of language. Second is the implication that a minority literature's productive political effect arises less from fixed programmes of action or the affirmation of stable group identities than from becomings that undo identities and open populations to uncertain possibilities. In recent years, a number of studies have appeared in which Deleuze and Guattari's concept of the minor is applied to the literatures of diverse minorities, and to varying degrees the authors have acknowl-edged and embraced the consequences of these challenges.[6] However useful "the minor" has proven to such analysts, what is certain is that the promises and challenges of the concept are of a piece, and a selective appropriation of its components induces a fundamental modification of the concept. Minor literature's blend of the aesthetic and the political, as well as its anti-identitarian, open-ended politics of becoming, arise directly from its presuppositions about language, for the minor is above all a minor practice, a deterritorialization of relations of power that engages immanent lines of continuous variation within language and thereby induces becomings and generates possibilities for collective self-invention.

Notes

1. For an illuminating reading of this diary entry and Deleuze and Guattari's interpretation of it, see Robertson (1985: 12–28). See also my *Deleuze on Literature* (Bogue 2003b: 92–5).
2. Chana Cronfeld objects to Deleuze and Guattari's conception of minor literature on the grounds that it limits minor literature to works written in major languages, and hence denies minor status to "literatures in 'indigenous' minority languages" (1996: 12) such as Hebrew and Yiddish. I would argue that her rich study of modernist literature written in Hebrew, far from departing from Deleuze and Guattari, actually demonstrates the usefulness of their work and supports their basic thesis that any language, including Hebrew, may undergo a major or a minor usage.
3. Deleuze's (1993b) essay on Bene, which first appeared in a slim volume titled *Superpositions* (Bene & Deleuze 1979), also includes the text of Bene's *Richard III*, yet to be translated into English.

4. I discuss Bene's minor theatre at greater length in *Deleuze on Literature* (2003b: 115–49).
5. For an illuminating discussion of Deleuze and minor cinema, see Rodowick (1997: 139–69). I discuss Rouch and Deleuze at greater length in *Deleuze on Cinema* (Bogue 2003a: 150–54).
6. Among the many studies of minorities and minor literature written in English, see especially Lloyd (1987), JanMohamed & Lloyd (1990), Bensmaïa (1994), Potok (1998), D'haen (1999) and Zhang (2002). For discussions of the implications of the concept of becoming-woman for feminist studies, see the insightful essays in *Deleuze and Feminist Theory* (Buchanan & Colebrook 2000).

TEN

Style, stutter

Christa Albrecht-Crane

Gilles Deleuze's concepts of "style and stutter" are best contextualized through the premise that meaning is not simply given by or found in the world around us, but rather is produced by the symbolizing systems of a cultural and political structure. Thus meaning arises out of cultural texts and signifying structures and does not reside in the things themselves. Deleuze works in this theoretical space to conceptualize how meaning is continuously produced *and* changed. Deleuze's project finds ways to lessen or alter oppressive mechanisms of control, by focusing on the dimension of resistance. In so doing, Deleuze creates an extraordinary range of concepts that address how individuals in a culture function both within structures *and* against them. The concepts style and stutter directly attend to normative systems of linguistic conventions and articulate ways of resisting such systems by creating lines of (linguistic, cultural–political) rupture and escape. This articulation occurs in Deleuze's work both at an explanatory and experiential level; Deleuze's writing presents itself as an eclectic and complex line of creation and escape.

Deleuze centres his style and stutter concepts on discussions of literature, although he also applies them to music, cinema, the arts and signifying systems in general. Central to this approach is Deleuze's understanding of language. He conceptualizes language (like other systems of meaning-making) as being part of an "assemblage", the heterogeneous, contingent and complex arrangements of practices, bodies and formations with their particular, changing relations of movement and rest. As Deleuze and Guattari explain, "the concrete rules of assemblage thus operate along these two axes" (ATP: 505): a territorializing, norming axis, and an axis that tends towards excess and breaking away, or deterritorialization. In other words, social space is suffused by two different kinds of forces: forces that order social space, and forces that escape that ordering.

More specifically, territorialization (a concept that draws on the metaphor of the territory) functions through processes that organize and systematize social space. These processes impose a certain kind of order and categorization on the world; they include the categories we learn to live by. In most Western societies, territorializations manifest themselves in how culture reads and categorizes individuals in terms of "their" race, class, gender, nationality, religion, physical ability and so on. Such categories do not pre-exist society, but they structure social space according to certain culture-specific values. Territorializations provide us with social identities, with a social face. Thus, in culture individuals must be marked and made recognizable as man or woman, straight or gay, black or white, Christian or non-Christian, American or non-American. In fact, Deleuze calls this sort of social structuration a "molar line": a rigid, holistic, binary line that signifies how we are identified as social individuals. According to Deleuze and Parnet, "We are always pinned against the wall of dominant significations, we are always sunk in the hole of our subjectivity, the black hole of the Ego which is more dear to us than anything" (D: 45). Social production along identity lines is dear to us because it provides a sense of security, certainty and belonging: a rootedness to the territory of dominant social categories.

Language enters this territorialization as the central conduit to its effectivity. Social organization becomes articulated through language and makes sense to members of a society. Language, in its social function, is used to convey an agreed-upon connection between a signifier and a signified; in other words, language works through agreed-upon meanings that structure ways of seeing the world. Language provides the terms and meanings with which to establish and divide the world into human beings and animals, nature and society; it divides nature into plants and animals, plants into plant families, animals into species and human beings into races. Deleuze understands words to function as ordering words, or, as he puts it, as "order-words". With Guattari he writes, "when the schoolmistress instructs her students on a rule of grammar or arithmetic, she is not informing them, any more than she is informing herself when she questions a student. She does not so much instruct as 'insign,' give orders or commands" (ATP: 75). In supporting such a social ordering function, Deleuze and Guattari argue, "language is made not to be believed but to be obeyed, and to compel obedience" (ATP: 76). Adhering linguistically to social structures assures, in part, that individuals become successful members of their communities; as Deleuze and Guattari put it, "forming grammatically correct sentences is for the normal individual the prerequisite for any submission to social laws. No one is supposed to be ignorant of grammaticality; those who are belong in special institutions. The unity of language is fundamentally political" (ATP: 101). According to Deleuze and Guattari, then, to speak and to write in grammatically acceptable terms means to submit to the societal laws of one's culture, since grammar expresses the appropriate and accepted means of expression. If members of a culture do not submit to such laws (either as a way of actively refusing such laws or because they lack social skill and cultural power), they are defined as "out-laws", as social misfits, as other. In this way, language functions as a regulatory mechanism, defining who belongs and who does not, and in this regard, it is political.

This social aspect of language is evident in all facets of the social–educational system in much of present-day Western first world culture. For example, schools function to instruct and command students to learn and internalize the linguistic conventions of a society: schoolbooks and teachers proclaim and "in-sign" a standardized dialect to function as the norm of social respectability. The function of school instruction culminates in the repetition and commandments of linguistic "rules". Many practices support such norming structures. For instance, they are fixed in the documentation standards of various professional organizations in different fields and countries, or the adherence to writing genres and discourse communities, as well as through universalized instruction in "academic" writing throughout an individual's education. In other words, language regulates by including and validating certain usages and utterances, and excluding and devaluing others.

As Deleuze explains, for language to function as a regulatory mechanism, it must separate out *constants* that fix a certain expression in a language (such literal fixing happens through the numerous style manuals and grammar books, for example). The process of fixing a certain meaning or usage happens by way of selecting that usage from a multitude of possible usages. To put it another way, a certain usage of linguistic rule is extracted from a range of possible variables. As Deleuze (and Guattari) argue, "it is obvious that constants are drawn from variables themselves; universals in linguistics have no more existence in themselves than they do in economics and are always concluded from a universalization of a rendering-uniform involving variables" (ATP: 103). Thus, language functions as an ordering mechanism through a process of normalizing and streamlining variables that are made to function as order-words in their support of molar, territorializing social processes. Language provides a (conceptual) vocabulary with which to make a certain sense of the world and each other. The first thing a doctor proclaims at the birth of a baby is its gender: "It's a boy!" or "It's a girl!" Thus, an entire structuration mechanism is put into place by taking recourse to the ordering structure of gender, made available through a gender-specific vocabulary. Or, when girl brings boy home to meet the parents, the inevitable questions arise: "Who is he? What does his father do? Where does he come from?" The identification and fixation of boy in terms of lineage, territory and location is well under way, under the tutelage of categories articulated in language.

So far, Deleuze performs the conceptual work of analyzing social space in terms of its organization. However, in establishing this analysis Deleuze is more interested in how this system of control tends to break down rather than how it is maintained. As he puts it:

> there is no diagram [social system] that does not also include, besides the points which it connects up, certain relatively free or unbound points, points of creativity, change and resistance, and it is perhaps with these that we ought to begin in order to understand the whole picture.   (FCLT: 44)

Rather than focus only on how the territorializing work of culture takes place, Deleuze focuses on how it deterritorializes and breaks apart. And rather than seeing such breaking apart as a destructive mechanism, he argues that it is active, productive and affirmative. Deleuze emphasizes that deterritorialization makes new thinking possible. The Deleuzian assemblage holds the two forces of territorialization and deterritorialization in mutual presupposition, one depending on the other. Thus, while social production is supported by a molar use of language, simultaneously language constantly and actively escapes a molar function. Deleuze and Guattari write, *"you will never find a homogenous system that is not still or already affected by a regulated, continuous, immanent, process of variation"* (ATP: 103, original emphasis). Because the connection between signifier and signified is held together by convention, not by immutable or intrinsic laws, language is at the mercy of conventional fluctuation and variation.

Moreover, the conventional connections between signifier and signified held in language are never complete, absolute or timeless. Words and texts are not static conveyors of information. They are changing, fluid bodies, as any reader feels when she reads a "favourite" novel or watches a favourite film. The meaning of signs slips and moves as individuals use language. The molar, "major", function of language certainly remains at work, but Deleuze points to another function of language, which he terms "minor". Language is made to "stutter" when its molar function of representing order takes on a halting, stuttering characteristic, thereby opening up on to a realm that has remained unbound by societal structuring (and molar language). Evoking, sensing and pushing language towards this realm form the focal point of Deleuze's work.

Because language functions in a social sense through repetitive, conventional structures, Deleuze expresses the idea of language's slipperiness through a non-conventional style and eclectic usage. He uses a range of concepts and coins new words, or new meanings for established words, to address this alternative and coexistent realm of language. As he explains, "a concept sometimes needs a new word to express it, sometimes it uses an everyday word that gives it a singular sense" (N: 32). Deleuze makes *his* language stutter, thus revealing the conventionality of forms of expression readers usually take for granted. For example, he and Guattari begin *A Thousand Plateaus* in this way (the text in the English translation starts under a five-line musical score of a piano piece gone-amok by avant-garde composer Sylvano Bussoti):

> The two of us wrote *Anti-Oedipus*. Since each of us was several, there was already quite a crowd. Here we have made use of everything that came within range, what was closest as well as farthest away. We have assigned clever pseudonyms to prevent recognition. Why have we kept our own names? Out of habit, purely out of habit. To make ourselves unrecognizable in turn. To render imperceptible, not ourselves, but what makes us act, feel, and think. (ATP: 3)

What can a reader make of this opening? If we take Deleuze's overall project into account, then we understand that Deleuze and Guattari place language under variation, deviating from established syntactic and grammatical conventions, to make *and* show the point that language is grounded in a selective, habitual usage in the first place. Just as Busotti's musical score disrupts regularized music, so do Deleuze and Guattari's words interrupt conventional language use (and in so doing, conventional ways of thinking). The first sentence presents a conventional opening that is immediately thwarted and "up-set" by the second sentence ("Since each of us was several, there was actually quite a crowd"). This sentence points to the assumption, expressed in language, that texts are authored by a singular entity, and furthermore to the belief that personhood implies a stable, singular consciousness.

Thus, as the writers of the book, Deleuze and Guattari are express-ing that they are not singular minds authoring a master text; rather, in excess of how language conceives of agency, they express that we are multiple, various, co-mingled. Their text is thus not univocal, consist-ent, or coherent; as they say in the third sentence, they "have made use of everything that came within range", not sticking to conventional philosophical texts, but borrowing from music, literature, poetry and cinema, from everything and nothing in particular. And why did they keep their names, since names are utterly conventional in their social function? They respond, "out of habit, purely out of habit". In other words, their usage of names is habitual, cultural. They turn that habit upside-down in the next (grammatically incomplete!) sentence, declar-ing that they make themselves "unrecognizable in turn", not identifiable in terms of certain categories. Rather than being specific individuals, as language conventionally asks us to be ("Are you male or female?" "White or black?" "Student or teacher?"), they become "unrecognizable" in terms of identity-language, or "imperceptible", as they write in the next sentence, in terms of how they "act, feel, and think", all categories that are conventionally dictated by identity-language. Rather than writing *as* certain individuals, Deleuze and Guattari suggest that they also write as zones of energy, one might say, undercutting and escaping the language that demands submission. They do not yield to its rules because those rules are not absolutely binding.

In all his work Deleuze reveals the tendency of order-words to create constants and patterns out of a range of variables. Deleuze's writing, and his argument, can in fact be summarized as employing and discovering ranges of variables, multiplicities, that are not subsumed under molar processes. Thus, opposing the territorial aspect of order-words, Deleuze speaks of a "rhizome" as an open system that emphasizes the capricious, undifferentiated and "nomadic" character of life and language. The first chapter of *A Thousand Plateaus* is thus fittingly titled, "Introduction: Rhizome". In a rhizome, working by "principles of connection and heterogeneity" (ATP: 7), "there is no language in itself, nor are there any linguistic universals, only a throng of dialects, patois, slangs, and specialized languages. There is no ideal speaker-listener, any more that there is a homogeneous linguistic community" (ATP: 7). Here, Deleuze and Guattari emphasize the multiplicity of possibilities in terms of what language can do. He looks at the non-conventional and non-common in language to argue that seeing it as a rhizome better accounts for its variations. A molar use of language merely stabilizes variables because "there is no mother tongue, only a power takeover by a dominant language within a political multiplicity" (ATP: 7). In contradistinction, "a method of the rhizome type ... can analyze language only by decentering it onto other dimensions and other registers" (ATP: 8). Deleuze and Guattari thus urge the abandonment of the narrow, predictable constraints usually presented in dominant forms of language use.

Deleuze sees artists as working within this domain of creative, nonconventional use of social (linguistic, representative) space in order to allow other meanings and connections to surface. In particular, Deleuze is fascinated with writers and their creation of new connections and strange, new expressions, both in terms of form and content. He is particularly fond of American writers, because "everything important that has happened or is happening takes the route of the American rhizome: the beatniks, the underground, bands and gangs, successive lateral offshoots in immediate connection with an outside" (ATP: 19). For instance, Herman Melville's character Bartleby seems enigmatic to Deleuze in his repetition of the phrase "I would prefer not to". And, as Deleuze quotes Melville, "a gaunt and pallid man has uttered the formula that drives everyone crazy" (ECC: 68). This formula, says Deleuze, consists of a strange construction: it is grammatically and syntactically correct, yet ends abruptly in "not to", leaving open what it refuses. It "confers upon it the character of a radical, a kind of limit-function" (ECC: 68). The effect of this linguistic oddity is thus a challenge to conventional language use and social rules. Deleuze writes, "Murmured in a soft, flat, and patient voice, it attains to the irremissible, by forming an inarticulate block, a single breath. In all these respects, it has the same force, the same role as an *agrammatical* formula" (ECC: 68, original emphasis). Such "a limit, a tensor" (ECC: 69) marks the point at which language stutters, in this case to literally break off conventional understanding. Deleuze shows how in each case when Bartleby utters the phrase, "there is a stupor surrounding Bartleby, as if one had heard the Unspeakable or the Unstoppable" (ECC: 70). And Bartleby remains silent beyond uttering this phrase, "as if he had said everything and exhausted language at the same time" (ECC: 70). Bartleby does exhaust language, the language in which he functions as a copyist, a man, a citizen, and reveals the unspeakable immensity of what he can become, "being as being, and nothing more" (ECC: 71). He expresses "a negativism beyond all negation" (ECC: 71), or a negation with positive measures; he is no longer intelligible by conventional categories because he has rendered them meaningless.

In effect, the phrase that feels like a bad translation of a foreign language, as Deleuze writes, cuts out "a kind of foreign language within language" (ECC: 71). Such a language has the capacity to render doubts about the major language's absolute value. The arbitrary and habitual aspects of the system are thus thrown into relief. Deleuze sees in many American writers this capacity to evoke a richer range of linguistic and conceptual creation; he admires Walt Whitman, Thomas Wolfe, F. Scott Fitzgerald, William Burroughs, Henry Miller and e e cummings. Deleuze asks, "is this not the schizophrenic vocation of American literature: to make the English language, by means of driftings, deviations, de-taxes or sur-taxes (as opposed to the standard syntax), slip in this manner?" (ECC: 72).

From Proust, Deleuze draws the notion that "great literature is written in a sort of foreign language" (D: 5). Deleuze and Guattari continue,

> that is the same as stammering, making language stammer rather than stammering in speech. To be a foreigner, in one's own tongue, not only when speaking a language other than one's own. To be bilingual, multilingual, but in one and the same language ... That is when style becomes a language. That is when language becomes intensive, a pure continuum of values and intensities.
>
> (ATP: 98)

That is to say, when Bartleby utters his arresting phrase "I would prefer not to", he employs a different register of meaning than the one used conventionally. He evades meaning by opening himself up to not being understood, yet at the same time refusing the system and defining himself no longer by the identity-language around him. In that sense, he stutters, stammers, breaks off understanding, abandons a definitive space and enters a virtual realm of intensity, becoming anything-whatever: non-categorizable in the language of his peers and his culture. Thus, Melville "minorizes" language, as do other writers when they "invent a *minor use* of the major language within which they express themselves entirely; ... they make language take flight, they send it racing along a witch's line, ceaselessly placing it in a state of disequilibrium, making it bifurcate and vary in each of its terms, following an incessant modulation" (ECC: 109, original emphasis). Making language flee in this way characterizes a writer's "style", her way of making the major language stutter and stammer. According to Deleuze, "style becomes non-style" (ECC: 113), rendering traditional style grotesque and inventing flows that undercut and escape what has been conventionally defined as intelligibility. In *Anti-Oedipus*, Deleuze and Guattari write that style is "asyntactic, agrammatical: the moment when language is no longer defined by what it says, even less by what makes it a signifying thing, but by what causes it to move, to flow, and to explode" (AO: 133).

In writing about Kafka, another author whose style they greatly admire, Deleuze and Guattari tease out their concept of "minor literature" and, in so doing, explore style and stutter in their revolutionary potential. The book opens with these two sentences: "How can we enter into Kafka's work? This work is a rhizome, a burrow" (K: 3). Thus, from the very beginning Deleuze and Guattari focus on Kafka as a writer whose work should be read against the grain, as an opening, an intensification of perception that defies traditional interpretations and meanings. Moreover, Deleuze and Guattari write that in "The Metamorphosis", Kafka expresses a style, that is, placing writing into variation, moving language into a multiplicity out of which order-words have been stabilized. Style is a matter of finding "pass-words beneath order-words ... words that pass, words that are components of passage, whereas order-words mark stoppages or organized, stratified compositions" (ATP: 110).

Herein lies the revolutionary potential of Deleuze's concepts of style and stutter: to make possible new ways of thinking. As Deleuze and Guattari's contemporary Foucault put it in the Preface to their first book together, *Anti-Oedipus*,

> the book often leads one to believe it is all fun and games, when something essential is taking place, something of extreme seriousness: the tracking down of all varieties of fascism, from the enormous ones that surround and crush us to the petty ones that constitute the tyrannical bitterness of our everyday lives.
>
> (Foucault 1983: xiv)

Foucault's words powerfully address the twofold injunction of Deleuze's project. The first is to provide concepts with which to better understand and resist the dynamic and effects of official thought and conventional ways of ordering society (territorialization) which, by way of including only certain discourses, must exclude others. Secondly, Deleuze's project makes possible an understanding of how in everyday life, by way of using official language and ways of thinking, individuals themselves perpetuate and cling to potentially oppressive mechanisms. Exuberantly, he calls for resisting such oppressive functions through (linguistic) experimentation and creation, expressed in the concepts style and stutter. For, what is the aim of literature? Deleuze writes that its aim is "to set free, in the delirium, this creation of a health or this invention of a people, that is, a possibility of life" (ECC: 4). Deleuze emphasizes that to live fully means to seek and embrace the potential to engender change and imagine a different future by surpassing the conditions of official thought and accepted knowledge.

Through the concepts of style and stutter, then, Deleuze articulates a revolutionary, political aspect, one that links style and artistic creation to resistance. As he puts it, "creating isn't communicating but resisting" (N: 143). Deleuze argues for resistance through becomings, and vice versa, for instituting "a zone of proximity with anything, on the condition that one creates the literary means for doing so" (ECC: 1–2). For Deleuze, the process involves us in following language's own detours, detours that constitute "zones of vibration", regions "far from equilibrium" (ECC: 109), making "one's language stutter, face to face, or face to back, and at the same time to push language as a whole to its limit, to its outside, to its silence – this would be like the boom and the crash" (ECC: 113). This style and stutter animate the disequilibrium of language, crashing through fixed social organizations with seemingly tiny fragments of creative experimentation that lead to intensifying and enlarging life.

ELEVEN

Logic of sensation

Jennifer Daryl Slack

How well we have learned that the task before us is the search for meaning. As young children we are taught to accept that words have meanings, to recognize the moral of a tale, to search for the meaning of a poem or the significance of a story. As we become more sophisticated, we may even learn to probe the hidden meanings of visual imagery or the complex significance of non-representational art forms. At some point, however, we may stand perplexed in the inadequacy of our tools, perhaps before a work of abstract visual art or a plotless novel, where in wonder, frustration, or disgust we find ourselves unable to answer with familiar satisfaction the question, "What does it mean?" Or we may glimpse the fact that in our habitual search for the meanings of things we have learned not to ask certain "irrelevant" questions: what is the meaning of a hiccup? Of cool rain on warm skin? Of a tear? Of a scream? Of an angry expression? Of a barn on fire?

But even as I key these questions into my computer, I know, as Deleuze has written, "A story always slips into, or tends to slip into, the space between two figures in order to animate the illustrated whole" (FB: 6). So well have we learned to search for meanings that we cleverly demand of the scream: what made you erupt? Are you a scream of lost love representing recognition in a narrative of pain and abandonment? Are you a cry of happiness representing release in a narrative of joy? Or are you a moan that represents a physiological response to the biting wind of a cold February blizzard? Deleuze writes that this practised application of representation "implies the relationship of an image to an object that it is supposed to illustrate; but it also implies the relation-ship of an image to other images in a composite whole that assigns a

131

specific object to each of them" (FB: 6). Even though a scream "no more resembles what it signals than a word resembles what it designates" (FB: 93), we demand to know what narrative, what organization of intelligible relationships renders this response – a scream, a tear, a frisson – a knowable object, a figure that stands against a background of story constituted of other knowable objects.

The best of college classes teach this skill: what is the meaning or meanings of, in, behind, underlying this or that image, film, photograph, sign, story, poem, article, document, book, world event, political demonstration, policy decision, scientific finding, or test result? And even as every savvy student learns to banter with the claim that "there is no one correct meaning", they also already know that meaning is what matters in a pitched battle between "their" meaning and someone else's. We have learned well to navigate with what matters: narrative, symbolization, representation, signification, illustration, character, plot, theme, figure–ground, the animation of a subject against a background. And the singular scream, the tear, the cool rain on warm skin, the hiccup, the anger, the fire, and all the other singular moments and movements that constitute the possibilities of the everyday and the extraordinary are seriously slighted.

Deleuze's concept of the logic of sensation can aid navigation in a manner otherwise than territorialized, guided and constrained by matters of meaning and representation. Thinking with the concept of the logic of sensation deterritorializes, fractures and frees the flows of materials, forces, sensations and affects out of which we otherwise construct this edifice of subject and story. This logic invites us to make way for, to make space for, what is excluded, disregarded, minimized, relegated to a subjugated place in a story. As with all concepts in Deleuze's work, difficulties of understanding arise in that the very tools of explanation elevate the habits of representation. How then to *convey* without asking, "What does the logic of sensation *mean*?"

The initial task requires convincing you of the territorializing, exclusionary work of representation, which the initial paragraph in this essay intends to do. Reducing a hiccup to its meaning would seem an odd operation to perform. When a hiccup bursts upon a scene, it does so as a panoply of sensations affecting (for example) bodies (of both the hiccupper and others), a room, a conversation, a flow, as well as senses of seriousness, appropriateness and self. Oh, how to acknowledge or convey the violence of that hiccup? Surely not by dissecting its meanings, which can only categorize, compartmentalize, intellectualize, diminish and, in Deleuze and Guattari's terms, territorialize the full-blown richness and violence of that deterritorializing hiccup. And if we would do such disservice to a mere hiccup, imagine what greater disservice we would do to a film or a political demonstration by dissecting them thus. But how, then, does the logic of sensation open up a different kind of access? A different way of approaching hiccups, films, political demonstrations?

The path I take is to comment on Deleuze as he paints – that is, enacts – a logic of sensation in his commentary on the paintings of Francis Bacon in the book, *Francis Bacon: The Logic of Sensation*. In serpentine fashion, Deleuze explores Bacon's practice of painting without telling a story, which liberates "the figure" from the mode of representation and accesses sensation that exceeds meaning and representation. Deleuze's concept of the logic of sensation resonates with Bacon's painting practice (including Bacon's own commentary on that practice in Sylvester 1987). The way that Bacon paints, the way that Deleuze writes, and the concept of the logic of sensation connect in a complex rhythmic relation – an already rich accumulation and coagulation of sensation – that incites new ways for the artist as well as the philosopher in each of us to feel and live.

However, since there are differences between viewing Bacon, Bacon on Bacon, reading Deleuze, and Deleuze on Bacon, it is intriguing to note that an appropriate Deleuzian commentary on Deleuze commenting on Bacon would enact yet another layered rhythmic relation or logic of sensation. I can only modestly begin such a daunting task by drawing from *Francis Bacon* a picture of the conceptual space within which the logic of sensation works and painting ways of living with that picture. My goal honours the concept not to explain what the logic of sensation *means*, but to explore what it *does*, how it *works*. And just as a richly textured painting begins with materials, takes shape in the accumulation and convergence of mark making, and converges as a complex sensation, *this* picture emerges in the selfsame fashion.

Materials: rubrics

Deleuze's short foreword to *Francis Bacon* offers guidance for negotiating his essay on Bacon and for working with the concept of the logic of sensation. He states that he considers increasingly complex "rubrics", or "aspects" of Bacon's paintings that converge "in the 'coloring sensation,' which is the summit of this logic" of sensation (FB: 3). What work is performed by these rubrics or aspects that converge in a logic of sensation?

Tempting though it is to think of this simply as a matter of aspects coming together to give form to something else, such a reading would too easily support the habit of searching for intelligible objects and relationships that render something (a logic of sensation in this case) a knowable object or idea. "Aspect", a thoroughly non-corporeal term, too easily suggests a narrative: the aspect in question is subjugated by its designation *qua* aspect as mere placeholder or support in the story of the real subject of the narrative. "Rubric" is more helpful, for if we think of it as drawing on the etymology of the Latin term *rubrica*, or red chalk, or on its sense of the colour red or reddish, it is no mere place-holder. Rather, rubric asserts a sensation, an intensity, a "colouration". Rubrics, "givens" that converge in a logic of sensation, are always already sensations with intensities; they are coloured, textured, fla-voured, shaped; they are always already "accumulated" or "coagulated" sensation (FB: 33). As such they come in all sorts of guises: colours, noises, rhythms, odours, textures, longings, desires, practices, feelings, beliefs, gestures, knowledges and so on. For Deleuze on Bacon's paint-ings, rubrics involve pictorial elements, such as the relationship between figure and ground, the hue and flatness of colours, the movement of the paint.

In thinking about the film *The Matrix* (dir. A. Wachowski & L. Wachowski 1999) using the concept of rubrics, I found it especially generative to work with four that helped me enter, feel, catch the mys-tery of the sensations and intensities, flows and blockages at work in the film and in the enactment of adolescence: the senses of a person being lost or found, flat or deep; a practice of and a desire to learn without effort; feelings of the adolescent body; and the colour (or quality) of adolescent love (see Slack 2003). None is a placeholder or mere aspect of *The Matrix*. Rubrics are not things, objects, or ideas as such, but already affective movements, flows, blockages, intensities. None, whether simple or complex, whether addressed first or last, is inherently more significant than any other. Their names – not critical in themselves – were chosen to point in the direction of the aggregate of relevant sensations. Rubrics neither respond well to the demands of hierarchy nor correspond to the signifiers with which they are designated.

Convergence: mark-making

Rubrics converge in the space we call a painting, a film or a political demonstration. The philosopher in each of us, like the painter, encoun-ters the rubrics, and in their spatial convergence paints, thinks, acts, lives. But how does this spatial convergence come about? What does it do? How do these relationships work if they are not (merely) narrative in character, if they are not (merely) an organization of intelligible objects? The challenge was well put by Bacon, who, in discussing this challenge in terms of painting, spoke thus: "how can this thing be made so that you catch the mystery of appearance within the mystery of the making?" (Sylvester 1987: 105).

Rather than focusing on or attending to intelligible relations of objects or ideas, Deleuze pays attention in a different way: to "sensations", "forces", "matters of fact" and "events". Each of these otherwise everyday terms is coloured by the Deleuzean point of view. "Sensation", the more evocative term, is that which exceeds intellectual control and works directly on and through the nervous system. Whether visual, auditory, taste, proprioceptive and/or mental, sensation is of the flesh, of the body. It is "transmitted directly", avoiding the "detour" of a story. We do not *think* sensation, we *"become* in the sensation and something *happens* through the sensation" (FB: 31, original emphasis). Sensation is "in the body, and not in the air" (FB: 32). Sensation and force, Deleuze tells us, are closely related, but forces are invisible, "insensible" (FB: 48). Only when a force is "exerted on a body" does a sensation come into existence (FB: 48). Sensation is force made visible, audible and/or palpable, and is thus embodied. For Bacon the challenge is to paint the sensation that makes invisible forces visible: to paint pressure, contraction, elongation, a scream and so on. Not to paint something that represents these, but to paint the sensation on, in and of the body. Bacon is not interested, for example, in painting horror, but the "sound of the scream and the forces that sustain it" (FB: 51). Deleuze writes that "If we scream, it is always as victims of the invisible and insensible forces that scramble every spectacle, and that even lie beyond pain and feeling" (FB: 51). That is what Bacon paints, and that is what Deleuze would have us access: the invisible and insensible forces that scramble every spectacle, the sensations on, in and of the body that are otherwise disregarded, minimized and subjugated in the territorializing practices in which meaning and representation prevail.

As embodied fact, sensation is always located in particular places, corporeal expressions or "events". An event might be called a painting, a dance, a hiccup, a film or a political demonstration. As such, sensation may exist radically independent from the experience of a particular spectator: it *is* what is painted, drawn, written, expressed; but what is painted "is the body", as the experience of the sensation (FB: 31–2). An event, a particular combination of rubrics of variable intensity that coexist and connect, encompasses and constitutes a characteristic "rhythmic unity", a distinctive "thisness" that encompasses and constitutes participants, subjects and stories in particular forms. To experience the sensation as a spectator, one must "enter" the event, live the sensation in the body, become the sensation. "Painting the sensation" corresponds for Deleuze (and for Bacon) with "record[ing] the fact" (FB: 32; Sylvester 1987: 57–8), and "feeling the event" (see Stivale 2003b: 46–7). What we experience in the sensation, what we become in the sensation, and what we do with the sensation exceed whatever story and meaning we might attach to the fact, the event of the sensation.

Sensations are multiple; they happen in aggregate, in what Deleuze has called, in *L'Abécédaire de Gilles Deleuze*, "a entire complex web of sensations" (ABC: "I as in Idea"). In painting a picture, exploring a film or experiencing a political demonstration, sensations assail the body as part of, as well as apart from, the way we read story and meaning. The rubrics or aspects of the web are conjoined throughout *Francis Bacon* in relations of "convergence", "intersection", "coexistence", "correlation", "connection", "coupling", "confrontation", "proximity" or "co-precision." Noticeably absent in these depictions of relations are terms of cause and effect (one force effecting another), interpenetration (one identity engulfed by another) and hierarchy (one rubric more important than another). This is neither a systems approach, where the whole is greater than the sum of its parts, nor a structural causality, where aspects are causes and have no identity outside their effects. This web is, rather, a composite of asignifying traits, strokes, sensations of distinguishable quality or character with features that permit us to identify or recognize them. Painters might think of these traits as brush strokes or marks; in the Deleuzian sense each has its own intensive reality or facticity, its own affective register in and on the nervous system. Just beyond, outside, repressed by the habits of representation to hold *"reign over vision"* (FB: 12, original emphasis), thought and practice, these marks, sensations and rubrics flow with variable intensity. Together they constitute a *"bloc of sensations"* (WIP: 164), a map of relations among rubrics, but a map as large as the territory, a map that *is* the territory, a map that exceeds what habits of representation could conceivably comprehend, a map in which the rubrics fold on to one another to create complexity and possibility. The web of sensation is thus a sort of totality of sensation that exceeds the intellect, that cannot be "summed up" or "figured out", and that entails creative possibility even as it includes the sensation of subject, meaning and representation.

Watching the film *The Matrix* for the first time, I "felt the event", although I do not know for certain why it had that affect for me. As Bacon has put it, "It is a very, very close and difficult thing to know why some paint comes across directly onto the nervous system and other paint tells you the story in a long diatribe through the brain" (Sylvester 1987: 18). What's more is that feeling the event while reading Deleuze (not at the same time, but folded in space) helped me to feel the importance of *sensing* rather than *knowing* the logic of sensation. *The Matrix* has clearly affected very many spectators, spawning a virtual industry of *Matrix* commentary. But most of that commentary seeks the meanings of the film, critiques or defends its representations of gender, youth, violence and so on, analyses the degree of accuracy or inaccuracy in representing the world, assesses its predictive potential, or merely sets out to clarify or expand the story. What is *The Matrix* about? Like photorealism, a purported representational rendering of *The Matrix*, circulates, washes over us, and colonizes (or territorializes) our access to it, our ability to experience and explore sensation. Just as a recent issue of *Discover* asserts:

EVEN IF YOU HAVEN'T SEEN THE MATRIX OR ITS sequels, you most likely know the basic premise of the movie: It's the distant future, and intelligent machines rule the world, having learned to harness an omnipresent and previously underutilized source of electrical power – humans. The machines "grow" people in vast industrial farms and siphon off the small current of electricity generated by the bodies. You, me – we are battery.   (Burdick 2004: 15)

It is true; even if you haven't seen it, you know this is the meaning. At the very least, this is where we have to begin. What more we may find represented – a psychoanalytical conflict, a love story, a post apocalyptic world, a mythic tale, the battle between good and evil and so on – contributes to accessing the film in terms of filling out or "fleshing out" its meanings. Those meanings are not sensations, that is, not on, in and of the flesh.

Experienced another way, by entering the event and living its sensations in the body, *The Matrix* provides a different kind of access. In the section on "Materials" above, I mentioned four rubrics (of many others, certainly) with which one can traverse *The Matrix*, to "feel the event". These rubrics are not what this film is *about*. Instead they are the accumulated and coagulated sensations that coexist, converge, and fold on to one another. I invite you to encounter *The Matrix* from within the space of these sensations: within what adolescence *feels like*. The film is not *about* adolescence, but for reasons I could only begin to guess at, the film transmits sensations of adolescence directly onto the nervous system. They are enfleshed sensations that render visible the otherwise

invisible forces that work in adolescence, forces that are typically territorialized into forms of being adolescent. The sensations are there and
felt on, in and of bodies, even though every viewing experience may not
connect with them. Recall that to experience the sensation as a spectator, one must "enter" the event, live the sensation in the body, become
the sensation. The success and popularity of *The Matrix* points to the
likelihood that many of its viewers are spectators, that they feel the event
in spite of a lack of conscious awareness of how the film *works*. Rhythm
possesses bodies, bypassing the brain.

In entering the event, I sensed that the rubric "lost and found, flat and
deep" affectively paints a picture of the isolation, indifference, suspicion
and suffering of adolescence. For example, Neo, the main character is
"lost" in the everyday until he is "found" by the Resistance; but once
found he must accept suffering as a condition of his salvation. The rubric
"learning with eyes closed" affectively paints a picture of learning without teachers, rules or sustained effort. For example, characters learn
what might otherwise take years of hard work by simply and very
quickly having information injected into them machinically; thus learning feels machinic, is delivered on a need-to-know basis and is physically
easy, even if mentally fatiguing in the short term. The rubric "what the
body feels" affectively paints a picture of computer use, drug use,
criminality and a search for truth and freedom in a spirit-killing world.
For example, exhausting criminal computer hacking is precisely what
draws the Resistance to rescue Neo; the feel of criminality and of being
saved are thus coupled. The rubric "the colour of love" affectively paints
an escape through romantic love from isolation, from suspicion and
from annihilation. For example, Trinity's expression of love for Neo
brings him back to life; thus the unreal expression of romantic love is
the final saving power against death. While it is impossible in this short
space to map the way these four rubrics – to which I have barely done
justice – intersect rhythmically as they transverse the story of *The Matrix*,
let me at least assert that they conjoin as a logic, a web of sensation. They
are different from one another, on different levels Deleuze would say,
that resonate, vibrate and flow in rhythmic relation, transversing the
story, rather than being the story or providing a background for the
story. Indeed, I think they are far more interesting than the story, for they
access adolescence, that is, "the sum total of material effects belonging
to" (ATP: 260) adolescence, a seriously misunderstood affective
domain. Access to that affective domain can help us understand the logic
of sensation within which certain ways to live *make sense,* including the
fact that certain kinds of violence *make sense.* As Deleuze puts it opti-
mistically, in his commentary on a Bacon painting of wrestlers:

It is within this visibility that the body actively struggles, affirming the possibility of triumphing, which was beyond its reach as long as these powers remained invisible, hidden in a spectacle that sapped our strength and diverted us. It is as if combat had now become possible. The struggle with the shadow is the only real struggle. When the visual sensation confronts the visible force that conditions it, it releases a force that is capable of vanquishing the invisible force, or even befriending it. (FB: 52)

The logic of sensation: colouring

A logic of sensation, such as that enacted in a painting, in *The Matrix*, in Deleuze's essay, or in any event or singular moment, is never necessarily a completed project, fixed in time and space. An assembled logic of sensation might in fact work like what Deleuze calls a "diagram", a "relay" that, even as it completes or constitutes a "stopping point", "always has effects that go beyond it" (FB: 111). Thus we always have a plethora of opportunities to become spectators of and participants in sensations that have been there all along. Further, having come to appreciate the role played by routinely marginalized sensation, it makes sense, as Deleuze suggests, to seek out novel encounters with the intent of being open to new sensations, to access creatively productive possibility. Deleuze encourages searching for paintings, films, pieces of music or events that might touch, affect and insert us into the folds of an event, into the pulsing of a logic of sensation. The encounter is not entertainment, but intellectual discovery, an escape from philosophy through philosophy (ABC: "C as in Culture"). Without searching out such encounters, we are more likely to ride the crest of the "givens" and remain defined by and dependent on the ready made, the represented, the cliché: painting illustrations and representations with sonambulistic skill; seeing only through habits of meaning and representation; seeking only that which we already know; reproducing the same. Tom Conley, commenting on *Francis Bacon*, warns that "A perception of a reign of clichés in the mental and visual world alike gives rise to a politics" (2003: 143). Order is constituted in such clichés. In the face of clichés and the order of life-constraining politics, Deleuze challenges us to free possibility, to colour the world differently, to promote new political realities, to enliven life, to, as Bacon puts it, "bring back the intensity of . . . reality" (Sylvester 1987: 172). There is possibility in even the most oppressive conditions. As Brian Massumi notes, "there's an objective degree of freedom even in the most deterministic system.

Something in the coming together of movements, even according to the strictest of laws, flips the constraints over into conditions of freedom" (Massumi 2002b: 222).

To respond to Deleuze's challenge, to flip the constraints, we need first to feel the logics of sensation with which the order is assembled and, secondly, to free productive sensations, new colours, new logics. We all work with "givens", whether painter, film-maker, dancer, writer; or spectator, audience member, reader. Deleuze writes that "An entire battle takes place on the canvas between the painter and these givens" (FB: 81). Just so, an entire battle takes place in life between the philosopher in each of us and the givens with which we live. Encounters open the space to free what has been excluded, minimized, diminished and subjugated in life-stultifying, territorialized colourations. In the end – in the middle of this battle really – Deleuze does not do away with meaning and representation, for to give up territorialized order entirely would be *mere* chaos. But *more* chaos or catastrophe is, for Deleuze, a welcome move, for that is what marks out "possibilities of fact" and a "germ of order or rhythm" in relation to a new order (FB: 83). Unlocking new areas of sensation – new colours, noises, rhythms, odours, textures, longings, desires, practices, feelings, beliefs, gestures and knowledges – gives rise to new facts, new events, new rhythmic relations, new logics of sensation, in short: new ways to appreciate life and new ways to live. With Deleuze, then, we can take up the challenge to vanquish life-deadening clichés, befriend life-enhancing colours and rhythms that already pulse with unacknowledged intensity, and embrace the accidents, encounters and chaos that unleash creative possibility.

TWELVE

Cinema

movement–image–recognition–time

Felicity J. Colman

Is that everything? It seemed like he said quite a bit more than that.
Bob (Bill Murray) to translator,
Lost in Translation (dir. S. Coppola 2003)

The criteria for working with Deleuze's cinema books – *Cinema 1: The Movement-Image*, and *Cinema 2: The Time-Image* – might be summarized quite simply: how and where do we see, hear and sense the perception of being? What is learnt, what is lost, what is wasted, what is invented in the recognition of the narratives, concepts and structures of life, giving rise to images of meaning in the cinema? How does the activity of relationally generated thought-perception occur within the cinema, and how might it be analysed?

If a viewer selects a favourite colour, character, dialogue, moment, movement, sound or gesture from any film, that aspect, person or thing has its characteristic and/or its gesture given in the juxtaposition between the viewer's contextual perceptual space, aesthetic preferences, historical moment and that aspect, person or thing itself. The conjunction and coordination of this vast range of possibilities provide the pulsing channels of perceptual power (*puissance*), and becoming perception of and between entities. According to Deleuze, the cinema provides such passageways of thought, showing itself to be a profound and sometimes rigorous surface that covers the visible world.

Deleuze's cinema books engage four fundamental interrelational concepts with which to chart a philosophy of cinema: movement, image, recognition and time. This philosophy assembles an epistemological bracketing of the how and where of cinema, and an answer to the archaeological question of what it is in the present, what its history is, and what it can become. Common to Deleuze's generation of thinkers, the Second World War marks a divisive point of a shift in European culture of the mid-twentieth century, and it is with this rupture that Deleuze registers an historical *epistēmē* for films: a shift from an image of action to an image where movement takes place in the passageways of the perception of an absolute and autonomous optical or sound image (C2: 1–3).

The four integrated concepts that I examine here offer a practical philosophy for approaching film analysis, a model based on the film-maker's own praxis, and the cinema's generic skills of interface, captivity, association, imagination and invention. Deleuze breaks apart the cinematic event, explores the temporal demeanour of the filmic situation and describes the dimensional structure of its workings around these conceptual points of possibility. The result is a hybrid renegotiation of the practices of modernist art forms and philosophies of the twentieth century.[1]

In *Difference and Repetition*, Deleuze acknowledges that his philosophy is one that proposes "descriptive notions" (DR: 284). Yet Deleuze's conception of art forms refutes the Western philosophical pedigree of Platonic debates of mimesis (see "Plato and the Simulacrum" in LS: 253–66). Ever present in the poststructuralist and postmodernist discussions of architecture, music, literature, art and fashion of the 1960s–1990s, these debates concerned artistic mimetic practices such as appropriation, imitation, remodelling, sampling and simulation. Critical and philosophical deliberations surrounding mimetic procedures involve the breadth of philosophical thought on the question of truth and reality, metaphysical to metaethical anxieties, and aporetic systems of thought. Deleuze's conception of art is very much both a product and a rejection of this historical context of the mid-twentieth century, and its reliance upon challenging the orthodox configurations of originary structures.

Although begun in *Bergsonism* (1966) as "commentaries" and extensions of Henri Bergson's work on intuition as a methodology for apprehending temporal paradigms, Deleuze's description of the processes of the cinematic image resonate as core texts for the analysis of all screen-based sound and visual imagery.[2] The commentaries on Bergson are conduits for Deleuze into the cinematic form, although Deleuze's previous work on the relational movement between component parts and their wholes in *Empiricism and Subjectivity* (1953), the consideration of aesthetic judgement in *Kant's Critical Philosophy* (1963), and the divergent relations evidenced in repetition in *Difference and Repetition* (1968) provide background principles for his analytic approach towards specific films. It is Bergson's contention for the singularity of a durational point in time and space that may expand or contract that forms the basis for Deleuze's organic methodology for cinematic properties. In *Cinema 1*, two commentaries are presented on Bergson: "Theses on Movement" (Ch. 1) (three ways of apprehending the metaphysics of movement) and "The Movement-image and its Three Varieties" (Ch. 4) (on the image and image-movement). In *Cinema 2*, Deleuze presents two additional commentaries on Bergson: "From Recollection to Dreams" (Ch. 3) (on recognition, the opsign and sonsign), and "Peaks of Present and Sheets of Past" (Ch. 5) (on time and memory).

Cinema reveals the devices and the means of the production of the relationships generated through coexisting bodies, and the possible synergetic and catalytic effects of a shared topography of what Deleuze describes (after the American semiologist C. S. Peirce) as a "taxonomy" (C1: xiv) of "pre-linguistic images" and "pre-signifying signs" (C2: 262). The result presents criteria for approaching what is lost in the translation between movement and image, between the recognition or recollection of an image, and the passage and consolidation of an image through time.

As a means of reading through Deleuze's cinema books, I draw upon Sofia Coppola's film *Lost in Translation* (2003) for its configuration of sound and optical images of being-in-time, and its conjoined protagonists of film star and philosophy graduate.[3] For Deleuze, considering the cinema consists of thinking of the relationships generated through various forms of writing about life, about people's experiences, politics, pleasures, responses and attitudes towards the real world. He is guided in this endeavour equally by philosophical precursors, and his favourite film-makers, those whose films, for him, have made from these representations so many reasons to have faith in the world, and in the people and things within it. As Deleuze notes in *Cinema 2*:

> Belief is no longer addressed to a different or transformed world. Man is in the world as if in a pure optical and sound situation. The reaction of which man has been dispossessed can be replaced only by belief. Only belief in the world can reconnect man to what he sees and hears. The cinema must film, not the world, but belief in this world, our only link. Restoring our belief in the world – this is the power of the modern cinema (when it stops being bad).
>
> (C2: 172)

In what follows, I sketch Deleuze's four concepts as relational, aporetic, yet not equivalent, at once multi-directional and multi-dimensional. The verbal concepts of translation and loss – to be lost, in translation – I employ throughout this essay, as subtextual ground for the four key Deleuzian concepts of the cinema to be discussed here: movement, image, recognition and time.

Movement

4:20am, Park Hyatt Hotel, Tokyo, Bob wakes up and looks at the clock.   *Lost in Translation*

"Movement is a translation in space," notes Deleuze (C1: 8). For Deleuze, movement in the cinema is inextricably linked to semiotic technique, habit, creativity and generative creation. He questions how the cinema communicates the movement of abstract qualities (such as thought, perception, knowledge, time and space), without assuming that the audience has a vocabulary of abstract aesthetics with which to translate. Film occupies a hyperbolic space, a "cinematographic network" (C2: 237) for the assemblage and dispersal of fragments, and the creation and depiction of whole realms of experience and knowledge. Movement in the cinema is an interactive translation of complex cognitive processes, voyages of activity that can be association machines for power, flows of desire, disruption of learned cognitive processes. "Movement in space", as Deleuze describes it, "expresses a whole which changes, rather as the migration of birds expresses a seasonal variation" (C2: 237).

The cinema requires a viewer, and that viewer brings to the cinematic screen not only her eyes and ears, but also her embodied perception, memories, aesthetic and ideological and ethical preferences. Deleuze's conception of the cinematic viewer is one who is appended to the cinematic image through affections on the surface and within the events on screen. This spectator's presence organically reconfigures the screen events, her corporeal appendage providing an expanded consciousness, a swollen screen. Movement takes place through, and exists in, the non-determined subjectivity of spectatorial apprehension of the optical and sound images of the cinema.[4]

For Deleuze, the cinematic apparatus functions as a translator of the movements of images and consciousness of perception within temporal modalities of worlds (real, imagined, past, present and future). Deleuze's cinematic philosophy attempts to account for the accumulative process of recognition that takes place when you watch a film, a perception that can be gradual, instantaneous, built, stalled between thoughts, stifled by distractions, overlooked: "The camera would then appear as an exchanger or, rather, as a generalised equivalent of the movements of translation" (C1: 4–5). In the case of the cinema, it is useful to think of translation in terms of another of Deleuze's concepts: that of the crystal. In Deleuze's philosophy, the cinema represents a crystal translation of temporal modalities, and how they might affect and intensively move whole points of meaning.[5] The crystal is a geological and mathematical term that Deleuze employs for its structural habits of forming through aggregates open (prism) and/or closed (cube) crystallographic forms, some of which require other forms to complete them, some of which can be complete in themselves.

Think of that moment at the end of *Lost in Translation* when Bob (Bill Murray) whispers something to Charlotte (Scarlett Johansson), inaudible to the viewer who is external to the diegetic world. Bob and Charlotte are characters who have connected, a chance encounter given favourable odds through the contextual milieu of Western habits. They come together in an asymmetrically cohabited durational passageway of becoming. They review some of the aspects of social ameliorations, friendship, marriage, being, and then, due to their customs, other selves, obligations, they must separate. This point of departure also contains the evolutionary detour of time, the inaudible, but visible whisper: a crystalline moment of cinema, one where the image coalesces narrative information to an open-ended point on the time surface of the film that becomes a virtual passageway for sensory movement to take place. As Deleuze suggests, "Need is the manner in which this future appears, as the organic form of expectation" (DR: 73).

In Deleuze's modern cinema, the crystal refers to such nomadic translations of a point (with) in space. As Deleuze has insisted, nomadic movement entails motionlessness (cf. ABC: "V as in Voyage"), not moving around too much (N: 138). Nomadic movement occurs in these optical and sound images and "sensations" and "situations" (C2: 55, 62). This point can be an image and/or sound of an occasion (an event), or its consequential haecceity (sonorous and/or optical). The crystal-image of the cinematic process is one that collects, collates, and collages actual and virtual things together to perform a crystalline translation of categories of meaning. This is a different process to that concept of cinematic "montage", which is essentially a technical method of assemblage within the cinema (C1: 29–30; C2: 129–30). The cinema generates a threshold for crystalline translation to occur. Deleuze reads movement through thought sublimes: mathematical, dynamic and dialectic sublimes where the "crystalline narration" has arrested and "fractured" movement (C1: 53; C2: 128, 157).

A bracket of silence, a rhythmic pause in movement, creates a memorable moment, the eternity of a lover's touch. The words the audience never hear in *Lost in Translation* are a sonsign, a silent phonic threshold and passage containing possible trajectories of desire and duration that have broken with the action-image movement of classical cinema. The movement of the sonsign and opsign are moments that do move the film-time forward, and provide semiotic indices for creating, sustaining and shifting meanings. This is movement that is not linear or chronological, but rather is aleatory, curved, textured, displaying how the cinema holds time captive within its crystalline regard, its nomadic movement of sensory meaning; it is a movement of thought-image.

(Sound)-image

Meow, meow, meow. *White fluffy kitten held by Sylvia (Anita Ekberg), in Rome.* *La Dolce Vita* (dir. F. Fellini 1960)

Seeing things can be done at a conceptual level as well as a sensorial level. A sound may make us "see" an image, or sensation; the sound of a kitten crying, for example, may invoke a familial hearth, a childhood haunt, a tactile or psychological association. A smell, a taste, a touch – all have the Proustian ability to constitute "vision" through association, which Deleuze calls "the law of the image" (C2: 210). Deleuze divides his two cinema books to focus upon cinema's representation of two specific kinds of images, the movement-image, and the time-image. In turn, these two are divided and discussed in terms of the particular type of image and its compatible signs of meaning. In *Cinema 1*, Deleuze names three key activities of the classical cinema's construction of images: action, affect and perception (C1: 64–5). These images are evidenced in certain "types" of films, each contributing to the sociopolitical constitution of things assembled within the film (whether person, kitten or thing): a relational image. In *Cinema 2*, the experience of the modern cinema begins, according to Deleuze, with the Italian neo-realist genre of film. With the advent of the neo-realist style, a syntax of coalesced time-images within the myriad surfaces of the cinema emerges.[6]

Deleuze's philosophy of cinema describes the semiotics of the cinematic image in terms of its affective–perceptual–active nature, in relation to the type of shot used, and then in relation to the spatial affect of the whole. To address the time-image, Deleuze describes the differences between the visual and/or optical image (which he names the opsign), the sound image (sonsign) and the haptic–tactile image (tactisign) (C2: 13, 92, 251). From the vectors created by image-signs, Deleuze describes the two poles of "reflecting surface and intensive micro-movements" (C1: 88), which become an "automatic image" (C2: 178) of "between"; or, citing Maurice Blanchot, Deleuze describes these vectors as "a vertigo of spacing", a whole image that exists in the between spaces of edited images and sounds (C2: 180).

Through the cinematic techniques of *mise en scene*, spatial awareness built through sound, lighting, dialogue, actions and movement of characters and things, film-makers create what Deleuze summarizes (after Bertold Brecht) as "the gest" of the image (C2: 192). The gest is the relational knot of "attitudes" of entities as they come together on film, whether optical, sonic or haptic; the gest forms the essential associations for the creation of the image by the film-maker (C2: 192–3). For Deleuze the image and self-reflexive narratives of film imagery engage in the construction of meaning through images of life cycles, forming a "re-linkage" that forms one part of the cerebral construction of the cinema as the "image of thought" (C2: 215). The gest is a theatricalization of the body, according to Deleuze, the body being an important component for the relationship between image and thought: "a topological cerebral space" (C2: 211). Deleuze says, "The gest is necessarily social and political . . . bio-vital, metaphysical and aesthetic" (C2: 194).

The image is the cinema's power, its ability to reproduce and cause intellectual and chemical affections to arise, to be aroused, to force us to acknowledge, through physical sensations, perceptions of the world through participation. Deleuze paraphrases film theorist Jean-Louis Schefer on the character and nature of the power and delusional nature of the cinematographic image: "As soon as it takes on its aberration of movement, [the image] carries out a *suspension of the world* or affects the visible with a *disturbance*" (C2: 168, original emphasis). This disturbance, as Deleuze suggests throughout the cinema books, takes on the forms of an image of movement – an "insertion of duration into matter" (B: 94), and/or an image of time – a virtual "coexisting" aggregate (B: 93). The cinema loves to play with the false images of thought, the suggestions of a dream, a fantasy, of the unbearable, of "a little time in the pure state" of the cinematic experience (C2: 169). The power of the falsity of images is linked by Deleuze to the process of memory, of recollection, as I shall discuss in the following section. The power of the image also rests with its affective ability, and our judgement of that image and its affectivity upon the body, an embodiment of the image (B: 25).[7] In thinking through the affectivity of the image (affect in the sense of Spinoza's (1982 [1677]: 77) use of the word – to take on something), Deleuze also polemically engages with Sartre's work on the emotions and the imaginary.[8] "'Every image', Sartre said, 'is surrounded by an atmosphere of world'" (C2: 63). Where is the atmosphere, the attitude, of the image in *Lost in Translation*, and how is it to be interpreted?

The framing devices directors use for their narratives are often an image of a physical site. This image is imbued with a spatial logic that resonates as a conceptual site and enables space and scope for the viewer's own perceptions to develop. Given an image as a structure for the whole, a viewer can think within the filmic text. For example, in David Lynch's infamous television series *Twin Peaks* (1990–91), one could say that the physical site was Laura Palmer's body, wrapped in plastic. In Danis Tanovic's film about the folly of war, *No Man's Land* (2000), the physical site is of a living human body lying upon a spring-loaded bomb. In both scenarios, the site is an image, invoked as a conceptual space, and we the audience are in pursuit of that space, that (dead/soon-to-be dead) body; that terrible thought. The site becomes image, which becomes thought. In *Lost Highway* (dir. Lynch 1997), the image of the highway as a physical site unifies the *noir* narrative of recollection. In *Lost in Translation*, the framing devices for the narrative are the body of the young woman, the body of an older man and the city. These are generic images that provide the framing devices, conceptual pursuits, spatial discourses for countless films. Coppola's film utilizes the physical layout of both bodies (of the woman, of the city) as a remembered topography to uphold and/or reinforce the imaginary content of these images. Coppola presents these images as congregates of meaning, rather than infinite, or limitless, virtual sites. The limits of the woman's body and the limits of the city are represented by the film's affective soundtrack, an understated sweetness that performs a grace one imagines in such bodies. Difference in the cinema's activities comes from the relational image, altering and reconfiguring the unidimensionality of paradigms, of signs, even icons, as Jean-Luc Godard observed, "*to describe* is to observe mutations" (quoted by Deleuze, C2: 19, original emphasis).[9]

In a central scene in *Lost in Translation*, Fellini's film *La Dolce Vita* (1960) plays on the television in Bob's hotel room. Also known as *This Sweet Life*, the film works as a time-image, the dialogue in Italian, with Japanese subtitling on the screen. Bob and Charlotte sit in front of the television, drinking saki. Charlotte smiles and turns to Bob. Although they have never even kissed, or held hands at this point in their relationship, they engage in a reminiscence common to lovers, of where they first met, what was said, details of an intimate circuit of meaning:

Image: *Sylvia (Anita Ekberg) holds a crying kitten she has found, stroking its fur and holding it close to her face.*

Sound: *Crying kitten and voice-over of* CHARLOTTE: You know the first time I saw you, you were wearing a tuxedo at the bar.

Image: CHARLOTTE [sitting on the floor, lower than Bob, arms resting on his bed, saki cup in focus]: You were very dashing [She smiles, closing her eyes at the end of the sentence]. I liked the mascara [She gently laughs into her saki].

Sound: *Kitten cries.*

Image: BOB [shakes his head in the negative]: But the first time I saw you was in the elevator.

Image: *Bob lying on bed, Charlotte sitting on floor, their faces turned to each other, close.*

CHARLOTTE: Really?

BOB: You don't remember?

They discuss the first meeting, and Charlotte's smile that Bob (and the viewer) noticed in the elevator, but that Charlotte no longer recalls. Then, they turn back away from the closeness of their faces, the "affection-image" (cf. C2: 32) of each other's face evident in their expressions, and back towards the television and *La Dolce Vita*. Within that film, Sylvia frolics in the Trevi Fountain in Rome on screen, calling out for her would-be lover to join her rapture. Two time-images simultaneously operate in this scene, a past and a present. The inferences of *This Sweet Life* now become coupled with those in *Lost in Translation*, and the circuit of generic images of bodies forms an "aggregate ensemble" of a rearticulated–remembered–recognizable desire (ABC: "D as in Desire"). As Deleuze reminds us, *"Repetition changes nothing in the object repeated, but does change something in the mind which contemplates it"* (DR: 70, original emphasis).

Recognition

If at times she showed me these marks of affection, she pained me also by seeming not to be pleased to see me, and this happened often on the very days on which I had most counted on the realisation of my hopes.   Proust, *Swann's Way* (1981 [1913]: 438)

The narrative characterization of Charlotte in *Lost in Translation* is of a young woman, a philosophy graduate of an expensive American university. She has moved from one city to live in another and partake of a heteronormative relationship of marriage. She is presumably economically dependent upon her working husband for her material needs. She leads a privileged leisure existence. Living in the Park Hyatt Hotel in Tokyo while her fashion photography husband works, she is thus free from the constraints of work, and home routines, yet bound by a relationship to an economic patriarchy that she deferentially acknowledges. It is Charlotte's emotive and phenomenologically observed existence that the camera shows to the audience: her differences in kind, her differences in strategies of engaging with the world, within her world's boundaries and exclusions. She is pensive, mostly reserved in her speech, does not engage in much small talk, asks big questions, listens to self-improvement instructional tapes, knits, smokes cigarettes, wears twin-sets and see-through briefs in her hotel room, slightly oversized coats and contemporary dress for outside. Her gait is uneven, her smile is distant, she is well groomed, white, blonde, petite. The gest she provides to the narrative whole is that of an observer, a listener, a *mise en scènic* reflection for the noise around her: a traditional role for her gender.

However, one aspect of the thought-imagery of Coppola's narrative is on Charlotte's apparent passivity, and her character's consciousness of her constitution within the world, her recognition of the need to become, to be, something, someone, somewhere. At times, she appears to have trouble recognizing herself, a representation of her knowledge of the world. Her attempts at communication fail – she is unable to transform feelings into words in reaction to experiences, for example over the telephone early in the film – and this is due to her evident fear of losing her ability to feel when confronted by a powerful affection-image:

CHARLOTTE [alone in her hotel room, talking into the phone, barely holding back tears, her voice affected by emotion]: It's great here, it's really great … umm, I don't know, I went to this shrine today, and umm, there were these monks and they were chanting. And I didn't feel anything [wiping tears from her face], you know, and umm, I don't know I even tried ikebana, [shaking her head in the negative] and John [her husband] is using these hair products and I don't know who I married.

Charlotte's attempted translation of feeling into language fails to convey the crisis to her friend on the phone who also seems too preoccupied to cope fully with Charlotte's emotive expression.

However, the audience is empathetic, due to the relational-images that have described her thoughts to us previously: a hard-edge focus on a tree tied with white knotted markers; an isolated figure against a relief of the cityscape – signals of other thoughts, other lives, other desires, other trajectories. As Deleuze notes, "memory is voice, which speaks, talks to itself, or whispers, and recounts what happened" (C2: 51). Through recollection, the audience can visualize her identity, along with auditory cues for her character given on screen; Charlotte's "cinemato-graphic presence" and "luminosity" (C2: 201) are given through the use of hand-held camera character-point-of-view shots (the audience see through her, at times, unsteady and slow to focus eyes), edited together with clearly focused imagery of the world around her. In this sense, Charlotte's presence is recognizable through the way her being affects the manner in which we, the audience, and other entities in her world (notably only Bob), envisage her topography of life.

In *Bergsonism*, Deleuze describes the process of intuition – an essen-tial component for the movement of meaning in the cinema (C2: Ch. 3) – as recollection, or recognition. In terms of understanding the artistic praxis of film-makers, Deleuze's Bergsonian approach is appropriate, given that most artists (film-makers, visual artists, creative writers) work *intuitively*, based on personalized formulas. Recognition and self- and intertextual acknowledgment by artists aware of the generative connec-tions forming from the conceptual and ideological dimensions of their practice allow the differences between praxis and the interpretive language of an image (intuition, datum, memory) to generate what we search for in this world (B: 103).[10] Recognition occurs through complex processes, and is not just a matter of viewing an image on a screen. Rather, that image must contain the processes of thought within it to be affective, actionary, perceivable. As Deleuze writes, "Something in this world forces us to think. This something is an object not of recognition but of a fundamental *encounter* ... It is not a quality but a sign" (DR: 139–40). The audience, and Bob, see Charlotte's gest as a recognizable entity through the many close-up shots of her face: a recognizable icon–encounter–event within the non-specific surfaces and spaces of the city (cf. C1: 109–10). What kind of circumstantial sign does she represent; what does Bob recognize in her smile by "association" (ES: 103)? One might observe, as Deleuze does, after his Bergsonian reading of Hume, that "the subject is constituted within the given" (ES: 104), and Bob immediately sees in Charlotte (in the sense of "*connaissance*", at once knowledge and recognition) the wonder of life (B: 14). Recognition of things, then, according to Deleuze might be summarized thus: "Intui-tion is the *jouissance* of difference" (DI: 33, translation modified).

151

Time

This magic moment, so different and so new
Was like any other, until I met you[11]
    "This Magic Moment" (1972), D. Pomus & M. Shuman,
as performed by Lou Reed on the soundtrack of *Lost Highway*
    (dir. D. Lynch 1997)

Recognition of a moment in time is often achieved through the aware-ness of loss, a feeling of loss that may not even be articulated. Rather, it may just present itself in an empty space, a moment of colour, a sound, an empty room, the chronos intrinsic to forehead furrows, a lack of wonder and joy. The Proustian search for lost time may provoke that clichéd "Cartesian diver in us," as Deleuze notes of the "ordinary" cinematic viewer (C2: 169). But to Proust's discernment of the creation of art, of thought, of essences, Deleuze adds Bergson and Hume's approach to the temporal consciousness of subjectivity.[12] "Subjectivity, then, takes on a new sense, which is no longer motor or material, but temporal and spiritual: that which 'is added' to matter, not what distends it; recollection-image, not movement-image" (C2: 47; Deleuze's reference is to Bergson's *Matter and Memory*). Recognition of possible futures, of new and aberrant signals of the future, are revealed by the image in situations of time, or of what Deleuze describes, after Nietzsche, as "detours" in evolution (C2: 43). So for Deleuze, aside from the mechanical aspect of the temporal workings of the apparatus, two possible states of time exist in the cinema: an organic time, and a crystalline time. Deleuze's sense of the latter corresponds to many twentieth-century modernist notions of the multiplicity of temporality, perceivable and representable through superimposed layers.[13] The organic and the crystalline senses of time are co-dependent: "What Fellini says is Bergsonian: 'We are con-structed in memory; we are *simultaneously* childhood, adolescence, old age and maturity'" (C2: 99, original emphasis).

According to Deleuze, in philosophical thought "Time has always put the notion of truth into crisis" (C2: 130). In the cinema, time provides the fundamental axes of possibilities of the construction and meaning of imagery.[14] Bergson's work on the links between the temporal variabil-ity of matter and the therein-created provisional difference of things, provide formative ideas for Deleuze's philosophy of the hows and whys of the concepts of the living world. Yet why did the cinema shift from producing a self-moving image to an image of temporality? As Deleuze says in his essay "Mediators" (1985),

Cinema is not by its very nature narrative: it becomes narrative when it takes as its object the sensory-motor schema. That's to say, someone on the screen perceives, feels, reacts. It takes some believing: the hero, in a given situation, reacts; the hero always knows how to react ... This all came to an end with World War II. Suddenly people no longer really believed it was possible to react to situations. (N: 123)

The cinematic screen will often show us recollection-images with which we as viewers have no possible historical or cultural connection, yet they may retain a power to affect us, or they may remain virtual in their non-recognition (C2: 54–5). Such images become time-images through their "disturbances" of thought, of memory, through their display of a "temporal 'panorama'" (C2: 55).

Time, in a Deleuzian reading of cinema, is all about the process of the becoming of things, and attending to the conditions of this experience. "Duration is not merely lived experience; it is also experience enlarged or even gone beyond; it is already a condition of experience" (B: 37). Deleuze is not interested so much in the final reading of a film's meaning, but in the syntactical construction of the filmic construction of a "magic moment" itself, taking us by surprise.[15] Deleuze cautions against the reading of a narrative into the cinema, noting that "whether explicitly or not, narration always refers to a *system of judgement*" (C2: 133, original emphasis). The cinema's epistemic kinesis is "fractured" by the direct presentation of time and "I is another ['*Je est un autre*'] has replaced Ego = Ego" (C2: 133). This is where the visual and auditory language of cinema exceeds that of the written or spoken word: the crystalline time-images where words are unnecessary, and pre-linguistic signifiers open alternatives for engaging with the world.

In *Lost in Translation*, Bob and Charlotte come together by chance, through their embodied reactions to the standard markings of time. Their interconnections begin as their fractured normative rhythms make duration into a common network, a shared ground of unknown and unpredictable moments of time-images. Insomnia distends each moment, enabling each character in their surrounding territory to further stray from the kind of relationship their deterministic chronological selves might have produced. Charlotte, well versed in pushing the limits of the temporal modalities of idleness and banality, takes pleasure in the dilation of the everyday, its intricacies, and variations. Until he encounters Charlotte, Bob emphatically fights to eliminate time, to speed it up, to get away from Tokyo as quickly as possible. After they spend some time together, clubbing and performing karaoke, Bob's involvement with the world changes. He works to extend time, to follow the becoming surrounding him, becoming in-time, as-time, in relation to Charlotte, but also to his altered self-awareness.

In an essay written at the same time as the cinema books, "On Four Poetic Formulas that Might Summarize the Kantian Philosophy", Deleuze describes this derivation of the I and the Self in time with a quotation from Arthur Rimbaud – "I is an other": "Time can thus be defined as the Affect of the self by itself, or at least as the formal possibility of being affected by oneself" (ECC: 31). Bob's struggle with duration, within the pull of chronological time, is ultimately a "form of interiority", but not that time is "specifically interior to us; it is we who are interior to time, and for this reason time always separates us from what determines us by affecting it. Interiority constantly hollows us out, splits us in two, doubles us, even though our unity subsists" (ECC: 31). Yet, because time continues, so does the doubling, the folding, so that *"time is constituted by a vertigo or oscillation*, just as unlimited space is constituted by a sliding or floating" (ECC: 31, original emphasis).

For Deleuze, the how and where of being is to be located in what he terms the "any-space-whatevers" of modern cinema (C1: 111), as the cinematic concept represents signs of meaning (of being, of life) that are in the perpetual process of translation: subtle, disconnected, and always incomplete in terms of their implication for the whole. The site of the cinema produces possible "modes of existence" (C1: 114), "an infinite set" (C1: 59), "a non-localizable relation [of time]" (C2: 41), "an underground fire which is always covered over" (C2: 279). Within and on this space, we find the time-image events and bodies of the modern cinema.

Conclusion

Modes of life inspire ways of thinking; modes of thinking create ways of living. (PI: 66)

The cumulative thesis of the cinema books rests upon the discovery or discrete awareness of cinematic moments and sounds – Deleuze will call these "just the one idea" of the film (N: 38–9) – wherein a formal and/ or affective change occurs. A position is moved. The degree zero is pinpointed; your position in the rhythm, in the dance, is noted, paused; duration is situated. This moment is not necessarily a corporeal configuration, although the cinema always has eyes upon its form to enable the modality of corporeal morphological relations to occur. In 1950 Gaston

Bachelard would describe this temporal pause as "temporal psychological phenomenon" (2000 [1950]: 49).

At the beginning of this essay I described the questioning of the perceptual process to be the channel for working with Deleuze's cinematographic philosophy. The thought-image of the cinema provides bridges across this channel, by which we might access the activity and reactivity of temporal platforms of being: vessels perpetrated and represented in the hyper-textuality of the cinematic form. Like Deleuze and Guattari's conception of the "Body without Organs" (ATP: plateau 6), Deleuze's discussion of time relates to the conception of subjectivity, consciousness and the possible constitutions (past, future) of the nature of being. The BwO is a way of apprehending the power of an assemblage of subjectivity, of self, of causing intensities to pass; it is an egg, say Deleuze and Guattari, the "full egg" that precedes the formation of the organism and its strata; the "intense egg" of transforming energy and group displacement; and the "tantric egg" that passes over thresholds into new gradients (ATP: 153). Thus, the BwO is not space, it is matter, and above all, it is the potential energy of becoming through intensities. If we think of the surface of the cinema as a receptive, sensory egg, an organ for perceiving activities and/or events of the world, then we might locate a vitality of perception that will re-connect us to the political and aesthetic world. For as Deleuze insists, "Truth is production of existence" (N: 134, translation modified).

Notes

1. The books are produced at a specific theoretical juncture, 1983 and 1985 (for their French publication, translated into English in 1986 and 1989), and as such, they evidence an economy of poststructuralist thought that historically situates and informs their methodologies of cinematic and philosophical analysis. For discussion and application of the cinematic concepts generated by Deleuze's cinema books, refer to Shaiviro (1993), Rodowick (1997), Flaxman (2000), Kennedy (2000), Pisters (2003).
2. Ronald Bogue (2003a: 194–6) notes the application of Deleuze's theories to the theatre and television. See also Patricia Pisters's (2003) discussion of the use of Deleuze's cinema theory in relation to "contemporary media culture".
3. *Lost in Translation* has a number of divergent readings; for example, see the *Lost-in-Racism* website www.lost-in-racism.org (accessed Dec. 2004). For a review/synopsis of the film see Samara Allsop (2004).
4. Bergson's thesis on movement and change provides a vital background for Deleuze's contention for the movement of bodies as entities, within wholes, or universes (Bergson 1911: 5). As Deleuze discusses in the first chapter of *Cinema 1*, every time a new element is introduced into the whole, the dimensions and qualities of that whole and everything within it always change. The only given

state of a thing exists as an illusory description because all things are subject to flux and change imposed by movement in space. The transformations and "translations" of space are those moments of difference that occur as the result of durational change. Deleuze describes moments of intuition as being move-ment, not duration (B: 32–3). With the developments in modern astronomy, physics, geometry, calculus and cinema, the movement of bodies is known not by "instants" but by elements within a section that can be determined (C1: 8–11).

5. Bergson's (1911: 249–64) concept of the "genesis of matter" is given agency through the crystal metaphor.

6. For a quick breakdown on the different types and categories of sign, activity and Deleuze's filmic examples in *Cinema 1* and *Cinema 2*, see Patricia Pisters "Appendix A" (2003: 227–8).

7. For an extended discussion on Deleuze and affect, see Barbara M. Kennedy's chapter titled "Towards an Aesthetics of Sensation" (2000: 108–22). For a dis-cussion of subjectivity and affect in Deleuze's use of Spinoza's concept of affect, see Rei Terada's chapter titled "A Parallel Philosophy" (2001: 90–127).

8. See Jean-Paul Sartre *The Imaginary* (2004 [1940]) and *Sketch for a Theory of the Emotions* (1962 [1939]).

9. For a Deleuzian reading of cultural difference and memory in the cinema, see Laura U. Marks (1999).

10. In a broad range of his writings, Deleuze takes this evolutionary approach to the development of ideas – from the virtual to the actual – as a process of differen-tiation that occurs through the passage of converting memory and duration to intuition – an understanding of the choices of life (PS: 41–4; B: 95–102; C1: 113–14).

11. "This Magic Moment" lyrics, www.elyrics4u.com/t/this_magic_moment_lou_reed.htm (accessed Jan. 2005). The second line of the original version, by D. Pomus and M. Shuman, reads "until I kissed you".

12. See Deleuze's progression of this idea through his essays: "The Image of Thought" (PS: 94–102), "The Image of Thought" (DR: Ch. 3), "Thought and Cinema" (C2: Ch. 7) and "Cinema, Body and Brain, Thought" (C2: Ch. 8).

13. For a historical summary of this position see historian Reinhardt Koselleck (1995 [1979]: 92–104).

14. If the recognition of the possibility of another movement, another image, another recollection, another future is produced in the crystalline (sonsignic–opsignic) moments of the cinema, then Deleuze's interest in the paradoxical nature of temporality and its relationship to the cognition of the structures and coordination of existence and meaning stem from Bergson's thesis in his book *Creative Evolution* (1911) on the protean development of matter to the cata-lytic effects of temporally mediated events. Bergson's use of the entropic nature of time enabled Deleuze to reassess many clichéd statements concerning time, and refigure them, according to the temporal laws of entropy and what would develop (with Guattari) into the understanding of rhizomatic processes of relativity (ATP: 10–12).

15. For elaboration on Deleuze's open and continual semiotic approach, and concepts of "firstness, secondness, thirdness" beyond the scope of this essay, refer to the work of C. S. Peirce: see Merrell (1997). For a discussion of Peirce in Deleuze, see Bogue (2003a: 78–9, 86, 99–101).

III

Folds

THIRTEEN

From affection to soul

Gregory J. Seigworth

> To assume that there was a power of being affected which defined the power of being affected of *the whole universe* is quite possible ...   (Deleuze 1997c: 9, emphasis added)

What follows is a story of affect as a set or series of encounters: affectionate encounters with enemies and allies, often proximate, sometimes more distant, and quite regularly both at the same time. Although this essay moves, in large part, by proper names (Guattari, Deleuze, Lacan, Lyotard, Foucault), it is simultaneously a story of affect's different modes of existence. Each encounter shifts slightly in its emphasis, while progressively navigating through the chief forms – and un-forms – of affect. It should be remembered that these affectional modes (as points, lines, vaporous atmospheres and planes) are, by their nature, perpetually tangled up in one another. However, it always takes far more than two or three to tangle, even if we begin with and between (seemingly) two: Guattari *and* Deleuze.

Brief prelude: affect as passion, or, when Felix *and* Gilles met

> ... passion dissolve[s] persons not into something undifferentiated but into a field of various persisting and mutually interdependent intensities ... Love's a state of, and a relation between, persons, subjects. But passion is a subpersonal event that may last as long as a lifetime ... It is very difficult to express, to convey – a new distinction between affective states.   (N: 116)

In endeavouring to understand what may have first drawn Guattari and Deleuze to each other in the summer of 1969, one could do infinitely worse than begin by wondering about the role played by "affect". After all, Guattari proposed (first in 1964) his conception of psychoanalytical practice as "transversality" – by enlarging the milieu of encounter to include affective qualities that went beyond, not only the psychically interpersonal, but also beyond the altogether too narrow realm of the human – to serve as a rather deliberate alternative to Jacques Lacan's focus upon the processes of "transference" between analyst and analysand. Meanwhile, Deleuze – whose *Expressionism in Philosophy: Spinoza* was published in 1968 – had set himself the task of retrieving affect from Spinoza's *Ethics* where it had long been mutilated and reduced in translation as "affection" or "emotion". But Deleuze's project here was not just a one-for-one replacement of the mistranslated "affection" with affect.[1] In fact, there is not one type of affect in Spinoza but two (*affectio* and *affectus*), and, then, not only two but, before and beneath them both, a third (affect as blessedness–beatitude or soul), and then, in a lightning flash, not just three but a multitudinous affectivity beyond number (a plane of immanence).

Never susceptible to pinning down, affect is that moment of singularity (sometimes Deleuze and Guattari will use the term "haecceity", or thisness) where a universe pours in, flows out – an unlimited One-All, universal-singular. To paraphrase Deleuze and Guattari: like an egg as it cracks open, affect flees on all of its sides at once. An affection dissolved between two, thereby a multitude (an infinite expanse of desert to be populated): affect as subpersonal event, as passionate line of flight.

Diverging Spinozan paths

As the color of the human soul as well as the color of human becomings and of cosmic magics, affect remains hazy, atmospheric, and nevertheless perfectly apprehensible to the extent that it is characterized by the existence of threshold effects and reversals in polarity.   (Guattari 1996a: 158)

Things never pass where you think, nor along the paths you think.
(D: 4)

When reflecting upon the impulses that guided the writing of their first book together, Guattari remarks that, for both himself and Deleuze, "our objections to Freud in *Anti-Oedipus* were very much bound up with our objections to Lacanism" (AO: 50). For while Sigmund Freud had, for some time, seriously endeavoured to give an accounting of affect (most especially in his earliest "scientific psychology" up through *The Interpretation of Dreams*), Jacques Lacan regarded any sustained analytical attention to affect as thoroughly misguided. The clearest moment in Lacan's direct assault on affect comes during the last day of his seminars in 1953–54. Following a question from Serge Leclaire about Lacan's ongoing alternation of silence and "direct attacks" in regard to affect, the master declares to his followers: "I believe that is a term ['the affective'] which one must completely expunge from our papers" (1988: 275). And it is with considerably more flourish that, a few weeks earlier in the same seminar, Lacan tells his audience that they must stop pursuing the affective as if it:

> were a sort of coloration, a kind of ineffable quality which must be sought out in itself, independently of the eviscerated skin which the purely intellectual realization of a subject's relationship should consist in. This conception, which urges analysis down strange paths, is puerile ... The affective is not like a special density which would escape an intellectual accounting. (*Ibid.*: 57)

But it is precisely down these "strange paths" that Deleuze and Guattari – both together and in their solo writings – chose to tread, although they would agree with Lacan on one point: that "affect escapes intellectual accounting" by *not* passing where you think, or, that is, where there is an image of thought.

Hence, as Deleuze tells the audience of his own seminars: "Every mode of thought insofar as it is non-representational will be termed affect" (1997c: 1). An affective path cannot be threaded through those places where representations or images of thought are predominant or hold sway. For affect is something more or other than a mode of thought: an affect, first as Spinoza's *affectio*, is the transitive effect undergone by a body (human or otherwise) in a system – a mobile and open system – composed of the various, innumerable forces of existing and the relations between these forces. More succinctly, *affectio* (affection) is the state of a body in as much as it affects or is affected by another body. Affect, then, cannot be converted into or delimited by the discursive, by images or representations, by consciousness or thought. Equally significant too, as we shall see, is the notion that affect has its own autonomy (not only from the intellect but from affectional–corporeal tracings as well), and this was the route that Lacan (and most subsequent Lacanians) refused to accept as viable.

161

It is intriguing, though, to wonder, as Lacan biographer Elizabeth Roudinesco (1997: 52–6) does, about Lacan's own passionate and idiosyncratic encounter with Spinoza. The walls of Lacan's boyhood bedroom were covered in diagrams and coloured arrows that charted the supple architecture of Spinoza's *Ethics*, while the epigraph of Lacan's thesis is a quote from Book 3 (proposition 57) of *The Ethics*, about how the affects of one individual differ from those of another to the same degree that their essences differ. The main problem for Lacan, as Roudinesco points out, is that he did not realize in his earliest readings of Spinoza (during the early 1930s) that, in *The Ethics* (and in his quoted thesis epigraph in particular), Spinoza had used two words for designating affect: *affectus* and *affectio*. The French translator Charles Appuhn had unfortunately rendered both as "affection", thus collapsing the key distinction for Spinoza between "the state of a body as it affects or is affected by another body" (*affectio*) and "a body's continuous, intensive variation (as increase-diminution) in its capacity for acting" (*affectus*). As Deleuze and Guattari derive from this latter formulation of affect (as *affectus*), a dimension of subjectivity opens up – a lived intensity that is simultaneously neutral, or, impersonal (an intimate exteriority) – that Lacan's work, during this time, could not bring into account.

Roudinesco remarks, then, that it would take Lacan "twenty years" (or, if the seminar of 1953–54 is any indication, a little longer than that!) to start to square Spinoza's affect with "his theoretical revisionism of Freudianism as a whole" (Roudinesco 1997: 55). But, even then, Lacan would invite Deleuze to his apartment a few months after the publication of *Anti-Oedipus* to ask him (without success) to consider becoming a disciple. Later, he would tell friends that Deleuze and Guattari had plagiarized his seminars, and, further, that they had pilfered his idea of a "desiring machine" (*ibid.*: 348).

Machining desire, or a general mechanics of the Soul

Subjectivity is never ours, it is time, that is, the soul or the spirit, the virtual . . . it was initially the affect, that which we experience in time; then time itself, pure virtuality, which divides itself in two as affector and affected, "the affection of self by self" as definition of time.   (C2: 82–3)

In the early pages of his *Heidegger and "the Jews"*, Lyotard initiates a discussion of what he says even Freud knew would be widely regarded as "pure nonsense, an affect that does not affect consciousness. How can one say it affects? What is a feeling that is not felt by anyone?" (1990: 12). More pointedly, *where* in a corporeal topography of the human psyche, with its capacity to affect and be affected, would such an affect reside? The short answer: in lost time. Following Lyotard further, this is what Deleuze finds so incredibly compelling about Marcel Proust's *A la recherche du temps perdu*: "a past located this side of the forgotten, much closer to the present moment than any past, at the same time that it is incapable of being solicited by voluntary and conscious memory – a past Deleuze says that is not past but always there" (Lyotard 1990: 12). And, thus, the oft-repeated mantra that Deleuze extracts from Proust – "real without being actual, ideal without being abstract" – that comes to serve as Deleuze's shorthand formula for the virtual.[2]

From one (rather human) standpoint, the virtual can be understood, in part, as what has happened: as subsistent past, in full affective-accumulation, on this side of forgetting. However, crucially, the virtual is also always in contact and actively–affectively participating with what is happening and about to happen contemporaneously (as becoming): in excess of consciousness, an affective-accumulation continually pressing toward its differentiated actualization in the future. The virtual is perhaps easiest to consider as what transpires in those passing everyday moments that never really present themselves to our conscious minds, generally because such moments (in their various contexts and variable durations) arrive with insufficient force or otherwise descend with an intensity that is altogether dispersed or atmospheric. As they slip well beneath the thresholds of consciousness, these intensive passages of affect (*affectus*) are, Lyotard writes, "'in excess' like air and earth are in excess of the life of a fish" (1990: 12). In fact, these low-level gradient changes in the passages of intensity are so much in excess that the word "moment" is not entirely adequate. This ongoing process of affective-accumulation (as time lost to time itself) makes up most of our days, as the between-moments (of any-space and any-time-whatevers) that come to constitute "a life".

Lyotard maintains that the soul is always exceeded, even as it is continually constituted and reconstituted by these passages of affective intensity; and he argues that this kind of metaphysics of a system of forces and force-relations "definitely needs a general mechanics" directed "toward the determination of the state of the soul itself" (1990: 12). To which he adds, "Deleuze has, in a sense, done nothing other than investigate and unfold its possibilities" (1990: 12), an assessment that Deleuze would hardly have disputed at all. Spinoza's distinction of *affectio* and *affectus* had provided a way to approach "soul" that departed rather radically from more traditional discourses of eternal salvation (or damnation). Speaking about Spinoza with Parnet, Deleuze concludes:

> the soul is neither above nor inside, it is "with", it is on the road, exposed to all contacts, encounters, in the company of those who follow the same way, "feel with them, seize the vibration of their soul and their body as they pass", the opposite of a morality of salvation, teaching the soul to live its life, not to save it.   (D: 62)

A life, and how to live it: through the modification of a body's affects by its contact with bodies outside it (*affectio*) to the melodic variation (*affectus*) that carries a body along "the road", it then moves through and beyond both, to a steady accumulation of affective-encounters (neither above nor inside, but virtually alongside). This accumulation opens no longer to a prescribed and transcendent morality but on to an immanently everyday ethics. It is no surprise, then, that Foucault would enthusiastically proclaim Deleuze and Guattari's *Anti-Oedipus* to be read as a "manual or guide to everyday life" (1977: xiii).

Flee: affect and power

To flee, but in fleeing to seek a weapon.   (D: 136)

Despite the enthusiasms Deleuze and Foucault shared for one another's work, it is relatively easy to mark some key distinctions – around the whole matter of affect – between their writings, and that's for two reasons: first, because there are so few significant differences between them; secondly, because they themselves, at different times, addressed rather directly those few points that separate their work, if often through only the very subtlest of shadings.

For example, they had different means of avoiding too-ready subsumption into the two of the major intellectual currents of their time: phenomenology and structural Freudo-Marxism (or, in many ways, "Lacanian-Althusserism"). In a 1981 interview, Foucault (1991: 31) said that the key sequence of figures in his own awakening and escape were first Blanchot, followed by Bataille and then Nietzsche, while, two years later in another interview (1996: 351), he stated that as he saw it, for Deleuze, it was Hume first, and then Nietzsche (although Foucault probably should also have added, at least, Bergson and Spinoza). Throughout their careers, Foucault and Deleuze were both evidently influenced by the work of Blanchot, Nietzsche and Spinoza. But the more telling names are those that do not fit particularly well into the other's itinerary: for instance, Bataille for Deleuze or Hume for Foucault. Consider, then, how Foucault attends to the themes of transgression and the violences that regularly circulate in the vicinities of "truth", the intricate, capillary linkages of knowledge and power, and the ethico-aesthetics of limit-experiences. Meanwhile, Deleuze's interests are sustained by matters more closely affiliated with the affective or passional: the ruptures, flows and assemblages of desire, the pragmatics of force, the continual hingings and unhingings of habits and territories.

When Deleuze registers some of the fundamental differences between himself and Foucault, he does so, as ever, by making these differences productive: most immediately, through the affects and ethics of Spinoza. In a succinct set of notes entitled "Desire and Pleasure" from 1977 (written with the intention of being privately passed to Foucault), but not published until 1994 in France, Deleuze sketched out several of the points along which he and Foucault coincided and, even more revealingly, those relatively few but significant points where they diverged. This essay also provides some useful elaboration of a small but critical endnote about Foucault located in Deleuze and Guattari's *A Thousand Plateaus* (ATP: 530–31, n.39).

In both this minor footnote and the notes in "Desire and Pleasure", Deleuze and Guattari lodged two primary disagreements with Foucault. First, assemblages are – for them – assemblages of desire before they are assemblages of power.

> If I speak, with Félix, of the desiring-assemblages, it's that I am not sure that micro-systems can be described in terms of power. For me, the desiring-assemblage marks the fact that desire is never a "natural" nor a "spontaneous" determination ... Systems of power would thus be a component of assemblages ... [However] systems of power would never motivate, nor constitute, but rather desiring-assemblages would swarm among the formations of power according to their dimensions. (Deleuze 1997a: n.p.)

Power, thus, is the stratified dimensions of an assemblage; power arrives as the coming-to-formation and sedimentations that follow in the temporary arresting of an assemblage. Power is something like a coagulation or scabbing on the skin or surface of the social rather than the immanent breaks, flows and movements of desire.

This perspective brings us to the corollary: in any critical analysis of the social field that links various of these assemblages with their discursive and non-discursive elements, "lines of flight ... are primary", that is, they are "not phenomena of resistance or counterattack in an assemblage, but cutting edges of creation and deterritorialization" (ATP: 531). The first rule of the social is that it flees on all sides at once: "the first given of a society is that everything flees" (Deleuze 1997a). In Deleuze and Guattari's view, any critical discourse that focuses on power in its initial move will, nearly by default, call up an attendant and too-symmetrical posture from acts of resistance as the occasion and site of their joint, interlocking exercise, even as Foucualt himself gamely tries to circumvent this state of affairs in his essay "The Subject and Power" (2000). Resistance falls, almost inevitably, into a "reactive" role as block and/or friction, and, further, such a conception only hastens a romantic anthropomorphization of power's possibilities. Hence, Deleuze's refusal to simply trumpet, unproblematically, the programmes and protestations of "the marginals" (D: 139): a real point of disagreement with Foucault.

Here, then, is where Deleuze's notion of the immanence and perpetual flowings and fleeings of the social field can be more fully grasped, again, through his reading of Spinoza's affect. Against dialectical reasoning and various structuralist dualisms, Deleuze discovers a "narrow gorge like a border or frontier" where a multiplicity can be divulged. Casting, then, both "power" and "desire" in relation to affect, Deleuze makes a concise but illuminating equation between these terms, claiming that the "first difference would thus be that, for me, power is an affection of desire" (1997a: n.p.). That is, power is the *affectio* of the encounter between two (or more) bodies, whether collective or individual. As outlined above, this affection (as *affectio*) is the most basic of affect's three primary modes as found in the Spinozan undercurrents of Deleuze's philosophical thought. When one is able to trace out in this way how Deleuze draws distinctions and connections between these three modes of affect, we can follow a similar trajectory across nearly all of his writings on other philosophers and their philosophical planes, as well as those books written in his own voice. It is an implicit (and sometimes explicit) movement through the vicissitudes of affect that continually guides Deleuze's thought.

To summarize:

- *Affectio* An affection of a body by or upon another; actualization as the "state of a thing", that is, affect turned "effect". Thus, to say that "power is an affection of desire" is, indeed, to say that power is an effect of desire, one of its (desire's) arrested, although resonating, modes of existence
- *Affectus* Affect as a line of continuous variation in the passage of intensities or forces of existence; affect as "becoming", a continual

inclining or declining slope or greater or lesser degrees of intensity or potentiality

- *Affect* as entirely active or as absolute survey. Pure immanence at its most concrete abstraction from all becomings and states of things. The autonomy of affect as outside any distinction of interiority or exteriority. In Deleuze's view, this is affect as virtuality, "soul" or "a life".

Returning more immediately to Deleuze's conceptualization of power as seen now in the light of affect, Deleuze's influential 1962 re-reading of Nietzsche in *Nietzsche and Philosophy* relies, in part, on drawing an affectual distinction between power as *pouvoir* (power acted out in reaction, reversal and ressentiment, i.e. power separated from what it can do) and power as *puissance* (potential, the power to act, the sensibility of force). There is also a great deal of affinity to be discovered between this pair of terms and similar dualities (with their own unique gorges) such as Bergson's virtual–actual and Spinoza's *potestas–potentia*.[3]

Because there is a Spinozan system of expression subtending the way that each of these concept pairs is split or shifted like a load, a third element circulates between potential and its actualization, between what expresses and what is expressed, be it Nietzsche's eternal return, Bergson's élan vital, Spinoza's beatitude, Leibniz's vinculum or Deleuze's "a life". This element serves not to close up potential and its actualization, but to leave them perpetually open to the Outside. In this regard, Pierre Macherey describes the perpetually mobile-architecture of Deleuze's philosophy quite effectively when he writes that what

Deleuze finds in Spinoza is a logic of univocity, where things are thought in their being, since the act of thinking something is the same act that produces it, by which it comes to be. So that expression is nothing to do with designating or representing anything ... [and hence] the act of expression that permits a synthesis of what is expressed and what expresses it is by definition the altogether positive affirmation of a power ... [O]ne might even say [here is] a logic of life or a logic of movement, essentially different from the traditional logics of representation that, in their quest for static identity, are constantly threatened by negativity, and therefore dependent on a transcendent principle.   (1996: 146–7)

Affect (in the encountering of bodies as *affectio*), movement (in the melodious intensive variation of *affectus*), *immanence* or soul as revealed in the myriad virtualities of (a) life: what one discovers, then, in Deleuze and Guattari's work is the attempt to grasp power positively not only as an effect or in its effects. More crucially, however, the task is to take account of power in its affectivity and producibility, in its expressibility.

Indeed, for Deleuze and Guattari, nothing much is advanced by finding everywhere the effects of power; something more is at stake when the task is, rather, to understand the virtual machine(s) and immanent assemblages that make the effects of power our actuality. The "world," Deleuze said, "does not exist outside of its expressions" (FLD: 132). Power, even at its most circumscribed and insistent (as either *pouvoir* or *puissance*), cannot begin to cover the full range of world-as-expression. With affect, Deleuze and Guattari seek a means to address the "whole" universe of expression in a way that no other logic allows.

In their last book together, *What is Philosophy?*, Deleuze and Guattari practically tick off, in sequential fashion, these progressive variations of affect: "The affect goes beyond affections [*affectio*] no less than the percept goes beyond perceptions. The affect is not the passage from one lived state to another [that is, *affectus*] but man's non-human becoming [*affect as expressive world*]" (WIP: 173). We may liken this series of beyondings – from *affectio* to *affectus* to immanently expressive world (soul) – to an increasing expansion or widening out: from the affective capacity of bodies (corporeal or incorporeal) to interval (as place of passage between intensive states or continuous variation) and, finally, to plane of immanence: as "the absolute ground of philosophy" (WIP: 41). The plane of immanence is

A LIFE and nothing else . . . A life is the immanence of immanence, absolute immanence: it is complete power, complete bliss . . . *A* life is everywhere, in all the moments that a given living subject goes through and that are measured by given lived objects: an imma-nent life carrying with it the events or singularities that are merely actualized in subjects and objects . . . A life contains only virtuals. It is made up of virtualities, events, singularities.

(PI: 27–31, original emphasis)

Locating the plane of immanence is not unlike discovering the intricate weave and meshings of a whole fabric of cloth, constantly moving, folding and curling back upon itself even as it stretches beyond and below the horizon of the social field (without ever separating from it or departing it). Trace out the story of affect and its encounters, and you will arrive at this plane of immanence: always there, always to be made, never still. It is affectionately yours, and, through it, the *whole* of the universe.

Notes

1. In a 1978 lecture on Spinoza, Deleuze says: "In Spinoza's principal book, which is called *The Ethics* and which is written in Latin, one finds two words: affectio and affectus. Some translators, quite strangely, translate both in the same way. This is a disaster. They translate both terms, affectio and affectus, by affection. I call this a disaster because when a philosopher employs two words, it is in principle because he has a reason to" (1997c: 1).
2. In *Proust and Signs*, Deleuze writes: "This ideal reality, this virtuality, is essence, which is realized or incarnated in involuntary memory" (PS: 60). See also Deleuze's reading of Spinoza, where essence and soul are intimately linked.
3. On the distinction *potestas–potentia* see Kenneth Surin's essay in this volume.

FOURTEEN

Folds and folding

Tom Conley

Folds and folding count among the most vital and resonant terms in Deleuze's copious and varied writings. The modest monosyllable, "pli", that refers both to a twist of fabric and to the origins of life, bears a lightness and density that mark many of the philosopher's reflections on questions of *being* and on the nature of *events*. Like the "events" of May 1968 in Paris, in 1988 the publication of *Le Pli: Leibniz et le baroque* [*The Fold: Leibniz and the Baroque*] became an event in itself and has since been a point of reference for the oeuvre in general. The intention behind the book, states the terse endnote on the back cover, is to show how, in the Baroque age that extends from the Counter Reformation to the Neo-Baroque in contemporary times, the fold can be taken as a figure and a form bearing almost infinite conceptual force. Leibniz's philosophy of the monad can be labelled "Baroque" because in the world of his fragmentary writing "everything folds, unfolds, refolds" (Deleuze, *Le Pli*, back cover). The soul is conceived as a monad, an enclosed space in a room without either doors or windows that draws its "clear perceptions" from a dark background (*Le Pli*, back cover). Deleuze notes that the German philosopher's response to the Cartesian concept of the soul can be understood by analogy with the inside of a Baroque chapel, whose inner walls are erected with slabs of black marble. "Light arrives only through openings imperceptible to the viewer inside." Thus, he adds, the "soul is replete with obscure folds" (*ibid.*). Implied is that the soul he finds in the chapel also inhabits the neo-Baroque worlds of poetry, literature, painting and music that include the work of near-contemporary creators from Mallarmé, Proust and Boulez to Hantaï. It is further suggested that the timeless question of the relation of the body to the soul, a theme central to philosophy from Plato to Alfred North Whitehead, has its most effective and pervasive figure in both the fold and its continuous process of folding.

The hypothesis is not only daring but also, for students of philosophy and aesthetics, at once unsettling and compelling. It requires reconsideration of the Cartesian split between body and spirit that has been at the foundation of ontology and epistemology. Deleuze's choice of the figure is neither arbitrary nor solely a project of a lifelong critical assessment of Leibniz. The fold belongs to a personal style and idiolect that develops along different paths in the writings that extend from the early work on empiricism and subjectivity to both *What Is Philosophy?* (1991) and his last book of essays on literature, *Essays Critical and Clinical* (1993), which appeared two years before his death. The aim of this short essay is to examine how and where folds and folding emerge in the writing and to assess their relation both to his study of Leibniz and his aesthetics in general. It can be speculated that the fold is a culminating and commanding figure in the philosophy and that the poet is found to be the double of the philosopher.

Folds in *Foucault*

The most terse and telling formulation of the fold is found in "Foldings, or the Inside of Thought (Subjectivation)". In this last chapter of *Foucault*, Deleuze examines Foucault's three-volume study of the history of sexuality, in which Foucault, he says, took sexuality to be a mirror of subjectivity and subjectivation. Deleuze broadens the scope by subsuming sexuality in a matrix of subjectivity. Every human being thinks as a result of an ongoing process of living in the world and by gaining consciousness and agency through a constant give and take of perception, affect and cognition. Subjectivity becomes an ongoing negotiation of things perceived, both consciously and unconsciously, within and outside of the body. He builds a "diagram", principally from Foucault's *The History of Sexuality* 1 (1978) and *The History of Sexuality: The Use of Pleasure* (1985), on the foundation of the earlier writings, to sketch a taxonomy and a history of the project. In *Archaeology of Knowledge* (1972), Foucault had contended that the "self", the "I", is always defined by the ways it is "doubled" by "another", not a single or commanding "other" or Doppelgänger, but simply any of a number of possible forces. "It is I who live my life as the double of the other" (FCLT: 98, translation modified),[1] and when I find the other in myself the discovery "is exactly like the invagination of another tissue in embryology, or the operation of a lining of a garment: twisting, folding over, stopping" (FCLT: 98, translation modified). For Foucault, history was the "doubling of a becoming" (FCLT: 98, translation modified). By that he meant that what was past or in an archive was also passed – as might a speeding car be overtaken or "doubled" by another on a highway – but also mirrored or folded into a diagram. History was shown to be what sums up the past but that can be marshalled for the shaping of configurations that will determine how people live and act in the present and future. Whether forgotten or remembered, history is one of the formative doubles or others vital to the process of subjectivation.

Therein begins Deleuze's rhapsody of folds and foldings. When a doubling produces an inner and an outer surface – *doublure* in French, meaning at once a lining stitched into a piece of clothing, a stand-in in a cinematic production, and even a "double", as Artaud had used the term in his writings on theatre – a new relation with being is born. An inside and an outside – a past (memory) and a present (subjectivity) – are two sides of a single surface. A person's relation with his or her body becomes both an "archive" and a "diagram", a collection of subjectivations and a mental map charted on the basis of the past and drawn from events and elements in the ambient world. Deleuze asserts that four folds, "like the four rivers of Hell" (FCLT: 104, translation modified), affect the subject's relation to itself: the first is the fold of the body, what is surrounded or taken within corporeal folds; the second is "the fold of the relation of forces", or social conflict; the third is the "fold of knowledge, or the fold of truth insofar as it constitutes a relation of veracity with our being" (FCLT: 104, translation modified), and vice versa; the fourth is the fold of "the outside itself, the ultimate" (FCLT: 104, translation modified) fold of the limit of life and death. Each of these folds refers to Aristotelian causes (material, efficient, formal and final) of subjectivity and has a variable rhythm of its own. It is necessary, Deleuze reminds us, for us to enquire of the nature of the four folds before we reflect on how subjectivity in our time is highly internalized, individualized and isolated. The struggle for subjectivity is a battle to win the right to have access to difference, variation and metamorphosis.

The human subject can only be understood "under the condition" (the formula, it will be shown, is a crucial one) of the fold and through the filters of knowledge, power and affect. The fold, a form said to obsess Foucault, is shown as something creased between things stated or *said* and things visible or *seen*. The distinction opened between "visible" and "discursive" formations is put forward in order to be drawn away from intentionality (as understood in Heidegger and Merleau-Ponty) that would ally subjectivity with phenomenology. Things spoken do not refer to an original or individual subject but to a "being-language," and things visible point to a "being-light" that illuminates "forms, proportions, perspectives" that would be free of any intentional gaze (FCLT: 109, translation modified). Anticipating his work on Leibniz, Deleuze notes that Foucault causes intentionality to be collapsed in the gap between "the two monads" (FCLT: 109, translation modified) of seeing and speaking. Thus phenomenology is converted into epistemology. To see and to speak is to know, "but we don't see what we are speaking of, and we don't speak of what we are seeing" (FCLT: 109, translation modified). Nothing can precede or antedate knowledge (*savoir*), even though knowledge or knowing is "irremediably double" (FCLT: 109, translation modified) – hence folded – as speaking *and* seeing, as language *and* light, which are independent of intending subjects who would be speakers and seers.

At this juncture the fold becomes the very fabric of ontology, the area of philosophy with which Deleuze claims staunch affiliation.[2] As a doubling or a lining the fold separates speech from sight and keeps each register in a state of isolation from the other. The gap finds an analogue in the hermetic difference of the sound and image track of cinema. From such a division knowledge is divided into pieces or "tracks" and thus can never be recuperated in any intentional form (FCLT: 111, translation modified).[3] The divided nature of communication has as its common metaphor the crease or fold between visibility and orality. It is no wonder that in his studies of difference and resemblance Foucault begins at the end of the sixteenth century, at the moment when writing evacuates its force of visual analogy from its printed form.[4] At that point, when print culture becomes standardized and schematic reasoning replaces memory in manuals of rhetoric, or when words are no longer analogous to the things they seem to embody or resemble, signs begin to *stand in* for their referents and to be autonomous "doubles" with respect to what they represent.

To demonstrate how the fold is a figure of subjectivation Deleuze calls history into the philosophical arena. He asks in bold and simple language: What can I do? What do I know? What am I? The events of May 1968 rehearsed these questions by enquiring of the limits of visibility, of language and of power. They brought forwards thoughts about utopia, and hence of modes of being that would enable resistance in repressive political conditions and foster the birth of ideas vital for new subjectivities. In a historical configuration *being* is charted along an axis of knowing. Being is determined by what is deemed visible and utterable; by the exercise of power, itself determined by relation of force and singularities at a given moment in time; and by subjectivity, shown to be a "process" or the places "through which passes the fold of the self" (FCLT: 116, translation modified). History is no sooner doubled or "folded over" by *thinking*. A grid or a new diagram makes clear the opposition by setting forward variations of power, knowledge and subjectivity (in French as *savoir*, *pouvoir*, *soi*). The latter is conceived as a fold. Foucault, Deleuze advances, does not divide a history of institutions or of subjectivations but of their *conditions* and of their *processes* within creases and foldings that operate in both ontological and social fields.

There is opened a dramatic reflection on the character of thinking, which belongs as much to Deleuze as to Foucault. Historical formations are "doubled" and thus define as such the epistemic traits of knowledge, power and subjectivity: in terms of knowledge, to think is to *see* and to *speak*; in other words, thinking takes place in the interstices of visibility and discourse. When we think we cause lightning bolts to flash and "flicker within words and make us hear cries in visible things" (FCLT: 116, translation modified). Thinking makes seeing and speaking reach their own limits. In what concerns power, thinking is equivalent to "emitting singularities", to a gambler's act of tossing a pair of dice on to a table, or to a person engaging relations of force or even conflict in order to prepare new mutations and singularities. In terms of subjectivation, thinking means "folding, doubling the outside with its co-extensive inside" (FCLT: 118, translation modified). A topology is created by which inner and outer spaces are in contact with each other.

History is taken to be an *archive* or series of *strata* from which thinking, a diagram replete with *strategies*, draws its force and virtue. To make the point clear Deleuze alludes indirectly to "A New Cartographer" (FCLT: 23–44), an earlier chapter that anticipates much of the spatial dynamics of *The Fold*. When we "think" we cross all kinds of thresholds and strata and follow a fissure in order to reach what, he says, Melville calls a "central room" wherein, we fear, no one will be and where "the soul of men might reveal an immense and terrifying void" (FCLT: 121, translation modified). Thinking is figured as a moving line; it is indeed "Melville's line" (FCLT 122), with its two free ends, which also resembles the poet Henri Michaux's line of "a thousand aberrations", a line moving at a growing molecular speed, a "whiplash of a crazed chariot-eer" (FCLT: 122, translation modified), which leads to what the same poet calls "*life in the folds [la vie dans les plis]*", and ultimately to a central room where there is no longer any need to fear its emptiness because the self (a fold) is found inside. "Here we become masters of our speeds, more or less commanding our molecules and singularities, in this zone of subjectivation in the embarkation of the inside and the outside"

(FCLT: 123, translation modified).[5] The dazzling vision in these sentences arches back to what Deleuze had stated about how the history of forms or an archive is "doubled" (passed or folded over) by a becoming of forces, where any number of diagrams – or folded surfaces of thought – are plied over each other. He calls it the torsion of the "line of the outside" that Melville described, an oceanic line without beginning or end, an oceanic line that turns and bumps about diagrams. The form of the line was "1968, the line 'with a thousand aberrations'" (FCLT: 44).

A line of divide

In the paragraph concluding "A New Cartographer" (first written as an article in *Critique* in 1975 before appearing in *Foucault*), Deleuze rehearses the words found at the end of *Foucault*. The line affiliated with Melville, implied also to be Michaux's, emblematizes what Deleuze calls Foucault's treble definition of writing, a writing that his own reading seems to be doubling: "writing is struggling, writing is resisting; writing is becoming; writing is mapping" (FCLT: 44, translation modified). The definition is rewritten in the final sentence of *The Fold*. Deleuze asserts that our subjectivity is Leibnizian because we are always "folding, unfolding, refolding" (FLD: 137). In the mode of a diagram, when the stratum from *Foucault* is superimposed onto that of *The Fold*, to fold means to write, but in the same treble sense. In a thetic movement folding resists itself; in an antithetical counterpart unfolding means becoming; and, finally, refolding – far from being a synthetic term assuring resolution – signifies the tracing of new maps and diagrams.

What Deleuze finds in the Foucaldian principle of writing as being and of folding as subjectivation informs much of his reading of Leibniz. Without the background of ontology shown as a series of folds in *Foucault*, some of the conclusions in the dense, rich and often obscure pages of *The Fold* might otherwise seem impenetrably obscure. Already Melville's open line and Michaux's line of a thousand aberrations led to what Deleuze called a central room, from which earlier anticipations of fear are seen, in the final sentences of both books, to be evacuated. It would not be wrong to compare this room to the room of "folds" that inaugurates his study of Leibniz. The room is the monad itself that has neither entrance nor windows, and that light penetrates only through openings imperceptible to the persons who, both inside and as "this zone of subjectivation", are more or less "the commanders of their speed, of their molecules and of their singularities" (FCLT: 123, translation modified).

The Fold begins with a description of the inner space before its walls are decorated with folded curtains and a veil stretched across its interior. The "Baroque House" becomes the allegory that opens and encapsulates the space of the study that follows. The Baroque is not an essence but a *trait*, a line that creates folds by twisting and turning them to infinity, "fold after fold ... fold according to fold" (FLD: 3). The house is divided into two labyrinthine floors. The folds of the soul occupy a second floor and the folds of matter reside on the first or public floor. The upper level is a double room or even a *camera obscura* adorned with a suspended canvas, "diversified by folds" as if it were a living skin. These folds (with springs or cords on the opaque canvas) represent innate knowledge, which is moved to action when, under the solicitude of matter, "vibrations" spring through "a few tiny openings" on the lower floor. Thus folds assure a strange but indeed physical communication between matter and soul. They take the form of veins in marble that resemble an "undulating lake stocked with fish" (FLD: 4, translation modified). The veins are innate ideas in the soul, like folded figures or virtual statues that can be extracted from a block of veined stone. Body and soul are marbled in different ways.

The architectural metaphor describing the *habitus* or living space of Deleuze's study is developed from the "central and obscure chamber" in the work in *Foucault* on subjectivation and on the folded nature of being constituting the "self". The insistence on Foucault's obsession with doubling leads to a reading of subjectivity that diverges from the prospect of a self that has little or no agency in the isolation that Foucault finds prevailing in contemporary societies. When he remarks that it is incumbent upon the self to "draw singularities from a space of the inside [*espace du dedans*]", and that thinking – what makes possible the agency of the self – is tantamount to doubling the outside with a coextensive inside (FCLT: 118), Deleuze suggests that the upper room and its folded furnishings become the imaginary space where subjectivation can be realized. The Baroque room, a space in which thinking takes place, is the site where new folds and folding (the forces and products of thinking) can be felt and harmonized.

Much of *The Fold* equates subjectivation with a continuous process of folding. For Deleuze, Leibniz's closed room is a site not only of mental variation in the vagaries of thinking, but also of a consciousness of possibility, as in Foucault's concept of history not as a chronology of events, but of their conditions of possibility. Truth is taken not to be a variation according to a perceiving subject, but the *condition* in which the truth of a variation appears to the subject (FLD: 20). The subject perceives variation at a paradoxical point of remove and of coincidence. Variation traverses, as might a wave of sound or of light, both the body and the soul. The most compelling figure of this difficult concept (that bears on early scientific cartography engineered by triangulation) is the figure of the city-view. Leibniz invokes the city-view to illustrate perception of variation. If a person were standing on a hillside behind a great city, such as Montmartre behind Paris before the eyes of Leibniz, the viewer would have been at the summit of a conic section, and the base would have included the agglomeration of streets and buildings seen below. From an Icarian (or ichnographic) perspective, Paris would be in the ambit of a circle, and from a bird's-eye view, taken from the slope of Montmartre, the city would be seen within the frame of an ellipse. Point of view would be neither the one nor the other, but the possibility of thinking the two (and others) at once, that is, of folding their variation into a labyrinthine totality of strategic – hence stratified – perspective.

> What is grasped from a point of view is ... neither a determined street nor its definable relation with the other streets, that are constants, but the variety of all the possible connections between the circuit from one given street to another: the city as a labyrinth that can possibly be ordered.   (FLD: 24, translation modified)

The work on point of view opens the closed or otherwise imperceptible folds of thinking (of seeing and of speaking) seen in the earlier study of Foucault. Point of view reflects on the condition of closure, and not on the closure of the dark chamber of the soul. Reading Leibniz through Heidegger, Deleuze pries open the monad so that it can fold in both inward and outward directions. If closure is "the condition of being for the world", it follows that any point of view on closure also holds for the "infinite opening of the finite" (FLD: 26, translation modified), assuring the world of the condition or possibility of beginning taking place over and again within the space of each monad. The fold, however rich or obscure its abstraction, allows the world to be placed within the subject (as monad) so that the subject can be in and of the world at large. "It is the torsion that constitutes the fold of the world and of the soul" (FLD: 26, translation modified). The fold grants a decisive opening for the subject and its subjectivation. The soul, the elusive object of modern philosophy, now becomes "the expression of the world" because "the world is what is expressed by the soul".

Predicates and events

Thus the fold allows the body and soul of the subject to be and to become in the world through "intensions" (and not, as it was shown in the rejection of phenomenology, of intentions) felt about "extensions" in space. Because inside and outside are conjoined by the point of view of the soul on the world, the apprehension of the condition of possibility of variation allows the subject to think about how it inflects and is inflected by the mental and geographical milieus it occupies. Here, along the line of divide between Deleuze's studies of Foucault and of Leibniz, are found two other and no less decisive concepts. One has to do with *predication* in its relation to subjectivity, and the other to the way that an *event*, understood in a strong philosophical sense, is figured by means of the fold. At the beginning of the second part of *The Fold*, Deleuze parrots a truism found in the deterministic circles of post-Cartesian literature and philosophy. "Everything has a reason" (FLD: 41). It can be a reasoned assertion but also a cry or a shriek, just as any speaker can shout, "I think, therefore I am" with defensive anxiety. "Everything that happens has a reason!" Deleuze interrogates causality by calling an event: that which happens (with or without an apparent *cause* or reason) to a thing, to a *chose*. "Sufficient reason would be what includes the event as one of its predicates" (FLD: 41, translation modified). Telescoping his argument, we can say that the passage from the event to the thing follows the trajectory of the movement from "seeing" to "reading": what is *seen* about or on the thing is *read* in its concept or notion (FLD: 41) as a signature, in other words, as that which assures the identity of both the event and the predicate.

It follows that every predicate or action is already in the subject (the nature of things also being the nature of the concept of the thing). If "everything [*tout*] has a reason", then reason is already folded into the concept of the everyday or of the ineffable nature of things. The event is indeed the micro-perception of the folded nature of things. And if the task of philosophy entails the construction of events, the latter are made manifest in the inclusions and inflections of the subject in the predicate and vice versa.[6] Agency is implied to be the action of folding, and the event of agency would amount to the sensation and perception of the condition of folding that makes the statement (the subject melded into the predicate) possible.

Later in *The Fold*, in a dazzling chapter entitled "What is an Event?", Deleuze refines the point even further. An event is not only "a man is crushed" but also the "Great Pyramid" itself and its duration for any quantum of time (FLD: 76, translation modified). To perceive the conditions of possibility of the Great Pyramid is to have a point of view upon it that makes it virtually happen without having to happen. When Deleuze poses a perversely sly question, "What are the conditions of an event so that everything may be an event [*quelles sont les conditions d'un événement pour que tout soit événement*]?" (FLD: 76, translation modified), he makes its articulation the event itself. The conditions are seen in the *tout* or subject that is read as the notion folded into the *événement*: an event is the perception of the fact that *all* or everything is what is glimpsed when an event "takes place". That is why Deleuze appears led to remark that for Leibniz (and for Whitehead) an initial component or condition of any event is *extension*, such that it is "all" (*tout*) and its effects are its parts (FLD: 77). Secondly, a vibration or a luminous wave turns inwards as much as it moves outwards because it bears *intensions*, intensities or degrees in the soul. The latter, in turn, is located in its third component, the subject, which is an individual "prehending" the two previous components who is being equally "prehended" by them. At a given moment Napoleon's soldiers "prehend the Great Pyramid when they sense, at the same time, that it is prehending them" (FLD: 78, translation modified). Deleuze notes that "echoes, reflections, traces, perspectives, thresholds and folds" qualify as prehensions when they are seen in their conditions of possibility, in other words, as "prehensions of prehensions" (FLD: 78, translation modified). The event would be a "nexus of prehensions" (FLD: 78), inseparably the objectivation of one prehension and the subjectivation of another. It would be at once public and private, potential and actual, entering into the becoming of another event and the subject of its own becoming (FLD: 78, translation modified).

At this juncture in his reading it is clear that the fold is what opens the otherwise closed condition of the event in its traditional philosophical sense. It includes the perception of the world as an open whole in flux and movement. The most telling confirmation of the concept of the fold-as-event is found in the pages where Deleuze shows how poetry combines subject and predicate in the creases between seeing and reading. The event of a poem takes place in the vibrations that Deleuze coaxes his reader to find in the doubling of his words and those of Mallarmé. The fold-that-is-the-world is what Mallarmé calls *l'unanime pli* [the unanimous fold], but also a lady's fan, an *éventail*, the subject of a collection of 18 short poems that, when unfolded and shaken, makes things rise and fall:

all the particles of matter, ashes and mist by which visibility is perceived as if through the mesh of a veil, following the creases that allow us to see stone in the opening of their inflections, "fold after fold," revealing the city, but also its absence or withdrawal, a conglomeration of dust, hollow collectivities, and hallucinating assemblies.[7]   (FLD: 30, translation modified)

Everything is seen in the swish of the *éventail*. Deleuze adds that the "fold is inseparable from wind" ventilated by the fan [*ventilé par l'éventail*]. "The fold is no longer the matter through which we see but the soul in which we read" the world (FLD: 31, translation modified). The event is endowed with the wind (*vent*) that we see creased in the word *éventail*. The effect of the event is found both in what we see in the unfolding and in what we read at the sight of its alluvial pattern of folded paper or parchment. The drift of the word betrays the intensions and extensions of the event in a process of molecularization, in the convections of matter and their vibrations in the domain of thought. The poet sums up what Deleuze calls the "operations" and action of the fold when the words are seen and read, explicating their own conditions of the possibility of melding, perception, being, sensation and subjectivity.

Folding and becoming

Other trajectories could be taken in a treatment of folds and folding in Deleuze's writings. It could be measured against a "plane of immanence that cuts into chaos" in his last work on philosophy (see WIP: 156, translation modified). It could be followed along the axis of seeing and reading images that is drawn through the two volumes on cinema.[8] In all events, the fold has its most dramatic and inclusive treatment in the passage from the work on being, subjectivity and epistemology extending from the end of *Foucault* to the entirety of *The Fold*. *Foucault* is a threshold and even a "user's guide" for what dilates and becomes a poetic and philosophical principle in a work that may be Deleuze's most personal and sensitive writing, his reading of Leibniz and the Baroque in *The Fold*. The passage of the fold from one work to the other attests to a style of writing that in itself is always folding, unfolding and refolding. Some concepts and figures shift emphasis or are metamorphosed when they migrate from one work to another. They show that in Deleuze's world everything is folded, and folds, in and out of everything else. The development of the fold demonstrates that philosophy finds in the fold the expression of a continuous and vital force of being and of becoming.

Notes

1. Here and elsewhere, for the purpose of the arguments of this article, all translations from the French are mine, including revisions of my translation of *Le Pli* as *The Fold: Leibniz and the Baroque* (1993).
2. Alain Badiou emphasizes the point in *Gilles Deleuze, The Clamor of Being* (1999).
3. Foucault's distinction and Deleuze's emphasis upon its conceptual power owe much to Maurice Blanchot's "Speaking Is Not Seeing," a dialogue of two voices (1993: 25–32).
4. Foucault takes up the distinction at the end of the first chapter and start of the second of *The Order of Things* (1970). It is evinced in many other historical studies, notably Jean Céard and Jean-Claude Margolin, *Rébus de la Renaissance: Des images qui parlent* (1984).
5. Departure is made from Séan Hand's elegant English translation of *Foucault* (1988), which calls *embarkation* a "boat" as the "interior of the exterior". For this reader the emphasis is on action, on embarking, not on the mode of conveyance, even though the boat is a privileged figure in Foucault's work on heterotopias in "Of Other Spaces" (a lecture first presented in 1967, first published in 1984 (Foucault 1998)) and, of course, the *stultifera navis* at the outset of *Madness and Civilization* (1973).
6. That sentience can be seen in a single grammatical construction attests to its ubiquity: "What is included in the notion as subject is always an event marked by a verb, or a relation marked by a preposition: I am writing, I am going to Germany, I'm crossing the Rubicon" (FLD: 52, translation modified).
7. Mallarmé's "fan" poems are in Mallarmé, *Oeuvres completes* (1945: 107–10).
8. Deleuze writes in *Cinema 1: The Movement-Image* (1983) that the frame is "as legible as it is visible" (C1: 12) and, in *Cinema 2: The Time-Image* (1985), that the image is shown to be "as legible as it is visible" (C2: 22).

FIFTEEN

Critical, clinical

Daniel W. Smith

The last book Deleuze published before his death in 1995 was a collection of essays entitled *Critique et Clinique* (1993), which included articles devoted to "clinical" analyses of various philosophers (Plato, Spinoza, Kant, Nietzsche and Heidegger) and literary figures (Artaud, Beckett, Carroll, Alfred Jarry, Kerouac, D. H. Lawrence, T. E. Lawrence, Masoch, Melville and Whitman) (see ECC). The idea that artists and philosophers are physiologists or symptomatologists, "physicians of culture", was a notion first put forward by Nietzsche, for whom all phenomena are signs or symptoms that reflect a certain state of forces.[1] Deleuze took this Nietzschean notion in new directions in his writings, using it to explore the complex relationships between psychiatry and medicine, on the one hand, and philosophy, art and literature, on the other. "The critical (in the literary sense) and the clinical (in the medical sense)," he once wrote, "may be destined to enter into a new relationship of mutual learning" (M: 14).

Deleuze first posed the question of the relationship between the "critical" and the "clinical" – in his 1967 book *Masochism: Coldness and Cruelty* – in the context of a concrete question: why were the names of two literary figures, the Marquis de Sade and Leopold von Sacher-Masoch, used as labels in the nineteenth century to denote two basic "perversions" in clinical psychiatry? What made this encounter between literature and medicine possible, Deleuze suggests, was precisely the distinctive status of symptomatology within the context of medicine itself. The field of medicine can be said to be made up of at least three different activities: symptomatology, or the study of signs and symptoms; etiology, or the search for causes; and therapy, or the development and application of a treatment. While etiology and therapeutics are integral parts of medicine, symptomatology marks a kind of neutral point, pre-medical or sub-medical, that belongs as much to art, literature and philosophy as it does to medicine. "I would never have permitted myself to write on psychoanalysis and psychiatry," Deleuze once admitted, "were I not dealing with a problem of symptomatology. Symptomatology is situated almost outside of medicine, at a neutral point, a zero point, where artists and philosophers and doctors and patients can encounter each other" (DI: 134, translation modified).

What accounts for this peculiar status of symptomatology? The medical diagnosis of a physician is always an act of judgement: it requires a genuine gift and an art, a "flair" that can only be obtained through long experience with numerous patients. Kant, however, had famously distinguished between two types of judgement, both of which are operative in the practice of medicine. In a "determinate" judgement, the general (the concept) is already given, and the problem is to determine the particular case to which it applies; in a "reflective" judgement, by contrast, only the individual case is given, and the problem is to find the general concept to which it corresponds. One might think that doctors make "determinate" judgements: they have learned the concepts of illnesses, and simply need to apply them to their patients. But in fact medical diagnoses are examples of reflective judgements, since in relation to an individual case the concept itself is not given, but is entirely "problematic". What a doctor confronts in an individual case is a symptom or group of symptoms, and his diagnostic task is to discover the corresponding concept (the concept of the disease). No doctor would treat a fever or headache as a definite symptom of a specific illness; they are rather indeterminate symptoms common to a number of diseases, and the doctor must interpret and decipher the symptoms in order to arrive at the correct diagnosis. If one seeks an example of a determinative judgement in medicine, it must be located instead in the therapeutic decision: here the concept is given in relation to the individual case, but what is difficult is its application (counter-indications in the patient, etc.).[2]

Although there is no less art or invention in determinative judgements than in reflective judgements, it is nonetheless in reflective judgements that Deleuze tends to locate the aspect of medicine that most interests him: the function of "concept creation". Illnesses are occasionally named after typical patients (e.g. Lou Gehrig's disease), but more often than not it is the doctor's name that is given to the disease (e.g. Parkinson's disease, Alzheimer's disease, Creutzfeldt-Jacob disease). The principles behind this labelling process, Deleuze suggests, deserve careful analysis. The clinician obviously does not "invent" the disease, but rather is said to have "isolated" it. He or she distinguishes cases that had hitherto been confused by dissociating symptoms that were previously grouped together and juxtaposing them with others that were previously dissociated. In this way, the physician creates an original clinical concept for the disease: the components of the concept are the *symptoms*, the signs of the illness, and the concept becomes the name of a *syndrome*, which marks the meeting place of these symptoms, their point of coincidence or convergence (e.g. Tourette's syndrome, Asperger's syndrome, Korsakov's syndrome, etc.). Deleuze has defined philosophy as the activity of creating concepts, but the creation of concepts is equally evident in medicine, if not more so. When a clinician gives his or her name to an illness, it constitutes an important advance in medicine, in so far as a proper name is linked to a determinate group of symptoms or signs. If diseases are usually named after their symptoms rather than their causes, it is precisely because a correct etiology depends first and foremost on a rigorous symptomatology.

It is true that, in numerous instances, the symptomatological description of the cases themselves is sufficient, without the invention of a corresponding concept. The remarkable case of Phineas Gage, who survived severe destruction of his prefrontal lobes, initiated important avenues of research in neurology.[3] In the case of Johann Schneider, reported by Goldstein and Gelb (1918), the patient could scratch his nose but not point to it, which seemed to reveal a distinction between concrete practice and the "abstract attitude" (categorization).[4] Merleau-Ponty would take up the Schneider case while developing his theory of the "corporeal schema" in the *Phenomenology of Perception* (2002). Oliver Sacks's famous "Man Who Mistook His Wife for a Hat" seemed to manifest the opposite condition: he maintained the "abstract attitude", but had lost the concrete ability to even recognize his wife's face (prosopagnosia) (1970: 8–22). In all such instances, the symptomatologies of case studies pose specific problems for which neurology must seek the etiological bases. This is why Deleuze can write that "etiology, which is the scientific or experimental side of medicine, must be subordinated to symptomatology, which is its literary, artistic aspect" (M: 133).

The history of medicine can therefore be regarded under at least two aspects. The first is the *history of diseases*, which may disappear, recede, reappear or alter their form depending on numerous external factors: the appearance of new microbes or viruses, altered technological and therapeutic techniques, changing social conditions. But intertwined with this is the *history of symptomatology*, which is a kind of "syntax" of medicine that sometimes follows and sometimes precedes changes in therapy or the nature of diseases: symptoms are isolated, named, renamed and regrouped in various manners. From the latter viewpoint, the plague and leprosy were more common in the past not only for historical and social reasons, but because "one tended to group under these headings various types of diseases now classified separately" (M: 16). The cultural repercussions of medicine tend to resonate most strongly in the domain of symptomatology. After the Second World War, for instance, there came the discovery of illnesses derived from "stress", in which the disorder is not produced by a hostile agent, but rather by non-specific defensive reactions that either run amok or become exhausted. Following the war, medical journals were filled with discussions of stress in modern societies, and new ways of grouping various illnesses in relation to it. More recently, there has been the discovery of "auto-immune" diseases, in which defence mechanisms no longer recognize the cells of the organism they are supposed to protect, or external agents make these cells impossible to distinguish from others. AIDS, Deleuze suggests, lies somewhere between these two poles of stress and auto-immunity (see N: 132–3). It is not difficult to see how these new "styles" of disease (diseases with carriers rather than sufferers, images rather than symptoms) end up getting reflected in arenas such as global politics and strategy, where the risk of war is seen to come not only from potential external aggressors (the terrorist as an "unspecified" enemy) but from defence systems going out of control or breaking down. In a similar vein, Susan Sontag has analysed the symptomatological myths that tend to surround diseases such as tuberculosis ("consumption"), cancer and, most recently, AIDS (see Sontag 1978, 2001).

The initial idea behind Deleuze's "critique et clinique" project is that writers and artists, like doctors and clinicians, can themselves be seen as profound symptomatologists. Sadism and masochism are clearly not diseases on a par with Parkinson's or Alzheimer's disease. Yet if Krafft-Ebing, in 1869 (in work that would culminate in his well-known *Psychopathia Sexualis* of 1886), was able to use Masoch's name to designate a fundamental perversion, it was not because Masoch "suffered" from it as a patient, but rather because his literary works isolated a particular way of existing and set forth a novel symptomatology of it, making the contract its primary sign. Freud would make use of Sophocles in much the same way when he created the concept of the "Oedipal complex", or of Shakespeare when he wrote about Hamlet. "From the perspective of Freud's genius," Deleuze writes, "it is not the complex which provides us with information about Oedipus and Hamlet, but rather Oedipus and Hamlet who provide us with information about the complex" (LS: 237). As Deleuze explains:

Authors, if they are great, are more like doctors than patients. We mean that they are themselves astonishing diagnosticians or symptomatologists. There is always a great deal of art involved in the grouping of symptoms, in the organization of a *table* [*tableau*] where a particular symptom is dissociated from another, juxtaposed to a third, and forms the new figure of a disorder or illness. Clinicians who are able to renew a symptomatological picture produce a work of art; conversely, artists are clinicians, not with respect to their own case, nor even with respect to a case in general; rather, they are clinicians of civilization.

(LS: 237, translation modified)

At one point, Deleuze goes so far as to suggest that artists and writers can often go *farther* in symptomatology than doctors and clinicians, precisely "because the work of art gives them new means, perhaps also because they are less concerned about causes" (DI: 133). No doubt this explains why, in their writings on schizophrenia, Deleuze and Guattari frequently appeal to the writings of literary figures rather than the work of clinicians. "We have been criticized for over quoting literary authors," they commented. "But is it our fault that Lawrence, Miller, Kerouac, Burroughs, Artaud, and Beckett know more about schizophrenia than psychiatrists and psychoanalysts?" (ATP: 4).

One can readily see that Deleuze's approach to literature is almost the exact opposite of most "psychoanalytic" interpretations of writers and artists, which generally tend to treat authors as real (or at least possible) patients, whose work is then seen either (regressively) as a kind of "working out" of their unresolved conflicts, or (progressively) as a kind of "sublimation" of those conflicts. Artists are treated as like clinical cases, as if they were themselves patients, and what the critic seeks in their work is a sign of neurosis, as if it were the secret of their work, its hidden code. In such cases, there is no need to "apply" psychoanalysis to the work of art, since the work itself is seen to constitute a successful psychoanalysis, either as a resolution or a sublimation. "All too often the writer is still considered as one more case added to clinical psychology, when the important thing is what the writer himself, as a creator, brings to clinical psychology" (DI: 133). Part of the problem is that psychoanalytic interpretations are often tied to an "egoistic" conception of literature: "Everyone seems, and seems to themselves, to have a book in them, simply by virtue of having a particular job, or a family even, a sick parent, a rude boss ... It's forgotten that for anyone, literature involves a special sort of exploration and effort, a specific creative purpose that can be pursued only within literature itself" (N: 130). Or, as Blanchot puts it, literature exists only in the condition of a third person that strips us of the power to say "I" (the neuter) (1993: 384–5).

Deleuze's 1967 essay on masochism, *Coldness and Cruelty*, provides one of the clearest examples of his symptomatological approach to literature. At a conceptual level, the book provides an incisive critique of the clinical notion of "sadomasochism", which presumes that sadism and masochism are complementary forces that belong to one and the same pathological entity. Psychiatrists were led to posit such a "crude syndrome", Deleuze argues, because they relied on hasty etiological assumptions (concerning the nature of the "sexual instinct"), and hence were content with a symptomatology much less precise and much more confused than the one found in Masoch himself. Because the judgements of the clinicians are often prejudiced, Deleuze's strategy in *Coldness and Cruelty* was to adopt a *literary* approach that attempted to provide a differential diagnosis of sadism and masochism based on the literary works from which their original definitions were derived. The results of Deleuze's analyses are twofold. On the clinical side, Deleuze shows that sadism and masochism are two incommensurable modes of existence whose symptomatologies are completely different from each other (a sadist would never tolerate a masochistic victim, nor would a masochistic torturer be a sadist). On the critical side, he shows that the clinical symptoms of sadism and masochism are themselves inseparable from the literary techniques and styles of Sade and Masoch. "Symptomatology is always a question of art," Deleuze writes.

> The clinical specificities of sadism and masochism are not separable from the literary values peculiar to Sade and Masoch. In place of a dialectic that all too readily perceives the link between opposites, we should aim for a critical and clinical appraisal able to reveal the truly differential mechanisms as well as the artistic originalities. (M: 14)

At the time, Deleuze saw *Coldness and Cruelty* as the first instalment of a series of literary–clinical studies: "What I would like to study (this book would merely be a first example) is a articulable relationship between literature and clinical psychiatry" (DI: 133, translation modified). The idea was not to apply psychiatric concepts to literature, but on the contrary to extract non-pre-existent clinical concepts from the works themselves. When asked in an interview why he had only treated Sade and Masoch from this point of view, Deleuze replied:

There are others, in fact, but their work has not yet been recognized under the aspect of a creative symptomatology, as was the case with Masoch at the start. There is a prodigious table [*tableau*] of symptoms corresponding to the work of Samuel Beckett: not that it is simply a question of identifying an illness, but the world as symptom, and the artist as symptomatologist.

(DI: 132, translation modified)

Twenty-five years later, in 1992, Deleuze would finally publish an essay analysing the symptomatology of Beckett's work around the theme of "The Exhausted".[5] But Deleuze also pursued the project in his writings on philosophical texts. When he asked, somewhat rhetorically, "Why is there not a 'Nietzscheism,' 'Proustism,' 'Kafkaism,' 'Spinozism' along the lines of a generalized clinic?" (D: 120) he seemed to be indicating that he considered his monographs on each of these thinkers to fall within the domain of the "critique et clinique" project. *Nietzsche and Philosophy* (1962), for instance, shows how Nietzsche set out to diagnose a disease (nihilism) by isolating its symptoms (*ressentiment*, the bad conscience, the ascetic ideal), tracing its etiology in a certain relation of active and reactive forces (the genealogical method), and setting forth both a prognosis (nihilism defeated by itself) and a treatment (the revaluation of values). Similarly, Deleuze's secondary doctoral thesis, *Expressionism in Philosophy: Spinoza* (1968), presents an analysis of the composition of finite "modes" in Spinoza, which includes both a clinical diagnostic of their passive state (human bondage), and a treatment for their becoming-active (the "ethical" task) (EPS: 11). In a sense, Deleuze can speak in philosophy of Spinoza's "modes" or Nietzsche's "will to power" in the same way that one speaks of Alzheimer's disease or Tourette's syndrome in medicine, that is, as a non-personal mode of individuation indicated by a proper name.

In this regard, one can see Deleuze's first collaboration with Guattari, *Anti-Oedipus: Capitalism and Schizophrenia* (1972), as a new direction in Deleuze's "critique et clinique" project. The book takes as its object an acute psychotic phenomenon that poses numerous problems for the clinical method: not only is there no agreement as to the etiology of schizophrenia, but even its symptomatology remains uncertain. In most psychiatric accounts of schizophrenia, the diagnostic criteria are given in purely *negative* terms, that is, in relation to the destructions the disorder engenders in the ego: dissociation, autism, detachment from reality. Whereas psychoanalysis would retain this negative viewpoint, in *Anti-Oedipus*, Deleuze and Guattari attempted an inverse approach: "We tried to reexamine the concepts used to describe neurosis in the light of the indications we received from contact with psychosis" (DI: 234). Following Karl Jaspers and R. D. Laing, they attempted to examine schizophrenia in its *positivity*, no longer as actualized in a mode of existence (an ego), but rather as a pure *process*, that is, as an opening or breach that breaks the continuity of a personality or ego, carrying it off on a kind of voyage through an intense and terrifying "more than reality" (AO: 24). They thus drew a sharp distinction between schizophrenia as a process ("breakthrough") and schizophrenia as a clinical entity ("breakdown"), which results from an interruption of the process. In short, Deleuze and Guattari attempted to *listen* to schizophrenic discourse, and to derive from it a "schizoanalytic" picture of the psyche. The result was their concept of the schizophrenic "Body without Organs", which has three aspects or components:

- *The anorganic functioning of the organs.* For the schizophrenic, bodily organs function primarily as unspecified elements of "machines", that is, they are experienced as parts that are connected to other parts: a tree, a star, a light bulb, a motor, another organ. In and of themselves, these organs or parts are completely disparate, foreign to each other, without any link, *pure singularities*; and yet they are made to function together in a complex machinic assemblage.
- *The Body without Organs.* In the midst of these organ-machines, a second theme appears: the Body without Organs as such, as it were, a liquid surface on which the anorganic functioning of the organs takes place; a non-productive or anti-productive surface that thwarts the productive activity of the organ-machines, at times making them stop dead in their tracks in a catatonic stupor. Yet the true enemies of the Body without Organs are not the organs themselves. The common enemy of both the organ-machines and the Body without Organs is the *organism*, that is, the organization that imposes on the organs a regime of totalization, collaboration, integration, inhibition and disjunction. In this sense, the organs of the organism are indeed the enemy of the Body without Organs, which attempts to *repulse* them, to denounce them as so many apparatuses of persecution. But the Body without Organs also *attracts* the organs, it appropriates them and makes them function *in another regime* than that of the organism. The organs are, as it were, "miraculated" by the Body without Organs, in accordance with this non-organic "machinic" regime that must not be confused either with organic mechanisms or the organization of the organism.

- *A relation in intensity*. But there is a third and final component to the description of schizophrenia: the theme of intensity. These two poles of the Body without Organs, never separate from each other – the vital anorganic functioning of the organs and their frozen catatonic stasis, with all the variations of *attraction* and *repulsion* that exist between them – translate the entire anguish of the schizophrenic and generate between them the various forms of schizophrenia: the paranoid form (repulsion), and its miraculating or fantastic form (attraction). This is *the intensive reality of the body*, a milieu of intensity that is "beneath" or "adjacent to" the organism and continually in the process of constructing itself. It is the proportions of attraction and repulsion that produce the various intensive states through which the patient passes, and thus the Body without Organs is something that is primarily *felt* under the integrated organization of the organism, as if the organs were experienced as *intensities* (or affects) capable of being linked together in an infinite number of ways. And in fact, as the organ-machines and the Body without Organs are really one and the same thing, Deleuze and Guattari's schizoanalytic model of the psyche is thus purely materialist: "In reality, the unconscious belongs to the realm of physics: the body without organs and its intensities are not metaphors, but matter itself" (AO: 283).

If, as Deleuze and Guattari suggest, schizophrenia appears as the illness of our era, it is not as a function of generalities concerning our mode of life, but in relation to very precise mechanisms of an economic, social and political nature. Our societies no longer function on the basis of codes and territorialities, but on the contrary on the basis of a massive decoding and deterritorialization. The schizophrenic is like the limit of our society, but a limit that is always avoided, reprimanded, abhorred. The problem of schizophrenia then becomes: how does one prevent the breakthrough from becoming a breakdown? How does one prevent the Body without Organs from closing in on itself, imbecilic and catatonic? How does one make the intense state triumph over the anguish, but without giving way to a chronic state, and even to a final state of generalized collapse, as is seen in the hospital? Is it possible to utilize the power of a lived chemistry and a schizo-logical analysis to ensure that the schizophrenic process does not turn into its opposite, that is, the production of the schizophrenic found in the asylum? If so, within what type of group, what kind of collectivity?

Anti-Oedipus thus adds a third and final component to Deleuze's conception of the "critique et clinique" project, an advanced symptomatological method that includes not only (i) the function of the proper name, and (ii) the assemblage or multiplicity of symptoms or signs designated by the name, but also (iii) the variations or "lines of flight" inherent in every such multiplicity, which account for the possibility of new discoveries and creations: "a process and not a goal" (AO: 133).

Like this direct engagement by Deleuze and Guattari with life through the symptomatological method, Deleuze's approach to literature is thus neither textual nor historical, but rather "vitalist", and as such is grounded in a principle of "Life" (Nietzsche, Bergson). It is always a question of evaluating, in a literary work, its possibilities of Life. But this also means that Deleuze's literary analyses are profoundly ethical, since it is Life itself that functions as an ethical principle in Deleuze's thought, and it is no accident that Foucault, in his American preface to *Anti-Oedipus*, called it "a book of ethics" (1983: xiii). Deleuze has frequently drawn a sharp distinction between morality and ethics. He uses the term "morality" to define, in general terms, any set of "constraining" rules, such as a moral code, that consists in *judging* actions and intentions by relating them to transcendent or universal values ("this is good, that is evil"). What he calls "ethics" is, on the contrary, a set of "facilitative" [*facultative*] rules that evaluates what we do, say and think according to the immanent mode of existence or possibility of life that it implies.[6] One says or does this, thinks or feels that: *what mode of existence does it imply?* This is the link that Deleuze sees between Spinoza and Nietzsche, whom he has always identified as his philosophical precursors. Each of them argued, in their own manner, that there are things one cannot do or think except on the condition of being weak or enslaved, unless one harbours a vengeance or resentment against life; and there are other things one cannot do or say except on the condition of being strong, noble or free, unless one affirms life. An immanent ethical distinction (good–bad) is in this way substituted for the transcendent moral opposition (Good–Evil). "*Beyond Good and Evil*," wrote Nietzsche, "at least that does *not* mean 'Beyond Good and Bad.'" (1968: 491). The "Bad" or sickly life is an exhausted and degenerating mode of existence, one that judges life from the perspective of its sickness, that devaluates life in the name of "higher" values. The "Good" or healthy life, in contrast, is an overflowing and ascending form of existence, a mode of life that is able to transform itself depending on the forces it encounters, always increasing the power to live, always opening up new possibilities of life.

Literature, likewise, is a question of health, and every literary work implies a manner of living, a mode of life, and must be evaluated not only critically but also clinically. "Style, in a great writer, is always a style of life too, not anything at all personal, but inventing a possibility of life, a way of existing" (N: 100). This does not mean that an author necessarily enjoys robust health; on the contrary, artists, like philosophers, often suffer from frail health, a weak constitution, a fragile personal life (e.g. Spinoza's frailty, Lawrence's hemoptysis, Nietzsche's migraines, Deleuze's own respiratory ailments). This frailty, however, does not stem from their illnesses or neuroses, but from having seen or felt something in life that is too great for them, something unbearable "that has put on them the quiet mark of death" (WIP: 172). But this something is also what Nietzsche called the "great health", the vitality that supports them through the illnesses of the lived. This is why Deleuze insists that writing is never a personal matter, it is never simply a matter of our lived experiences. "You don't get very far in literature with the system 'I've seen a lot and been lots of places'" (N: 134). Novels are not created out of our dreams and fantasies, our memories and travels, our sufferings and griefs, our opinions and ideas. It is true that writers are necessarily "inspired" by their lived experiences; but even in writers like Thomas Wolfe or Henry Miller, who seem to do nothing but recount their own lives, "there is an attempt to make life something more than personal, to free life from what imprisons it" (N: 143; cf. WIP: 171). Wolfe himself insisted that "it is literally impossible for a man who has the stuff of creation in him to make a literal transcription of his own experience" (1983: 20). For Deleuze, Life itself is an impersonal and non-organic power that goes beyond any lived experience, and the act of writing is itself "a passage of Life that traverses both the livable and the lived" (ECC: 1). In every great work of writing, then, one reaches the point at which "critique" and "clinique" become one and the same thing, when life ceases to be personal and the work ceases to be historical or textual: "a life of pure immanence" (DI: 141).

Notes

1. See, for instance, Nietzsche, "The Philosopher as Cultural Physician" (1873), in Brezeale (1979: 67–76), although the idea of the philosopher as a physician of culture recurs throughout Nietzsche's writings. For Deleuze's analysis of the symptomatological method in Nietzsche, see *Nietzsche and Philosophy* (NP: x, 3, 75, 79, 157).
2. On the distinction between determinative and reflective judgements, see Deleuze's comments in *Kant's Critical Philosophy* (KCP: 59–60), where, not insignificantly, he makes use of these medical examples.
3. See Damasio's (1995: 3–33) analysis of Phineas Gage's case.
4. For a recent assessment, see Marotta & Behrmann (2004).
5. Gilles Deleuze, "L'Épuisé", originally published as the postface to Samuel

Beckett's *Quad* (1992) (translated in ECC: 151–74), a revised version from the original translation by Uhlmann (1995).

6. *Règles facultatives* is a term Deleuze adopts from the sociolinguist William Labov to designate "functions of internal variation and no longer constants" (see FCLT: 146–7, n.18).

Chronology

Cited (and translated) from the ADPF Deleuze site: www.adpf.asso.fr/adpf-publi/folio/textes/deleuze/00intro.pdf (accessed Dec. 2004).

18 January 1925 Born in Paris

Secondary studies at the Lycée Carnot.

1944–48 Studies in philosophy at the Sorbonne, where he met François Châtelet, Michel Butor, Claude Lanzmann, Olivier Revault d'Allones and Michel Tournier.

Principal professors: Ferdinand Alquié, Georges Canguilhem, Maurice de Gandillac, Jean Hyppolite.

Regularly visited La Fortelle, a residential *château*, where Marie-Madeleine Davy organized encounters between intellectuals and writers at the time of the Liberation (1944), including Father Fessard, Pierre Klossowski, Jacques Lacan, Lanza del Vasto and Jean Paulhan.

1948 Earns the *agrégation* diploma in philosophy.

1948–57 Philosophy professor in *lycées* in Amiens, Orléans, and Louis-le-Grand (Paris).

1957–60 Assistant at the Sorbonne, in the history of philosophy.

1960–64 Research attaché at the CNRS (French national research centre, Paris).

1962 Meets Michel Foucault in Clermont-Ferrand, at the home of Jules Vuillemin.

1964–69 Associate professor (*chargé d'enseignement*) at the University of Lyon.

1969 Doctorate defended, with principal thesis *Difference and Repetition* (directed by Maurice de Gandillac) and secondary thesis *Expression in Philosophy: Spinoza* (directed by Ferdinand Alquié).

1969   Meets Félix Guattari and undertakes a joint research project.

1969   Professor at Paris VIII-Vincennes from which Michel Foucault had just departed and where Deleuze again encounters François Châtelet.

After 1969   Various leftist political activities.

1987   Retires from teaching.

Particular characteristics: travels little, never belonged to the Communist Party, was never a phenomenologist nor a Heideggerian, never renounced Marx, never repudiated May 1968.

Took his life in Paris on 4 November 1995.

References

Works By Gilles Deleuze

Deleuze, G. 1961. "De Sacher-Masoch au masochisme", *Arguments* 5(21), 40–46.

Deleuze, G. with Madeleine Chapsal 1967. "Mystique et masochisme", *La Quinzaine littéraire* 25, 12–13.

Deleuze, G. 1983. *Nietzsche and Philosophy*, H. Tomlinson (trans.). New York: Columbia University Press. [Originally published as *Nietzsche et la philosophie* (Paris: Presses universitaires de France, 1962).]

Deleuze, G. & F. Guattari 1983. *Anti-Oedipus: Capitalism and Schizophrenia*. R. Hurley, M. Seem & H. R. Lane (trans.). Minneapolis, MN: University of Minnesota Press. [Originally published as *L'Anti-Oedipe: Capitalisme et schizophrénie I* (Paris: Minuit, 1972).]

Deleuze, G. 1984. *Kant's Critical Philosophy*, H. Tomlinson & B. Habberjam (trans.). Minneapolis, MN: University of Minnesota Press. [Originally published as *La Philosophie critique de Kant* (Paris: Presses universitaires de France, 1963).]

Deleuze, G. 1985. "Les plages d'immanence". In *L'Art des Confins: Mélanges offerts à Maurice de Gandillac*, A. Cazenave & J.-F. Lyotard (eds), 79–81. Paris: Presses universitaires de France.

Deleuze, G. 1986. *Cinema 1: The Movement-Image*, H. Tomlinson (trans.). Minneapolis, MN: University of Minnesota Press. [Originally published as *Cinéma 1, L'Image-mouvement* (Paris: Minuit, 1983).]

Deleuze, G. & F. Guattari 1986. *Kafka: Toward a Minor Literature*, D. Polan (trans.). Minneapolis, MN: University of Minnesota Press. [Originally published as *Kafka: Pour une littérature mineure* (Paris: Minuit, 1975).]

Deleuze, G. & F. Guattari 1987. *A Thousand Plateaus: Capitalism and Schizophrenia II*, B. Massumi (trans.). Minneapolis, MN: University of Minnesota Press. [Originally published as *Mille plateaux: Capitalisme et schizophrénie II* (Paris: Minuit, 1980).]

Deleuze, G. & C. Parnet 1987. *Dialogues*, H. Tomlinson & B. Habberjam (trans.). New York: Columbia University Press. [Originally published as *Dialogues* (Paris: Flammarion, 1977).]

Deleuze, G. 1988a. *Bergsonism*, H. Tomlinson & B. Habberjam (trans.). New York: Zone Books. [Originally published as *Le Bergsonisme* (Paris: Presses universitaires de France, 1966).]

Deleuze, G. 1988b. *Foucault*, S. Hand (trans.). Minneapolis, MN: University of Minnesota Press. [Originally published as *Foucault* (Paris: Minuit, 1986)].

Deleuze, G. 1988c. *Périclès et Verdi*. Paris: Minuit.

Deleuze, G. 1988d. *Spinoza: Practical Philosophy*, R. Hurley (trans.). San Francisco, CA: City Light Books. [Originally published as *Spinoza: Philosophie pratique* (Paris: Presses universitaires de France, 1970).]

Deleuze, G. 1989. *Cinema 2: The Time-Image*, H. Tomlinson & R. Galeta (trans.). Minneapolis, MN: University of Minnesota Press. [Originally published as *Cinéma 2, L'Image-temps* (Paris: Minuit, 1985).]

Deleuze, G. 1990a. *Expressionism in Philosophy: Spinoza*, M. Joughin (trans.). New York: Zone Books. [Originally published as *Spinoza et le problème de l'expression* (Paris: Minuit, 1968).]

Deleuze, G. 1990b. *The Logic of Sense*, M. Lester & C. Stivale (trans.), C. Boundas (ed.). New York: Columbia University Press. [Originally published as *Logique du sens* (Paris: Minuit, 1969).]

Deleuze, G. 1991a. *Masochism: Coldness and Cruelty*, J. McNeil (trans.). New York: Zone Books. [Originally published as "Le Froid et le Cruel" in *Présentation de Sacher-Masoch* (Paris: Minuit, 1967).]

Deleuze, G. 1991b. *Empiricism and Subjectivity: An Essay on Hume's Theory of Human Nature*, C. V. Boundas (trans.). New York: Columbia University Press. [Originally published as *Empirisme et subjectivité. Essai sure la nature humaine selon Hume* (Paris: Presses universitaires de France, 1953).]

Deleuze, G. 1993a. *The Fold: Leibniz and the Baroque*, T. Conley (trans.). Minneapolis, MN: University of Minnesota Press. [Originally published as *Le Pli. Leibniz et le baroque* (Paris: Minuit, 1988).]

Deleuze, G. 1993b. "One Less Manifesto", A. Orenstein (trans.). In *The Deleuze Reader*, C. V. Boundas (ed.), 204–22. New York: Columbia University Press. [Originally published in C. Bene & G. Deleuze, *Superpositions* (Paris: Minuit, 1979).]

Deleuze, G. 1994. *Difference and Repetition*, P. Patton (trans.). New York: Columbia University Press. [Originally published as *Différence et répétition* (Paris: Presses universitaires de France, 1968).]

Deleuze, G. & F. Guattari 1994. *What Is Philosophy?*, H. Tomlinson & G. Burchell (trans.). New York: Columbia University Press. [Originally published as *Qu'est-ce que la philosophie?* (Paris: Minuit, 1991).]

Deleuze, G. 1995. *Negotiations, 1972–1990*, M. Joughin (trans.). New York: Columbia University Press. [Originally published as *Pourparlers 1972–1990* (Paris: Minuit, 1990).]

Deleuze, G. & C. Parnet 1996. *L'Abécédaire de Gilles Deleuze*, Pierre-André Boutang (dir.). Video Editions Montparnasse.

Deleuze, G. 1997a. "Desire and Pleasure", M. McMahon (trans.), www.arts.monash.edu.au/visarts/globe/issue5/delfou.html (accessed Jan. 2005). [Also published as "Desire and Pleasure", in *Foucault and his Interlocutors*, A. Davidson (ed.), 183–92 (Chicago, IL: University of Chicago Press, 1996). Originally published as "Désir et plaisir", *Magazine littéraire* 325 (1994), 59–65.]

Deleuze, G. 1997b. *Essays Critical and Clinical*, D. W. Smith & M. A. Greco (trans.). Minneapolis, MN: University of Minnesota Press. [Originally published as *Critique et clinique* (Paris: Minuit, 1993).]

Deleuze, G. 1997c. Seminar session on Spinoza, *DeleuzeWeb*, T. Murphy (trans.), www.webdeleuze.com/php/index.html (accessed Jan. 2005). [Original work published 1978.]

Deleuze, G. 2000. *Proust and Signs*, R. Howard (trans.). Minneapolis, MN: University of Minnesota Press. [Originally published as *Proust et les signes* (Paris: Presses universitaires de France, 1964).]

Deleuze, G. 2001a. "Immanence: A Life", A. Boyman (trans.). In *Pure Immanence: Essays on A Life*, 25–34. New York: Zone Books. [Originally published as "L'Immanence: Une Vie", *Philosophie* 47 (1995), 3–7. Reprinted in *Deux régimes de fous* (Paris: Minuit, 2003), 359–63.]

Deleuze, G. 2001b. "Nietzsche", A. Boyman (trans.). In *Pure Immanence: Essays on A Life*, 53–102. New York: Zone Books. [Originally published as *Nietzsche* (Paris: Presses universitaires de France, 1965).]

Deleuze, G. 2001c. *Pure Immanence: Essays on A Life*. New York: Zone Books.

Deleuze, G. 2003a. *Deux régimes de fous*. Paris: Minuit.

Deleuze, G. 2003b. *Francis Bacon: The Logic of Sensation*, D. W. Smith (trans.). Minneapolis, MN: University of Minnesota Press. [Originally published as *Francis Bacon: Logique de la sensation* (Paris: Editions de la différence, 1981).]

Delezue, G. 2004. *Desert Islands and Other Texts, 1953–1974*, M. Taormina (trans.). New York: Semiotext(e). [Originally published as *L'Ile déserte et autres textes* (Paris: Minuit, 2002).]

Other works

Alliez, E. (ed.) 1998. *Gilles Deleuze, une vie philosophique*. Le Plessis-Robinson: Institut Synthélabo.

Allsop, S. 2004. "More than This: Sofia Coppola's *Lost in Translation*", June 2004, http://cinetext.philo.at/magazine/allsop/lostintranslation.html (accessed Jan. 2005).

Althusser, L. 1971. "Ideology and Ideological State Apparatus". In *Lenin and Philosophy and Other Essays*, B. Brewster (trans.). London: New Left Books. [Originally published in *Lénine et la philosophie* (Paris: Maspero, 1969).]

Andrijasevic, R. & S. Bracke 2003. "Coming to Knowledge, Coming to Politics: A Reflection on Feminist Practices from the NextGENDERation network", http://multitudes.samizdat.net/article.php3?id_article=1189 and www.5thfeminist.lu.se/filer/paper_843.pdf (accessed Jan. 2005).

Ansell-Pearson, K. (ed.) 1997. *Deleuze and Philosophy: The Difference Engineer*. New York: Routledge.

Aristotle 1998. *Metaphysics*, Book Γ, Ch. 1, Clarendon Aristotle Series, Christopher Kirwan (trans.). Oxford: Clarendon Press.

Ashcraft, K. L. & M. E. Pacanowsky 1996. "'A Woman's Worst Enemy': Reflections on a Narrative of Organizational Life and Female Identity", *Journal of Applied Communication Research* 24, 217–39.

"Assemblage" (n.d.) *McGraw-Hill Encyclopedia of Science and Technology Online*. www.accessscience.com (accessed Jan. 2005).

Bachelard, G. 2000 [1950]. *The Dialectic of Duration*, M. M. Jones (trans.). Manchester: Clinamen Press.

Badiou, A. 1999. *Gilles Deleuze: The Clamor of Being*, L. Burchill (trans.). Minneapolis, MN: University of Minnesota Press. [Originally published as *Gilles Deleuze: La clameur de l'être* (Paris: Hachette, 1997).]

Balsamo, A. 1996. *Technologies of the Gendered Body: Reading Cyborg Women*. Durham, NC: Duke University Press.

Bataille, G. 1988. *The Accursed Share: An Essay on General Economy*, R. Hurley (trans.). New York: Zone Books.

Beckett, S. 1992. *Quad*. Paris: Minuit.

Bene, C. & G. Deleuze 1979. *Superpositions*. Paris: Minuit.

Bensmaïa, R. 1994. "On the Concept of Minor Literature: From Kafka to Kateb Yacine". In *Gilles Deleuze and the Theater of Philosophy*, C. V. Boundas & D. Olkowski (eds), 213–28. New York: Routledge.

Benveniste, E. 1971. *Problems in General Linguistics*, M. E. Meek (trans.). Coral Gables, FL: University of Miami Press.

Bergmann, J. R. 1993. *Discreet Indiscretions: The Social Organization of Gossip*, J. Bednarz, Jr. (trans.). New York: Aldine de Gruyter. [Originally published as *Klatsch: zur Sozialform der diskreten indiscretion* (Berlin: de Gruyter, 1987).]

Bergson, H. 1911 [1907]. *Creative Evolution*, A. Mitchell (trans.). New York: Henry Holt & Co. [Reprinted in 1983 (Lanham, MD: University Press of America).]

Bergson, H. 1994 [1986]. *Matter and Memory*. N. M. Paul & W. S. Palmer (trans.). New York: Zone Books.

Blanchot, M. 1993. *The Infinite Conversation*, S. Hanson (trans.). Minneapolis, MN: University of Minnesota Press. [Originally published as *L'Entretien infini* (Paris: Gallimard, 1969).]

Bogue, R. 2003a. *Deleuze on Cinema*. New York: Routledge.

Bogue, R. 2003b. *Deleuze on Literature*. New York: Routledge.

Bookchin, M. 1971. *Post-Scarcity Anarchism*. Berkeley, CA: Ramparts Press.

Boundas, C. V. & D. Olkowski (eds) 1994. *Gilles Deleuze and the Theater of Philosophy*. New York: Routledge.

Bréhier, E. 1928. *La Théorie des incorporels dans l'ancien stoïcisme*. Paris: Vrin.

Brezeale, D. (ed.) 1979. *Philosophy and Truth*. Atlantic Highlands, NJ: Humanities Press.

Broadhurst, J. (ed.) 1992. "Deluze and the Transcendental Unconscious", *Pli (Warwick Journal of Philosophy), vol. 4*. Coventry: University of Warwick.

Braidotti, R. 2002. *Metamorphoses: Towards a Materialist Theory of Becoming*. Cambridge: Polity Press.

Bray, A. & C. Colebrook 1998. "The Haunted Flesh: Corporeal Feminism and the Politics of (Dis)embodiment", *Signs* **24**(1), 35–68.

Bryden, M. (ed.) 2001. *Deleuze and Religion*. New York: Routledge.

Buchanan, I. (ed.) 1999. *A Deleuzian Century?* Durham, NC: Duke University Press.

Buchanan, I. & C. Colebrook (eds) 2000. *Deleuze and Feminist Theory*. Edinburgh: Edinburgh University Press.

Buchanan, I. & J. Marks (eds) 2000. *Deleuze and Literature*. Edinburgh: Edinburgh University Press.

Burdick, A. 2004. "The Biology of Batteries", *Discover* **25**(1), 15–16.

Canning, P. 2001. "Power". In *Encyclopedia of Postmodernism*, V. E. Taylor & C. Winquist (eds), 311–13. London: Routledge.

Céard, J. & J.-C. Margolin 1984. *Rébus de la Renaissance: Des images qui parlent*, 2 vols. Paris: Maisonneuve.

Charlton, J. I. 2000. *Nothing About Us Without Us: Disability, Oppression, and Empowerment*. Berkeley, CA: University of California Press.

Colebrook, C. 2000. "Introduction". In *Deleuze and Feminist Theory*, I. Buchanan & C. Colebrook (eds), 1–17. Edinburgh: Edinburgh University Press.

Conley, T. 2003. "Afterword: A Politics of Fact and Figure". In *Francis Bacon: The Logic of Sensation*, G. Deleuze; D. W. Smith (trans.), 130–49. Minneapolis, MN: University of Minnesota Press.

Conrad, J. 1984. *Chance: A Tale in Two Parts*. London: Hogarth Press.

Coppola, S. (dir.) 2003. *Lost in Translation*. American Zoetrope/Elemental Films.

Cousin, P.-H., L. L. Sinclair, J.-F. Allain, C. E. Love 1990. *Harper Collins French Dictionary* (College Edition). New York: HarperCollins.

Cressole, M. 1973. *Deleuze*. Paris: Editions Universitaires.

Cronfeld, C. 1996. *On the Margins of Modernism: Decentering Literary Dynamics*. Berkeley, CA: University of California Press.

Damasio, A. 1995. *Descartes' Error: Emotion, Reason, and the Human Brain*. London: Picador.

Delacampagne, C. 1999. *A History of Philosophy in the Twentieth Century*, M. B. DeBevoise (trans.). Baltimore, MD: Johns Hopkins University Press. [Originally published as *Histoire de la philosophie au XXe siècle* (Paris: Éditions du Seuil, 1995).]

D'haen, T. 1999. "'America' and 'Deleuze'". In *Traveling Theory: France and the United States*, S. Bertho & T. Hoenselaars (eds), 39–53. Madison, NJ: Fairleigh Dickinson University Press.

Feinstein, H. 2004. "Interview with Lars Von Trier", *See Magazine* (April), 22–8.

Flaxman, G. (ed.) 2000. *The Brain Is The Screen: Deleuze and the Philosophy of Cinema*. Minneapolis, MN: University of Minnesota Press.

Foucault, M. 1970. *The Order of Things*. New York: Pantheon. [Originally published as *Les Mots et les choses* (Paris: Gallimard, 1966).]

Foucault, M. 1972. *The Archaeology of Knowledge*, A. M. Sheridan (trans.). New York: Pantheon. [Originally published as *L'Archéologie du savoir* (Paris: Gallimard, 1969).]

Foucault, M. 1973. *Madness and Civilization*, R. Howard (trans.). New York: Vintage. [Originally published as *Histoire de la folie à l'âge classique; folie et déraison* (Paris: Plon, 1961).]

Foucault, M. 1977. *Discipline and Punish: The Birth of the Prison*, A. Sheridan (trans.). Harmondsworth: Penguin. [Originally published as *Surveiller et punir: naissance de la prison* (Paris: Gallimard, 1975).]

Foucault, M. 1978. *The History of Sexuality*, R. Hurley (trans.). New York: Pantheon. [Originally published as *La Volonté de savoir* (Paris: Gallimard, 1976).]

Foucault, M. 1980. *The History of Sexuality, Volume One*. R. Hurley (trans.). New York: Vintage. [Originally published as *La volonté de savoir. Histoire de la sexualité 1* (Paris: Gallimard, 1976).]

Foucault, M. 1983. "Preface". In *Anti-Oedipus: Capitalism and Schizophrenia*, G. Deleuze & F. Guattari; R. Hurley, M. Seem & H. R. Lane (trans.), xi–xiv. Minneapolis, MN: University of Minnesota Press. [Reprinted in English in *Power: Essential Works of Michel Foucault*, J. Faubion (ed.) (New York: The New Press, 2000), 106–10; republished in French in Foucault (1994), vol. 3, 133–6.]

Foucault, M. 1985. *The History of Sexuality: The Use of Pleasure*, R. Hurley (trans.). New York: Pantheon. [Originally published as *Histoire de la sexualité 2: L'usage des plaisirs* (Paris: Gallimard, 1984).]

Foucault, M. 1991. *Remarks on Marx*, R. J. Goldstein & J. Cascaito (trans.). New York: Semiotext(e). [Originally published in Italian as "Conversazione con Michel Foucault", *Il Contributo* 4(1) (1980), 23–84; republished in French in Foucault (1994), vol. 4, 41–95.]

Foucault, M. 1994. *Dits et écrits*, 4 vols. Paris: Gallimard.

Foucault, M. 1996. "How Much Does it Cost for Reason to Tell the Truth?", M. Foret & M. Martius (trans.). In *Foucault Live*, S. Lotringer (ed.), 348–62. New York: Semiotext(e). [Original interview conducted in German in 1983, republished in French in Foucault (1994), vol. 4, 431–57.]

Foucault, M. 1998. "Different Spaces". In *Aesthetics, Method, and Epistemology: The Essential Works of Michel Foucault*, vol. 2, P. Rabinow (ed.), R. Hurley (trans.), 175–85. New York: The New Press. [Reprinted in Foucault (1994), vol. 4, 752–62.]

Foucault, M. 2000. "The Subject and Power". In *Power: The Essential Works of Foucault 1954–1984*, P. Rabinow (ed.), 326–48. New York: The New Press. [Originally published in English in *Michel Foucault: Beyond Structuralism and Hermeneutics*, H. L. Dreyfus & P. Rabinow (eds) (Chicago: University of Chicago Press, 1982); republished in French in Foucault (1994), vol. 4, 222–43.]

Foucault, M. & G. Deleuze 1977. "Intellectuals and Power". In *Language, Counter-Memory, Practice*, M. Foucault; Donald Bouchard (ed.), 205–17. Ithaca, NY: Cornell University Press. [Originally published in *L'Arc* 49 (1972), 3–10; reprinted in Foucault (1994), vol. 2, 306–15.]

Freud, S. 1959. *Collected Papers*, vol. 3. New York: Basic Books.

de Gandillac, M. 1945. "Approches de l'amitié". In *L'Existence*, A. de Waehlens (ed.), 63–7. Paris: Gallimard.

Gatens, M. 1995. *Imaginary Bodies: Ethics, Power, and Corporeality*. London: Routledge.

Goldstein, K. & A. Gelb 1918. "Psychologische Analysen hirnpathologischer Falle auf Grund von Untersuchungen Hirnverletzer", *Zeitschrift fur die gesamte Neurologie und Psychiatrie* **41**, 1–142.

Griggers, C. 1997. *Becoming-Woman*. Minneapolis, MN: University of Minnesota Press.

Grosz, E. 1994. *Volatile Bodies: Toward a Corporeal Feminism*. Bloomington and Indianapolis, IN: Indiana University Press.

Guattari, F. 1984. "Anti-psychiatry and Anti-psychology". In *Molecular Revolution: Psychiatry and Politics*, R. Sheed (trans.), 45–50. New York: Penguin. [Originally published in *La revolution moléculaire* (Fontenay-sous-Bois: Recherches, 1977), 139–46.]

Guattari, F. 1995. "Everywhere At Once" [interview with M. Butel], C. Wiener (trans.). In *Chaosophy*, S. Lotringer (ed.), 27–35. New York: Semiotext(e). [Excerpt of interview originally published as "1985 – Entretien avec Michel Butel", in F. Guattari, *Les Années d'Hiver, 1980–1985* (Paris: Barrault, 1986), 80–121.]

Guattari, F. 1996a. "Ritornellos and Existential Affects", J. Schiesari & G. Van Den Abeele (trans.). In *The Guattari Reader*, G. Genosko (ed.), 158–71. Oxford: Blackwell. [Originally published as "Ritournelles et Affects existentiels", in *Cartographies schizoanalytiques* (Paris: Galilée, 1989), 251–67.]

Guattari, F. 1996b. "Microphysics of Power/Micropolitics of Desire", J. Caruana (trans.). In *The Guattari Reader*, G. Genosko (ed.), 172–181. Oxford: Blackwell. [Originally published as "1985-Microphysique des pouvoirs et micropolitique des désirs", in F. Guattari, *Les Années d'Hiver, 1980–1985*, 207–32 (Paris: Barrault, 1986).]

Guattari, F. 2000. *The Three Ecologies*, I. Pindar & P. Sutton (trans.). London: Athlone. [Originally published as *Les trois écologies* (Paris: Galilée, 1989).]

Hall, S. 1986. "On Postmodernism and Articulation: An Interview with Stuart Hall", L. Grossberg (ed.), *Journal of Communication Inquiry* **10**, 45–60.

Haraway, D. J. 1991. "A Cyborg Manifesto: Science, Technology, and Socialist-feminism in the Late Twentieth Century". In *Simians, Cyborgs, and Women: The Reinvention of Nature*, 149–81. New York: Routledge. [Reprinted from D. J. Haraway, "Manifesto for Cyborgs: Science, Technology, and Socialist Feminism in the 1980s", *Socialist Review* 80 (1985), 65–108.]

Harris, D. W. 1999. "Keeping Women in Our Place: Violence at Canadian Universities". In *Canadian Woman Studies: An Introductory Reader*, N. Amin *et al*. (eds), 264–74. Toronto: Ianna Publications.

Hay, J. 2000. "Unaided Virtues: The (Neo-)Liberalization of the Domestic Sphere", *Television & New Media* 1(1), 53–73.

Hegel, G. W. F. 1977. *Phenomenology of Spirit*, A. V. Miller (trans.). Oxford: Oxford University Press.

Howard, P. N. 2004. "Embedded Media: Who We Know, What We Know, and Society Online". In *Society Online: The Internet in Context*, P. N. Howard & S. Jones (eds), 1–27. Thousand Oaks, CA: Sage Publications.

JanMohamed, A. R. & D. Lloyd (eds) 1990. *The Nature and Context of Minority Discourse*. New York: Oxford University Press.

Jardine, A. 1985. *Gynesis: Configurations of Woman and Modernity*. Ithaca, NY: Cornell University Press.

Jones, D. 1990. "Gossip: Notes on Women's Oral Culture". In *The Feminist Critique of Language: A Reader*, D. Cameron (ed.), 242–50. New York: Routledge. [Reprinted from D. Jones, "Gossip: Notes on Women's Oral Culture", in *The Voices and Words of Women and Men*, C. Kramarae (ed), 193–8 (Oxford: Pergamon Press, 1980).]

Kafka, F. 1977. *The Diaries of Franz Kafka*, vol. 1, M. Brod (ed.), J. Kresh (trans.). New York: Schocken.

Kant, I. 1911. *The Critique of Judgment*, J. Meredith (trans.). Oxford: Clarendon Press.

Kant, I. 2002. *The Critique of Practical Reason*, W. Pluhar (trans.). Indianapolis, IN: Hackett.

Katz, J. E. & M. Aakhus (eds) 2002. *Perpetual Contact: Mobile Communication, Private Talk, Public Performance*. New York: Cambridge University Press.

Kaufman, E. & K. J. Heller (eds) 1998. *Deleuze and Guattari. New Mappings in Politics, Philosophy and Culture*. Minneapolis, MN: University of Minnesota Press.

Kelly, M. 1983. *Modern French Marxism*. Baltimore, MD: Johns Hopkins University Press.

Kennedy, B. 2000. *Deleuze and Cinema: The Aesthetics of Sensation*. Edinburgh: Edinburgh University Press.

Khilnani, S. 1993. *Arguing Revolution: The Intellectual Left in Postwar France*. New Haven, CT: Yale University Press.

Koselleck, R. 1995 [1979]. *Futures Past: On the Semantics of Historical Time*, K. Tribe (trans.). Cambridge, MA: MIT Press.

Kozinn, A. 2001. "Violinist Isaac Stern Dies at 81; Led Efforts to Save Carnegie Hall", *The New York Times*, 23 September, 1A:1, Column 5.

Kristeva, J. 1974. *La révolution du langage poétique; l'avant-garde à la fin du XIXe siècle, Lautréamont et Mallarmé*. Paris: Éditions du Seuil.

Lacan, J. 1966. *Écrits*. Paris: Éditions du Seuil.

Lacan, J. 1988. *Freud's Papers on Technique 1953–1954*, S. Tomasseli & J. Forrester (trans.), J. A. Miller (ed.). New York: Norton.

Latour, B. 1999. *Pandora's Hope: Essays on the Reality of Science Studies*. Cambridge, MA: Harvard University Press.

Lloyd, D. 1987. *Nationalism and Minor Literature: James Clarence Mangan and the Emergence of Irish Cultural Nationalism*. Berkeley, CA: University of California Press.

Lorraine, T. 1999. *Irigaray & Deleuze: Experiments in Visceral Philosophy*. Ithaca, NY: Cornell University Press.

Lost-in-Racism, www.lost-in-racism.org/ (accessed Jan. 2005).

Lyotard, J.-F. 1974. *Économie libidinale*. Paris: Les Éditions de Minuit.

Lyotard, J. F. 1990. *Heidegger and "the Jews"*, A. Michel & M. S. Roberts (trans.). Minneapolis, MN: University of Minnesota Press. [Originally published as *Heidegger et "les juifs"* (Paris: Galilée, 1988).]

MacCormack, P. 2001. "Becoming Hu-Man: Deleuze and Guattari, Gender and 3rd Rock from the Sun", *Intensities: The Journal of Cult Media* 1(1), www.cult-media.com/issue1/Amccor.htm (accessed Jan. 2005).

Macherey, P. 1996. "The Encounter with Spinoza", M. Joughin (trans.). In *Deleuze: A Critical Reader*, P. Patton (ed.), 139–61. Oxford: Blackwell.

Maggiori, R. 1991. "Deleuze–Guattari: Nous Deux", *Libération* 12 September, 17–19.

Maggiori, R. 1995. "Un 'courant d'air' dans la pensée du siècle", *Libération* 6 November, 8–10.

Mallarmé, S. 1945. *Oeuvres completes*, H. Mondor & G. J. Aubry (eds). Paris: Gallimard.

Marks, L. U. 1999. *The Skin of the Film: Intercultural Cinema, Embodiment and the Senses*. Durham, NC: Duke University Press.

Marotta, J. J. & M. Behrmann 2004. "Patient Schn: Has Goldstein and Gelb's Case Withstood the Test of Time?", *Neuropsychologia* 42, 633–8.

Marx, K. 1975. *Early Writings*, R. Livingstone & G. Benton (trans.). New York: Vintage.

Massumi, B. 1992. *A User's Guide to Capitalism and Schizophrenia: Deviations from Deleuze and Guattari*. Cambridge, MA: MIT Press.

Massumi, B. 2002a. *Parables for the Virtual: Movement, Affect, Sensation*. Durham, NC: Duke University Press.

Massumi, B. 2002b. "Navigating Movements". In *Hope: New Philosophies for Change*. M. Zournazi (ed.), 210–43. New York: Routledge.

Massumi, B. (ed.) 2002c. *A Shock to Thought: Expression after Deleuze and Guattari*. New York: Routledge.

Merleau-Ponty, M. 2002. *Phenomenology of Perception*, C. Smith (trans.), 2nd edn. New York: Routledge.

Merrell, F. 1997. *Peirce, Signs, and Meaning*. Toronto: University of Toronto Press.

Mullins, J. "Spin Doctors", www.newscientist.com/article.ns?id=mg16622444.700 (accessed Jan. 2005).

Negri, A. 2003. *Time for Revolution*, M. Mandarini (trans.). London: Continuum. [Originally published as *La costituzione del tempo* (Rome: Manifestolibri, 1997).]

Nietzsche, F. 1968. *On the Genealogy of Morals*. In *Basic Writings of Nietzsche*, W. Kaufman (trans.). New York: Modern Library.

Olkowski, D. 1999. *Gilles Deleuze and the Ruin of Representation*. Berkeley, CA: University of California Press.

Orenstein, P. 1995. *Schoolgirls: Young Women, Self Esteem, and the Confidence Gap*. New York: Anchor.

Patton, P. (ed.) 1996. *Deleuze: A Critical Reader*. Oxford: Blackwell.

Patton, P. 2000. *Deleuze and the Political*. London: Routledge.

Pipher, M. 1994. *Reviving Ophelia: Saving the Selves of Adolescent Girls*. New York: Ballantine Books.

Pisters, P. 2003. *The Matrix of Visual Culture*. Stanford, CA: Stanford University Press.

Pomus, D. & M. Shuman 1972. "This Magic Moment" lyrics. www.elyrics4u.com/ t/this_magic_moment_lou_reed.htm (accessed Jan. 2005).

Potok, R. N. 1998. "Borders, Exiles, Minor Literatures: The Case of Palestinian-Israeli Writing". In *Borders, Exiles, Diasporas*, E. Barkan & M.-D. Shelton (eds), 291–310. Stanford, CA: Stanford University Press.

Poxon, J. 2001. "Embodied Anti-theology: The Body without Organs and the Judgment of God". In *Deleuze and Religion*, M. Bryden (ed.), 42–50. New York: Routledge.

Pringle, R. 1988. *Secretaries Talk: Sexuality, Power and Work*. London: Verso.

Proust, M. 1981. *Remembrance of Things Past*. Harmondsworth: Penguin.

Rajchman, J. 2000. *The Deleuze Connections*. Cambridge, MA: MIT Press.

Rheingold, H. 2003. *Smart Mobs: The Next Social Revolution*. Cambridge, MA: Perseus Publishing.

Rilke, R. M. *Selected Poems of Rainer Maria Rilke*, R. Bly (trans.). New York: Harper & Row.

Robertson, R. 1985. *Kafka: Judaism, Politics, and Literature*. Oxford: Clarendon Press.

Rodowick, D. N. 1997. *Gilles Deleuze's Time Machine*. Durham, NC: Duke University Press.

Rose, N. 1999. *Powers of Freedom: Reframing Political Thought*. Cambridge: Cambridge University Press.

Ross, K. 2002. *May '68 and its Afterlives*. Chicago, IL: University of Chicago Press.

Roudinesco, E. 1997. *Jacques Lacan*, B. Bray (trans.). New York: Columbia University Press.

Roy, A. 2002. Lensic Performing Arts Center, Santa Fe, New Mexico, 18 September, www.lannan.org/docs/arundhati-roy-020918-trans-read/pdf (accessed Jan. 2005).

Sacks, O. 1970. *The Man Who Mistook His Wife for a Hat, and Other Clinical Tales*. New York: Simon and Schuster.

Sartre, J.-P. 2004 [1940]. *The Imaginary*, J. Webber (trans.). London: Routledge.

Sartre, J.-P. 1962 [1939]. *Sketch for a Theory of the Emotions*, P. Mairet (trans.). London: Methuen.

Shaviro, S. 1993. *The Cinematic Body*. Minneapolis, MN: University of Minnesota Press.

Simmons, R. 2002. *Odd Girl Out: The Hidden Culture of Aggression in Girls*. Orlando, FL: Harcourt.

Slack, J. D. 1989. "Contextualizing Technology". In *Rethinking Communication, Volume Two: Paradigm Exemplars*, B. Dervin, L. Grossberg, B. J. O'Keefe & E. Wartella (eds), 329–45. Newbury Park, CA: Sage Publications.

Slack, J. D. 2003. "Everyday Matrix: Becoming Adolescence". In *Animations (of Deleuze and Guattari)*, J. D. Slack (ed.), 9–29. New York: Peter Lang.

Slack, J. D. & J. M. Wise 2002. "Cultural Studies and Technology". In *The Handbook of New Media*, L. Lievrouw & S. Livingstone (eds), 485–501. Thousand Oaks, CA: Sage Publications.

Slack, J. D. & J. M. Wise (eds) (forthcoming). *Culture and Technology: A Primer*. New York: Peter Lang.

Smith, D. W. 1997. "'A Life of Pure Immanence': Deleuze's 'Critique et Clinique' Project". In G. Deleuze, *Essays Critical and Clinical*, D. W. Smith & M. A. Greco (trans.), xi–lvi. Minneapolis, MN: University of Minnesota Press.

Sontag, S. 1978. *Illness as Metaphor*. New York: Farrar, Straus and Giroux.

Sontag, S. 2001. *Illness as Metaphor and AIDS and Its Metaphors*. New York: Picador.

Sotirin, P. & H. Gottfried 1999. "The Ambivalent Dynamics of Secretarial 'Bitching': Control, Resistance, and the Construction of Identity", *Organization* 6, 57–80.

Spinoza, B. 1982 [1677]. *The Ethics and Selected Letters*, S. Shirley (trans.), S. Feldman (ed.). Indianapolis, IN: Hackett.

Spinoza, B. 2000 [1677]. *Ethics*, G. H. R. Parkinson (ed. and trans.). Oxford: Oxford University Press.

Stivale, C. J. 1998. *The Two-Fold Thought of Deleuze and Guattari. Intersections and Animations*. New York: Guilford.

Stivale, C. J. 2003a. "Deleuze/Parnet in *Dialogues*: The Folds of Post-Identity." *Journal of the Midwest Modern Language Association* 36(1), 25–37.

Stivale, C. J. 2003b. "Feeling the Event: Spaces of Affects and the Cajun Dance Arena". In *Animations (of Deleuze and Guattari)*, J. D. Slack (ed.), 31–58. New York: Peter Lang.

Sugano, M. Z. 1992. *The Poetics of the Occasion: Mallarmé and the Poetry of Circumstance*. Stanford, CA: Stanford University Press.

Sylvester, D. 1987. *Interviews with Francis Bacon*. London: Thames & Hudson.

Terada, R. 2001. *Feeling in Theory: Emotion after the 'Death of the Subject'*. Cambridge, MA: Harvard University Press.

The Matrix, film, A. Wachowski & L. Wachowski (dirs). Warner Brothers.

tom Dieck, M. 2002. "Entretien avec Martin tom Dieck", www.fremok.org/entretiens/tomdiecknouvelles.htm (accessed Jan. 2005).

tom Dieck, M. & J. Balzer 1997. *Salut, Deleuze!* Brussels: Fréon Éditions.

tom Dieck, M. & J. Balzer 2002. *Nouvelles aventures de l'Incroyable Orphée*. Brussels: Fréon Editions.

Uhlmann, A. (trans.) 1995. "Gilles Deleuze, 'L'Épuisé'", *SubStance* 78(3), 3–28.

Volosinov, V. N. 1986. *Marxism and the Philosophy of Language*, L. Matejka & I. R. Titunik (trans.). Cambridge, MA: Harvard University Press.

Wellesley College & American Association of University Women (AAUW) 1992. *How Schools Shortchange Girls: The AAUW Report: A Study of Major Findings on Girls and Education*. Washington DC: AAUW Educational Foundation, National Education Association.

Williams, R. 1975. *Television: Technology and Cultural Form*. New York: Schocken.

Wise, J. M. 2003. "Home: Territory and Identity". In *Animations (of Deleuze and Guattari)*, J. D. Slack (ed.), 107–27. New York: Peter Lang.

Wiseman, R. 2003. *Queen Bees and Wannabes: Helping Your Daughter Survive Cliques, Gossip, Boyfriends, and Other Realities of Adolescence*. New York: Three Rivers Press.

Wolfe, T. 1983. *The Autobiography of an American Novelist*, L. Field (ed.). Cambridge, MA: Harvard University Press.

Yoon, K. 2003. "Retraditionalizing the Mobile: Young People's Sociality and Mobile Phone Use in Seoul, South Korea", *European Journal of Cultural Studies* 6(3), 327–43.

Zhang, X. 2002. "Shanghai Image: Critical Iconography, Minor Literature, and the Un-Making of a Modern Chinese Mythology", *New Literary History* 33, 137–60.

Zourabichvili, F. 2003. *Le Vocabulaire de Deleuze*. Paris: Ellipses.

Index